SAT®

ELITE 1600

The Staff of The Princeton Review

PrincetonReview.com

Penguin
Random
House

The Princeton Review
24 Prime Parkway, Suite 201
Natick, MA 01760
E-mail: editorialsupport@review.com

Published in the United States by Penguin Random House LLC, New York, and in Canada by Random House of Canada, a division of Penguin Random House Ltd., Toronto.

ISBN: 978-1-101-88201-6
eBook ISBN: 978-1-101-88206-1
ISSN: 2373-9622

Editor: Aaron Riccio
Production Editors: Beth Hanson and Liz Rutzel
Production Artist: Deborah A. Silvestrini

Printed in the United States of America on partially recycled paper.

10 9 8 7 6 5 4 3 2 1

Editorial
Rob Franek, Senior VP, Publisher
Casey Cornelius, VP Content Development
Mary Beth Garrick, Director of Production
Selena Coppock, Managing Editor
Meave Shelton, Senior Editor
Colleen Day, Editor
Sarah Litt, Editor
Aaron Riccio, Editor
Orion McBean, Editorial Assistant

Random House Publishing Team
Tom Russell, Publisher
Alison Stoltzfus, Publishing Manager
Melinda Ackell, Associate Managing Editor
Ellen Reed, Production Manager
Kristin Lindner, Production Supervisor
Andrea Lau, Designer

Acknowledgments

Authors
Brian Becker
Kathryn Menafee
Amy Minster
Elizabeth Owens

Contributors
Aaron Lindh
Bobby Hood
Cat Healey
Anthony Krupp
Chris Knuth
V. Zoe Gannon

Project Managers
V. Zoe Gannon
Kathryn Menafee

National Content Director, High School Programs
Jonathan Chiu

Contents

Register Your

1 Go to **PrincetonReview.com/cracking**

2 You'll see a welcome page where you can register your book using the following ISBN: 9781101882016

3 After placing this free order, you'll either be asked to log in or to answer a few simple questions in order to set up a new Princeton Review account.

4 Finally, click on the "Student Tools" tab located at the top of the screen. It may take an hour or two for your registration to go through, but after that, you're good to go.

If you are experiencing book problems (potential content errors), please contact EditorialSupport@review.com with the full title of the book, its ISBN number (located above), and the page number of the error. Experiencing technical issues? Please e-mail TPRStudentTech@review.com with the following information:

- your full name
- e-mail address used to register the book
- full book title and ISBN
- your computer OS (Mac or PC) and Internet browser (Firefox, Safari, Chrome, etc.)
- description of technical issue

Book Online!

Once you've registered, you can...

- Access and print out online drills as well as the corresponding answers and explanations

- Find any late-breaking information released about the SAT

- Sort colleges by whatever you're looking for (such as Best Theater or Dorm), learn more about your top choices, and see how they all rank according to *The Best 380 Colleges*

- Check to see if there have been any corrections or updates to this edition

The **Princeton** Review®

Part I
Orientation

Chapter 1
Introduction to the SAT

The pursuit of a perfect or near-perfect SAT score is an impressive goal. Achieving that goal requires a thorough command of the material and strategies specific to the SAT. To begin your quest, learn everything you can about the test. This chapter presents an overview of the SAT, advice about when to take it, and a guide to reporting your scores.

WELCOME

So you think you can score a 1450 or better? We're all for it. The Princeton Review supports all students who want to do their best. We've written this book specifically for students who are in a position to score at the very highest levels. We believe that to achieve a perfect or near-perfect score, you have to know as much as possible about the test itself and, more importantly, know yourself.

You may know all of the basic facts about the SAT already, but even if you think you do, we encourage you to read through this chapter to be sure you know every single thing you can about the test you're going to conquer.

FUN FACTS ABOUT THE SAT

All of the content review and strategies we teach in the following lessons are based on the specific structure and format of the SAT. Before you can beat the test, you have to know how it's built.

Structure

The SAT consists of three main sections: Reading, Writing & Language, and Math. The Math is broken into two sub-sections, the first of which must be completed without the use of a calculator.

Reading	52 questions 65 minutes
Writing & Language	44 questions 35 minutes
Math	NO CALCULATOR 20 questions 25 minutes CALCULATOR 38 questions 55 minutes

There is also an optional essay section, for which you are given fifty minutes. This may seem like fewer sections than the previous SAT, but if you add it all up, you're looking at at least three hours of test-taking, and almost four if you complete the essay. Whew!

Scoring

The Reading and Writing sections are scored together on a scale from 200–800, and added to the total from the two Math sections (also on a scale from 200–800) for a total score between 400 to 1600. There are are also a series of sub-scores that point out how you did on specific types of questions, such as math problems that require data analysis or reading questions that focus on understanding words in context. All that really matters, however, is the overall score, which has a maximum of 1600.

Content

In Parts II–IV, we'll thoroughly review the content and strategies you need for each of the three main sections. Here is a brief overview of each section.

Reading

The Reading section contains five passages, for which there will be 52 multiple-choice questions (10 or 11 per passage). These passages can be anywhere from 500 to 750 words, may include associated data to be interpreted along with the text, and range from literature to social studies and science. One of the five passages will actually have two shorter, paired passages. Passage-based questions are *never* presented in order of difficulty; the order of questions tends to be chronological.

Writing

The Writing section consists of four passages, each with 11 associated questions, for a total of 44 multiple-choice questions. These tend to be shorter passages, somewhere between 400 and 450 words, but otherwise cover the same topics as the Reading section, as well as some career-oriented topics.

Math

The Math section features 58 questions, split between a no-calculator section (20 questions) and a calculator section (38 questions). There is no specific order of difficulty, but both sections feature grid-in questions at the end (5 and 8, respectively), and some students find the lack of multiple-choice options to be tricky.

Content on the Math section is drawn from arithmetic, pre-algebra, elementary algebra, intermediate algebra, plane geometry, and coordinate geometry. Some advanced topics, such as trigonometric ratios and radian measure are tested, but make up only a small percentage of all questions.

THE SAT SCHEDULE

In the United States, the SAT is offered seven times a year: October, November, December, January, March, May, and June. The March test is not offered in international locations.

Take the SAT when your schedule best allows. Many high scorers take their first SAT in the fall of their junior year. If you have more commitments in the fall from sports, plays, or clubs, then plan to take your first SAT in the winter or spring.

Many high school counselors advise waiting to take the SAT until spring because students may be unfamiliar with some of the more difficult material before then. Students in an honors track, however, will have covered all of the content by the end of sophomore year at the latest. Even if you aren't in an honors track, there are relatively few concepts that will be unfamiliar to you. We recommend taking your first SAT as early as your schedule allows.

REGISTERING FOR THE SAT

Go to **collegeboard.org** and create a student account. At **collegeboard.org**, you can view test dates, fees, and registration deadlines. You can research the requirements and processes to apply for extended time or other accommodations, register for the test, view your scores, and order score reports.

You can contact College Board customer service by phone at 866-756-7346 (or 212-713-7789 for international callers), but you cannot sign up for the test by phone if you are taking it for the first time.

Test Security

As part of the registration process, you have to upload or mail a photograph that will be printed on your admissions ticket. On test day, you have to take the ticket and acceptable photo identification with you.

Registration Tips

You have options for obtaining SAT score reports, copies of your test, and cancellation. We have recommendations on each.

Score Reports

When you register, supply the codes for any schools on your application list. If you want to add more schools to your list later, you certainly can. Since colleges are interested only in your highest scores, there is no benefit to withholding any scores from prospective colleges.

Test Information Release

If you take the SAT in October, January, or May, we recommend you sign up for the Question and Answer Service when you register. Six to eight weeks after the test, you'll receive a copy of the test and your answers. This service costs an additional fee and is available only for the dates above. You can order the Question and Answer Service up to five months after the test date, but it's easier to order at the time you register. It's a great tool to help you prepare for your next SAT.

How Many Times Should You Take the SAT?

We will be thrilled if you review the content in this book, take the SAT for the first time, and earn the score you seek. If you don't hit your target score the first time, take it again. In fact, we recommend that you enter the process planning to take the SAT two or three times. Nerves and anxiety can be unpredictable catalysts, and for many students, the first experience can seem harder than what you've seen in practice. Perception is reality, so we won't waste your time explaining that it only *seems* harder and different. That's why we recommend taking your first SAT as soon as your schedule allows. Get that first experience with a real test over with as soon as possible, and leave yourself enough time to take the test again. Subsequent administrations won't seem nearly as hard and daunting as the first.

While no one wants to take the SAT more than three times, it's not out of the question if you haven't reached the score you need. Just make sure you consider what you will do differently before taking the test again. Dedicate yourself to trying new strategies that you initially thought you wouldn't need.

Score Cancellation

You have the option to cancel your scores, either immediately (at the testing center) or soon after the exam. Usually, you should use this option only under extreme circumstances—you were violently ill, there was a punk band rehearsing in the next classroom, or something equally dramatic. Don't cancel your scores just because you feel like you had a bad day; you can always take the test again, and it's good to have a starting point to compare subsequent tests to. If you *really* feel you must cancel your scores, you have until 11:59 P.M. (EST) on the Wednesday after the exam. See the College Board website for more information.

HOW TO PREPARE FOR THE SAT

The following lessons cover the content and strategies for the Math, Reading, and Writing sections. Review all lessons, even in the subjects that you think you already have targeted as your strengths. We want to make sure you're thoroughly prepared, and we'll risk boring you a tad to cover content you may know. But we won't waste your time. All of the content and strategies we cover are necessary.

As we noted above, the easiest path to your best score is to maximize your strengths. Earn every point that you can from your strengths even as you acquire new skills and strategies to improve your weaknesses.

Practice, Practice, Practice

To achieve a great SAT score, you have to practice a lot! We recommend that you practice with both real SAT tests and Princeton Review practice tests.

You can also pick up a copy of the College Board's The Official SAT Study Guide, 2016 Edition, which contains four real tests, answer explanations, and scoring guides. That said, this same content can also be printed out for free from the College Board website at **collegereadiness.collegeboard.org/sat/practice/full-length-practice-tests**.

For more practice materials, The Princeton Review publishes *Cracking the New SAT and 500+ Practice Questions for the New SAT.* In addition, we recommend contacting your local Princeton Review office to investigate free practice test dates and follow up sessions. Visit princetonreview.com for more information, including a comprehensive list of all other available titles.

TEST TAKER, KNOW THYSELF

To earn a perfect or near-perfect score on the SAT, it's not enough to know everything about the test. You also need to know yourself. Identify your own strengths and weaknesses. Don't try to make yourself something you're not. You do not need to be a master of every subject to earn a top score on the SAT. You do need to be a master test taker. Stop the part of your brain that wants to do the question the *right* way. All that matters is that you get it right. *How* you get the question right doesn't matter. So don't waste time trying to make yourself into the math or reading genius you thought you needed to be.

Read more in the next chapter about the overall strategies, and read through all the lessons in individual subjects that follow. Be willing to tweak what you already do well, and be willing to try entirely new approaches for what you don't do well.

Summary

o Knowing the structure of the SAT is the first step to mastering the test.

o Take your first SAT as soon as your schedule allows.

o Order the Question and Answer Service if it's available for your test date.

o Plan to take the SAT 2–3 times.

o Take the SAT again if you do not achieve the best score you've hit in practice.

o Know your options about score reporting and cancellation.

o Practice on real SATs as much as possible.

o Use Princeton Review practice materials to supplement your preparation.

Chapter 2
Strategy, Pacing, and Scoring

To earn a perfect or near-perfect SAT score, you need strategies specific to the SAT. In this chapter, we'll provide an overview of the universal strategies. Each section of the SAT demands a specific approach, and even the most universal strategies vary in their applications. In Parts II–IV, we'll discuss these strategies in greater detail customized to the Writing & Language, Math, and Reading sections.

THE BASIC APPROACH

The SAT is different from the tests you take in school, and, therefore, you need to approach the SAT differently. The Princeton Review's strategies are not arbitrary. To be effective, strategies have to be based on the SAT and not just any old test.

Enemy #1: Time

Consider the structure of each section. On the Reading Test, for example. you'll have 65 minutes to answer 52 questions. Depending on how long it takes you to read the passages, which is why we encourage skimming and actively reading, that's not much more than a minute per question. Time is your enemy on the SAT, and you have to use it wisely and be aware of how that time pressure can bring out your worst instincts as a test taker.

Enemy #2: Yourself

There is something particularly evil about tests like the SAT. The skills you've been rewarded for throughout your academic career can easily work against you. You've been taught since you started school to follow directions, go in order, and finish everything. But treating the SAT the same way you would a school test won't necessarily earn you a perfect or near-perfect score.

On the other hand, treating the SAT as a scary, alien beast can leave our brains blank and useless and can lead to irrational, self-defeating behavior. When you pick up a #2 pencil, you tend to leave your common sense at the door. Test nerves and anxieties can make you misread a question, commit a careless error, see something that isn't there, blind you to what is there, talk you into a bad answer, and worst of all, convince you to spend good time after bad.

Work Smarter, Not Harder

When you're already answering most questions correctly, it can be difficult to change your approach. But to answer nearly *every* question correctly, you have to do something different. You can't just work harder. Instead, you have to work smarter. Realize what isn't working. Be open-minded about changing your approach. Know what to tweak and what to replace entirely. Determine when to abandon one approach and try another.

The following is an introduction to the general strategies to use on the SAT. In Parts II–IV we'll discuss how these strategies are customized for each section on the SAT.

SAT STRATEGIES

Pacing

The biggest mistake many high scorers make is to spend too *little* time on the easy and medium questions, and too *much* time on the hard ones. That might seem backward—the hard questions are hard (duh), so you need to spend as much time as possible on them, right?

The problem with this approach is that if you rush through the easy and medium questions, you are almost certain to make a few careless mistakes, which will have a devastating impact on your score. If you want to score in the high 700s on a section, you can't afford *any* careless mistakes. So here's the first step toward improving your score: *slow down* and spend enough time (but not a minute more) on the easy and medium questions to get *every* one of them right. With practice, you should have enough time for the hard questions as well, but you've got to get the easy and medium questions right first.

Personal Order of Difficulty (POOD)

Because the questions on the SAT aren't presented in order of difficulty, you'll want to create your own Personal Order of Difficulty (POOD). Don't be a slave to the order of the test. If you're stumped by a question, circle it and come back later. Do all the questions that are easy and medium *for you*, and save the hardest ones for last.

Process of Elimination (POE)

Multiple-choice questions offer one great advantage: They provide the correct answer right there on the page. Of course, they hide the correct answer amidst three incorrect answers. However, it's often easier to spot the wrong answers than it is to identify the right ones, particularly when you apply a smart Process of Elimination (POE).

The Best Way to Bubble In

Work a page at a time, circling your answers right in the booklet. Transfer all the answers from a single page to the bubble sheet at once. It's better to stay focused on working questions than to disrupt your concentration to find where you left off on the scantron. This will also help you remember to leave blanks for questions that you plan on coming back to. If you do this, you'll become more accurate at both tasks.

POE is a powerful strategy on the SAT. For some question types, you'll always use POE rather than wasting time trying to figure out the answer on your own. For other questions, you'll use POE when you're stuck. The SAT hides the correct answer behind wrong ones, but when you cross off just one or two wrong answers, the correct answer can become more obvious, sometimes jumping right off the page.

POOD, Pacing, and POE all work together to help you get as many questions right as possible.

Use Your Pencil
You own the test booklet, and you should write where and when it helps you. Use your pencil to literally cross off wrong answers on the page.

Scoring

There are two types of scores on the SAT: raw and scaled. Your raw score on the SAT is the number of questions you got right, period. Every time you answer an SAT question correctly, you get 1 raw point, regardless of the difficulty or type.

Because the questions on the SAT are constantly changing, the College Board scales the scores as it converts from the raw number of correct answers to your final 400–1600 score. However, these deviations tend to be minor, so you should be able to use the following conversion table, based on recently released data, to get an idea of how many questions you'll have to get right to reach your target score.

RAW SCORE CONVERSION TABLE 1   SECTION AND TEST SCORES

Raw Score (# of correct answers)	Math Section Score	Reading Test Score	Writing and Language Test Score	Raw Score (# of correct answers)	Math Section Score	Reading Test Score	Writing and Language Test Score
0	200	10	10	30	530	28	29
1	200	10	10	31	540	28	30
2	210	10	10	32	550	29	30
3	230	11	10	33	560	29	31
4	240	12	11	34	560	30	32
5	260	13	12	35	570	30	32
6	280	14	13	36	580	31	33
7	290	15	13	37	590	31	34
8	310	15	14	38	600	32	34
9	320	16	15	39	600	32	35
10	330	17	16	40	610	33	36
11	340	17	16	41	620	33	37
12	360	18	17	42	630	34	38
13	370	19	18	43	640	35	39
14	380	19	19	44	650	35	40
15	390	20	19	45	660	36	
16	410	20	20	46	670	37	
17	420	21	21	47	670	37	
18	430	21	21	48	680	38	
19	440	22	22	49	690	38	
20	450	22	23	50	700	39	
21	460	23	23	51	710	40	
22	470	23	24	52	730	40	
23	480	24	25	53	740		
24	480	24	25	54	750		
25	490	25	26	55	760		
26	500	25	26	56	780		
27	510	26	27	57	790		
28	520	26	28	58	800		
29	520	27	28				

CONVERSION EQUATION 1   SECTION AND TEST SCORES

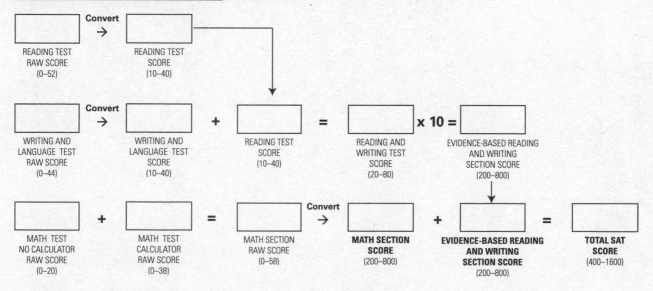

Should You Guess?

There is no longer any penalty for guessing, so think of this question another way: should you leave a question blank and have a 100% chance of getting it wrong, or guess and have at least a 25% chance of getting it right? Obviously you should fill something in. It can only help your score. Ideally, you'll have the time to make an educated guess, using POE to increase your odds, but if you've only got a minute or two left, pick a letter and bubble it in for all of the remaining choices.

BE RUTHLESS

The worst mistake a test taker can make is to throw good time after bad. You read a question, don't understand it, so you read it again. And again. If you stare at it really hard, you know you're going to just *see* it. And you can't move on, because really, after spending all that time it would be a waste not to keep at it, right?

Wrong. You can't let one tough question drag you down, and you can't let your worst instincts tempt you into self-defeating behavior. Instead, the surest way to earn a great SAT score is to follow our advice.

- Use the techniques and strategies in the lessons to work efficiently and *accurately* through the questions. Set a goal right now of zero careless mistakes.
- Know when to move on. If you're stuck, come back later.

In Parts II-IV, you'll learn how POOD, Pacing, and POE work in each section.

Summary

- Don't let your own worst instincts work against you on the SAT. Work Smarter, Not Harder.

- Identify your own Personal Order of Difficulty (POOD). Don't be a slave to the order of the test.

- Pace yourself. Don't rush through easy and medium questions only to make careless errors.

- Use Process of Elimination (POE) to save time, when you're stuck, or when you're out of time.

- If time does run out, make sure that you've at least guessed something for every multiple-choice question.

- Be Ruthless. If one strategy isn't working, switch immediately to another.

Part II
Reading

Chapter 3
Introduction to
SAT Reading

INTRODUCTION

When you read a book or watch a movie, you're typically able to make a choice. The questions you may typically ask yourself when checking the bookstore shelves or the movie listings may not only be "What would I like to see or read?" but also, whether you realize it or not, "How would I like to see or read?"

You are actually reading all the time, and how you read can take a tremendous number of forms. The basics are always the same: The letters combine to make words, and those words make sentences and paragraphs. Somehow in the middle of all of it, meaning is dumped into your brain. However, it's not quite that simple because ultimately what you read determines how you read.

Let's take an obvious example. What do you do differently when you read these two pieces of text?

> 1. *Tomorrow, and tomorrow, and tomorrow,*
>   *Creeps in this petty pace from day to day*
>   *To the last syllable of recorded time,*
>   *And all our yesterdays have lighted fools*
>   *The way to dusty death. Out, out, brief candle!*

> 2. *I saw Lisa the other day lol she told me the funniest thing oh and what are you doing this Fri?*

It's safe to say that we're looking at two very different things, so how we approach those two things will also be very different. (The first comes from Shakespeare's *Macbeth*, and the second comes from a text message.)

One big difference in your approach to these two texts is that you'll probably read the first example more carefully if you're reading and writing about it for an English class. Its language is unfamiliar, so understanding it is the first basic hurdle. Once you get through to a basic understanding of the words, there's the question of meaning. You might look at the repetition of the word "tomorrow" or try to find the referents for "this petty pace" or "brief candle." You could spend a lifetime reading these lines, as many scholars have, and find something new or newly meaningful each time.

You'll use a much different skill set on the other text. There's no reason to look at how the language is used here. The weird non-grammar of the passage isn't really worthy of attention either. This text message is all content, and all the basic information you need to receive from it is right there. You'll never have a reason to read it again.

Neither approach is better. They are just different.

Now how about the Shakespeare passage in different contexts? How, for example, would it change the way you read if

1. You read the "Tomorrow, and tomorrow, and tomorrow" speech in a class
2. You read the "Tomorrow, and tomorrow, and tomorrow" speech on an English test

We've already thought about how you'd read in the first instance. Now, in the second, you're reading the same speech, but this time you have to read it on a test.

There are a number of things you'd have to do differently this time. For one, you'll probably have to answer some questions about the text: You may be asked to analyze the language or literary devices, you may be asked to identify the speaker (Macbeth!), or you may be asked to tie the passage to some theme or larger question you discussed in class. The point, though, is that you're asked to be a more active participant in your reading than you were initially, and that's going to change how you read. There's also the fact that you'll have to read on a timed test, that you'll probably already be familiar with the passage, and that you're much more likely to assess than to understand.

You often apply these different styles of reading without even realizing it. One of the keys to success on the most difficult passages of the SAT is to be aware of what you do when you read. When you read a passage about a topic that's not of particular interest to you, you might skim, make assumptions, match words in the passage and the answer choices, and spend far too much time along the way. The best way to beat the SAT at its own game, to really crack the SAT, is to understand the peculiarities of SAT Reading and how it differs from other reading you do in school and out. The students who knock the SAT out of the park are those who have the self-awareness necessary to avoid the SAT's traps.

GENRES OF READING

We are all familiar with the genres of writing—romance, horror, and sci-fi are just three of the most popular. However, becoming a good, self-conscious reader is about realizing that there are genres of reading as well. What you're trained to do in your English classes is something we could call the genre of Literary Reading.

If you like to read, or if you do particularly well in your English classes, then you're probably already very proficient at Literary Reading. Above all, this genre is characterized by sophisticated interpretations. The papers that you write in high-school or college English classes require creative but convincing readings of the meanings of particular texts. There are some basic aspects on which everyone has to agree—plot, characters, narrative voice—but beyond that, the rein is relatively free. In many classes, you are actually encouraged to come up with your own interpretation, and you are evaluated on your ability to interpret a text in a personal way. This is why some people love to read novels in their spare time. Two people may read the same novel but have totally different reactions to it because literary reading is rooted in a kind of personalization. The students who do best in English classes, and those who go on to become English majors, are those who forge the closest personal connections to the material that they read, and are not necessarily those who understand the text in the most "correct" way. The best English students, in other words, are those who have mastered the genre of Literary Reading.

The Genre of SAT Reading

There's a simple reason that the best readers in an English class are not necessarily the best readers on an SAT: Literary Reading and SAT Reading are two different genres of reading. They require different skill sets.

It helps to remember what a standardized test is. Essentially, ETS needs to be able to promise that everyone—regardless of race, gender, region, or family income—can read a question and have an equal shot at getting the correct answer. If the SAT were testing Literary Reading, everyone would come up with a different answer, and the test would be impossible to score because it would no longer be standardized.

As a result, SAT Reading is much more characterized by *understanding* than by *interpretation*. Interpretation is personal to the reader. Understanding is all about what the text says. This is good news because it means that everything you'll need to answer the questions will be right in front of you in the text, but it also means that you have to stop approaching it the same way you've been trained to approach reading in your English classes all along.

Reading for understanding is tough! Let's take a paragraph from an SAT passage about the studio-recording device Auto-Tune:

> The first major hit to popularize Auto-Tune was Cher's "Believe," which was released in 1998. Since that time, the vocal pitch corrector has
> *Line* become almost a staple of popular music. A 2011
> 5 study said that 95% of Top 40 radio hits that year had used Auto-Tune to one degree or another. The technology is clearly here to stay, though its effects on the present and future of popular music are hotly debated. While some have argued that the
> 10 new technology has opened up new possibilities for popular music, others have responded that the technology has ripped music from its roots, creating an industry built on computer enhancement rather than musical talent.

This is part of a larger essay, but let's think for a moment about how we might answer a question about it on the SAT.

> **1**
>
> In this paragraph, what is the author's main point about Auto-Tune?
>
> A) The technology was useful in the late 1990s, but it is no longer useful.
>
> B) The technology has changed popular music for the worse.
>
> C) Popular music is now dominated by poor singers whose voices are modified.
>
> D) Popular music has been influenced by the introduction of Auto-Tune technology.

While this question seems fairly straightforward, it can actually be very difficult if you apply your Literary Reading skills. In Literary Reading, the major question is typically, "What does the author *mean*?" or "What is the author suggesting?" You can take those questions in a number of directions.

You could say, for example, that (A) is the correct answer because the author singles out Cher's "Believe," thus implying that this was an innovative use of Auto-Tune technology. The later discussion of the widespread use of the technology could also be said to imply that the author believes that Cher's use of AutoTune inspired many imitators and that popular music is now watered-down and dull.

But does the author actually *say* any of this?

How about (B)? The author clearly suggests that Auto-Tune is changing popular music, and he cites some critics who suggest that it is ruining music. We might say that the author is implying his own critique of Auto-Tune in giving more space to Auto-Tune's detractors than to its supporters.

But, again, even with all these smart reasons, can we actually choose this as our correct answer?

As for (C), the author does cite a statistic (the 2011 study) that indicates that popular music is now dominated by Auto-Tune. Because Auto-Tune does modify the voices of singers, couldn't we say that these singers must be poor? Seems logical, but is it definitely true?

In the end, however, only (D) is actually *stated* in the passage, so it is the only possible correct answer. We can even point to the lines that make it correct (*A 2011 study said that 95% of Top 40 radio hits that year had used Auto-Tune to one degree or another. The technology is clearly here to stay*). No intense thinking or reasoning is required.

This demonstrates the cornerstone of the genre of SAT Reading: Correct answers are always rooted firmly in the text and are based on what the author *actually says*, not what the author *could be perceived to say*. There will always be a word or phrase that offers direct, irrefutable support for the correct answer. If you find yourself *reasoning* rather than *identifying*, be careful!

So here's the thing that the administrators of the SAT will never admit but that is absolutely true, particularly for students like you who do well in school and are shooting for Verbal scores in the 700s.

> Thinking is not rewarded on the SAT.

We could debate the merits of this approach all day long. Ultimately, though, whether the test is better, worse, or equal to what you learn in school doesn't change the basic fact: SAT Reading is a genre of reading that will not change, but you can learn and perfect the skills necessary to master it.

So the first rule of the SAT Reading genre is as follows:

> Read to understand, not to assess. Read for information, not interpretation.

Answer Support and Selective Close Reading

As you will see in the next chapter, it's not a good idea to read every word of an SAT passage. It's best to let the questions guide you through the passage. You don't get points for reading the text—you get points for answering the questions. Read the parts of the text that will get you the points. Who cares about the rest?

When you do read, even though you'll be reading smaller chunks of text, make sure you are reading carefully. Every answer on this test will have specific support within the passage, and sometimes that support can hide in particular words or phrases. If you're skimming rather than reading carefully, you may miss these words or phrases altogether.

Take this selection from a recent PSAT.

> Daddy was seeing an awful lot of his new friend.
> One of the rooms in his house was all of a sudden
> full of her stuff; neither Sarah nor her brother was
> *Line* allowed in there anymore. It had started with a few
> 5 dinners and shopping trips, and now it seemed that
> their father's friend basically lived in the house and
> was shifting around some furniture that had been
> in place for as long as Sarah could remember.

34

The phrases "an awful lot" and "all of a sudden" serve to emphasize Sarah's

A) disapproval of her father's new girlfriend

B) wish that things could be as they once were

C) unwillingness to accept a new person into her life

D) surprise at a new development in her father's home

This question asks you to do exactly the kind of close reading that you should always do. Another way of asking the question would be, *Why does the author use the phrases "an awful lot" and "all of a sudden"?* One way to test the effectiveness of language is to take the word or phrase in question out of the passage.

So the first two lines would change to the following:

> *Daddy was seeing a lot of his new friend. One of the rooms in his house was full of her stuff.*

Now compare that to what it actually says.

> *Daddy was seeing an awful lot of his new friend. One of the rooms in his house was all of a sudden full of her stuff.*

Notice how the original lines add Sarah's voice to the third-person narration. Phrases like *an awful lot* and *all of a sudden*, in other words, come from Sarah herself, and they help to emphasize her surprise at how quickly things are moving between her father and his "new friend." Of the answer choices listed, (D) best captures the use of these terms.

Let's try a slightly more difficult passage.

To take one example, the name "Iraq" is not quite as applicable to all its citizens as the names "France," "Portugal," or "The United States" are
Line in their own regions. For many Westerners,
5 nationality is a given and ultimately trumps the more local identifications of town, city, or state. In Iraq, as the Bush administration learned, religious distinctions are more meaningful than national similarities. Approximately 65% of those living
10 in Iraq are Shia Muslims, but does this make it a Shia country? To an extent, maybe, but Sunni Muslims represent a powerful and vocal minority, and the northern regions of Iraq comprise a semi-autonomous region of a third group, the Kurds. The
15 Western notions of nation-above-all and religious coexistence don't hold up in countries like this because the value systems of these countries have developed so independently of Western notions.

12

What does the first sentence suggest about the name of the nation of Iraq?

A) The name of the country comes from the region in which the majority of Shias live.

B) The name of the country has less significance in Iraq than it does in other countries.

C) The name of the country does not apply to most citizens, who therefore frequently disregard the name.

D) The name of the country refers to an area that does not include the region of Kurdistan.

In this sentence, notice the difference that the words "quite as" make. Without them, the sentence would read as follows: *To take one example, the name "Iraq" is not applicable to all citizens….* Without the "quite as," therefore, this sentence is much more extreme, and the answer might be (C) or (D). As it is, though, the only answer that can work is (B).

Let's try another.

13

According to the author, how do Westerners identify with the towns, cities, or state in which they live?

A) These local identifications play some role, but the idea of belonging to a nation is more important.

B) These local identifications hold some importance but are trumped by religious identifications.

C) These local identifications are most important in European countries such as France and Portugal.

D) These local identifications are less important than both religious and national identifications.

The correct answer here is (A), but (B), (C), and (D) all contain some compelling parts, particularly if you have not read the passage closely. Choices (B) and (D) contain the words *religious identification* and (C) contains the names *France and Portugal*. Although all of these words may have appeared in the initial passage, the answer choices rearrange the words to say things that the passage doesn't say. Use the context clues if you're not sure what terms like *trumps* and *given* mean in this particular context. The sentences surrounding this one define those words specifically. Again, these passages can't really presume any outside knowledge at all, so anything that seems especially difficult or complicated will be defined in the passage itself. When you read, do so carefully, and make sure that you've read enough to know what the passage is saying.

In future chapters, we will discuss our particular approach to reading passages, but if you're looking for the very highest scores on this test, remember that SAT Reading is a genre of reading with its own particular set of rules.

Play to Your Strengths

You will get all five of the Reading passages at once. There is no reason that you have to do them in order! Remember, you will have one World Literature and two each of Science and History/Social Studies. Pick and choose your order! First do the passages where you're most likely to get points. If you love reading novels, Literature might be a great place to start. If you love data, see if you've got a Science passage with graphs.

To get a top score, you'll have to do all five passages, but starting with the passage you hate the least will help you to be efficient right off the bat. In turn, this will help you build momentum much more effectively than starting with a more challenging passage.

The following are some things to consider:

- **Type of passage**: There's always one literature passage and two each of science and history/social studies, but not necessarily in that order. One of the five will be a dual-reading passage.

- **Topic of passage:** The blurb will give you some basic information about the passage. If it makes you the least bit curious, that may help you decide whether to do the passage or skip it.

- **Types of questions**: You may find some question types easier than others, so skim those to see if there are a lot of line references and lead words, In general, those two question types help you to find what you're looking for relatively quickly, whereas other big-idea questions may require you to spend more time wading through the passage to find what you want.

READING INTRODUCTION EXERCISE

Questions 1-6 are based on the following passage.

The following passage is an excerpt from the memoir of a well-known African American singer and community leader. It is set in New York and Philadelphia in the 1920s.

I now had what amounted to a complex about music. Hopes had been raised too high, and when they crashed too low, I could not be
Line
objective. Perhaps I had not admitted it to myself,
5 but Town Hall in New York had represented the mainstream of American musical life, and I had plunged into it hoping to become one of the fortunate swimmers.

I kept rehashing the concert in my mind,
10 lingering on some points and thrusting others so thoroughly aside that I do not remember to this day which dress I wore, whether it was the one Mrs. Patterson had made over for me or a special one. I don't remember what financial
15 arrangements were made with the young man who managed the event, but I do know that I received nothing and that he must have lost money. I thought then, and still do, that I might have done better if I had not been told that
20 auditorium was full. If you are sensitive, and I was perhaps too sensitive, a misrepresentation like that can throw you off balance, particularly if you feel that you have a great deal at stake.

I stopped going regularly to Mr. Boghetti's
25 studio. I appeared once in a while, and things must have gone very indifferently. He realized how much the fiasco had shaken me, and he did not make an issue of my irregular attendance.

Mother and I talked about the whole thing,
30 and with her patience and understanding she helped me out of my trouble. I knew that the criticism was right and that I should not have given the critics the opportunity to write as they did. I kept reiterating that I had wanted so very
35 much to sing well enough to please everybody.

"Listen my child," Mother said. "Whatever you do in this world, no matter how good it is, you will never be able to please everybody. All you can strive for is to do the best it is humanly
40 possible for you to do."

As the months went by I was able again to consider singing as a career. "Think about it for a while," Mother advised, "and think of other things you might like to do."

50 I thought about it. It took a long time before I could confront singing again with enthusiasm, before the old conviction returned that nothing in life could be as important as music.

1

The passage as a whole best supports which explanation of the narrator's "complex about music" (lines 1-2) ?

A) A critical review of a performance caused her to change careers.

B) Becoming an accomplished singer was not her primary ambition.

C) A formidable experience led her to question her aspirations.

D) Performing in Town Hall was the pinnacle of her early musical career.

2

In line 8, "fortunate swimmers" refers to the author's

A) obsession with music.

B) desire to be a popular singer.

C) respect for other famous singers.

D) rapid change of fortune.

The use of the phrase "thrusting . . . aside" (lines 10-11) conveys a sense of the narrator's

A) distress.

B) resentment.

C) instability.

D) perseverance.

According to the passage, "misrepresentation" (line 21) refers to a discrepancy between

A) the narrator's actual proficiency at singing and her performance at the Town Hall.

B) the stated number of people in the attendance and the actual number.

C) the reaction of the audience to the Town Hall performance and the reviews of it.

D) the narrator's desire to please everybody and her inability to do so.

The third paragraph (lines 24-28) primarily focuses on

A) the importance of rehearsals.

B) the kindness of strangers.

C) a return to a musical career.

D) the consequences of a performance.

In line 33, the narrator's comment about having "given critics the opportunity" suggests that she

A) acknowledged that the unfavorable reviews were warranted.

B) intended to switch careers from music to journalism.

C) doubted that the critics who reviewed her did so objectively.

D) recognized the influence critics exert on a singer's career.

Summary

- SAT Reading is not the same as English Class Reading.

- Read to understand, not to assess.

- Read for information, not interpretation.

- Read only what you need, but read it carefully.

- Use the structure of the test to your advantage.

Chapter 4
Basic Approach to SAT Reading

In the Introduction, we talked about the genre of SAT Reading. In this chapter, we're going to discuss in more detail The Princeton Review's basic approach for attacking this peculiar genre.

Even for good readers, SAT Reading can be really tough. The difficulty can be summarized in the following ways:

- There's not enough time to read the passage and work the questions.
- Large parts of each passage don't seem to matter, so it's impossible to focus your reading.
- You end up reading a ton of stuff you don't need.
- The questions are written in a confusing way.
- It often seems like more than one answer can work.

We know what makes the SAT Reading section tough. Our Basic Approach is designed to address every single one of these issues!

The centerpiece of our approach will come as a relief. This section is a time-crunch for everyone, so here's our most important piece of advice.

> Don't read the passage until you know what you're looking for.

Think about it. Typically, you'll read the whole passage and then go to the questions, forget everything you just read, and read the whole passage again. Why not cut out that first step entirely? After all, you aren't scored on your ability to read quickly or to understand every aspect of the passage, as you might be in an English class. On SAT Reading, you get points for answering questions, so you'll want to get to those questions as quickly as possible and let them frame how you read.

Do the following:

1. **Read the Blurb**. The blurb may be only a sentence or two long, but it shouldn't be skipped. The blurb will help you identify the type of passage and tell you briefly what the passage is about.

2. **Select and Understand a Question**. Skip any confusing or time-consuming questions and do the questions that you understand first.

3. **Read What You Need.** Most answers will be located within a small window of about 10-12 lines. Find that window and read it carefully. You'll also be reading it with a specific goal in mind, which will help with efficiency.

4. **Predict the Answer.** Find something in the text that answers the question. Underline it whenever you can. Do not try to analyze or paraphrase. Stick with what's actually in the text.

5. **POE.** Find your answer by eliminating three bad answers. "Bad answers" are ones that are inconsistent with your prediction, or answers that contain one of ETS's common traps.

We'll work the Basic Approach through an SAT-style reading passage. We'll take it in chunks in exactly the way that we advise that you do on the test. It may feel like you're making a real leap of faith here, but you'll see that our technique contains everything you need.

Step One: Read the Blurb

The blurb is easy to ignore. It's usually a sentence or two long, and none of the questions will ask directly about it. Still, the blurb situates you within the passage. Because you won't be reading the passage in its entirety, the blurb may be the closest you get to a statement of the main idea. The blurb will also help you make a quick decision about when you want to do each passage as you work through the Reading test.

So, first things first, let's check out the blurb.

> The following passage was taken from the autobiography of Helen Keller, who was stricken with an illness that left her deaf and blind as a young child.

This blurb is only a sentence long, but it contains a good deal more than you may suspect. We know the passage is about Helen Keller. We also know that since it's an *autobiography*, it'll be in her own words. Chances are good the passage will have something to do with her experiences as a child unable to hear or speak.

Step Two: Select and Understand a Question

Your first impulse might be to try to do the questions in order. However, you don't have to do that just because the SAT presents the questions to you in a certain order. In fact, ETS has specifically said they will often put the general or main-idea questions first, followed by the specific questions. That means the very first question you get could ask *What is the main idea of the passage?* That's not a particularly efficient question to attempt first if you're trying to avoid reading the entire passage at once!

The students who perform best on the SAT are those who can make the test their own. We call this strategy POOD, or Personal Order of Difficulty, and because Reading has no Order of Difficulty, POOD is even more important.

Now, remember how little you've done on this passage so far. Maybe you've skimmed for a minute or so, but more than likely, you've read only the blurb. Do you think you're ready to answer a question like this one?

Skimming or Skipping: What's the Skinny?
Some people can benefit from a very quick skim of the passage here. We have found that most students work better with skipping the passage, but if you can use your skimming time wisely (that is, you don't just stare blankly at the passage for two minutes), go for it. Just remember that you don't get points for reading the passage. You get points for answering the questions, so that's where you should be spending most of your time.

The passage as a whole suggests that the narrator views language as

A) a necessary but frustrating part of life

B) the key to her appreciation of the world around her

C) a phenomenon that remains mysterious

D) the only method she can use to express her feelings

Absolutely not! This question asks about "the passage as a whole," but we haven't read a single line of it yet. Let's skip this question and come back to it when we've got a better sense of how the passage works.

The author's reference to being "at sea in a dense fog" (line 15) emphasizes that she felt

A) scared, because she felt like she was sinking in her dark, still life

B) angry, because she could not control her life

C) lost, because she had difficulty communicating with the world

D) confused, because her new teacher was trying to teach her too much.

SAT Reading questions will often not actually be questions. Start by turning the sentence into an actual question that begins with *what* or *why* and ends with a question mark. Something like this: *What does the author's use of the phrase "at sea in a dense fog" tell us about how she was feeling?*

Now we've got a question we can answer, and we know where to look for it in the passage. When you are selecting questions, take these things into account:

- **Line and paragraph references**. Both of these have the obvious advantage of directing you to the part of the passage that you need.
- **Lead words.** These are words that will "lead" you back to particular parts of the passage. Look in particular for proper nouns, italics, years and dates, or words in quotations—basically, anything you can easily scan for in the passage.
- **Chronology.** The SAT presents questions in chronological order through the passage. If you do the questions in order, you will work through the passage in order. That will help a great deal with your overall understanding of the passage.

- **Length of questions and answers**. Shorter questions and answers are usually easier on the SAT. There's less information to manage, and you can pay more particular attention to the words.

Now it's time to go to the passage.

Step Three: Read What You Need

Now that you know what you're looking for, you're ready to read. Mark the reference window (about 10-12 lines around the line reference or lead word), and read carefully. You've got enough time to do so, and you want to make sure you can pay attention to all the words you're reading.

Here's your window for this question.

> 15   Have you ever been at sea in a dense fog,
> when it seemed as if a tangible white darkness
> shut you in, and the great ship, tense and
> anxious, groped her way toward the shore with
> plummet and sounding-line, and you waited
> 20 with beating heart for something to happen? I
> was like that ship before my education began,
> only I was without compass or sounding-line,
> and had no way of knowing how near the
> harbour was. "Light! Give me light!" was the
> 25 wordless cry of my soul, and the light of love
> shone on me in that very hour.

The question asks about the phrase "at sea in a dense fog." Underline that phrase. Read carefully, looking for indicators that give you clues about *how the author was feeling*. Underline anything in the text that answers that question.

Step Four: Predict the Answer

Now that we've read our reference window, let's try to answer the question ourselves, using the text. Remember, we rewrote it like this:

> *What does the author's use of the phrase "at sea in a dense fog" tell us about how she was feeling?*

Look back at what you underlined in the window. You might have underlined *shut you in*, *groped her way toward the shore*, or *waited...for something to happen*. She goes on to say *I was like that ship...without compass*. Notice that at no point does the author explicitly say to the reader, "I felt like I was _____." However, there are many clues to help you figure out the answer to that question.

If the author is groping along without a compass, it's not a big leap to say that she is drifting, aimless, or lost.

Step Five: POE

Now, let's go back to the question and try to eliminate bad answers.

14

The author's reference to being "at sea in a dense fog" (line 15) emphasizes that she felt

A) scared, because she felt like she was sinking in her dark, still life

B) angry, because she could not control her life

C) lost, because she had difficulty communicating with the world

D) confused, because her new teacher was trying to teach her too much.

Because we've already predicted an answer, this question becomes significantly easier! We just need to eliminate anything that has nothing to do with our prediction. It might make sense that she's scared or angry or confused, but none of those have anything to do with drifting or being aimless or lost. Given the answer we came up with (*the author feels lost*), we won't be distracted by the others, and the answer must be (C).

Sometimes you won't be able to guess the answer with such precision, so make sure you're using POE aggressively, and above all, don't think! Strange as it is to say, thinking can be your enemy on the SAT. Any of these answers could be plausible in an English class, and your English teacher might encourage you to come up with your own interpretation. However, in the SAT genre of reading that we discussed in the Introduction, thinking and interpreting can get you into big trouble.

When eliminating answers, remember that **a correct answer must have support in the passage**. Always be ready to double-check your answer by asking yourself, "Where did I see that in the passage?" or "How can I prove that answer using the text?"

POE Criteria

The SAT can throw you a few curveballs, so be on the lookout for three special kinds of trap answers.

- **Mostly Right/Slightly Wrong**. These answers look just about perfect except for a word or two that don't match what's in the text. Remember: don't just read the passage carefully. Make sure you read the full question and each answer choice very carefully as well.

- **Could Be True**. These answers might initially look good because they make sense or seem logical. You might be able to support these answers in an English class, but they lack the concrete support from the text to make them correct SAT answers.
- **Deceptive Language**. The SAT will give you answer choices with words that look exactly like what you saw in the passage, but the words are put together in such a way that they don't actually say what you need them to say. Make sure you're reading carefully and not just matching words.

Try another question using the Basic Approach.

> Miss Sullivan had tried to impress it upon me
> that "m-u-g" is mug and that "w-a-t-e-r" is water,
> but I persisted in confounding the two. In despair
> 55 she had dropped the subject for the time, only to
> renew it at the first opportunity. I became impatient
> at her repeated attempts and, seizing the new doll,
> I dashed it upon the floor. I was keenly delighted
> when I felt the fragments of the broken doll at
> 60 my feet. Neither sorrow nor regret followed my
> passionate outburst. I had not loved the doll. In
> the still, dark world in which I lived there was no
> strong sentiment or tenderness.

18

The passage suggests the author broke the doll in order to

A) express her frustration at her inability to understand her teacher's lesson

B) lash out at her teacher's failure to instruct her properly

C) reveal the extent to which she felt enraged by her situation

D) see if her teacher would become angry at her childish actions

Rearrange the question into an actual question. You want to answer the question *Why does the author break the doll?* When you read your window, you find that she had *persisted in confounding* mug *and* water, and when her teacher tried again to teach her, the author *became impatient at [the] repeated attempts* and broke the doll.

Choice (D) can be eliminated right away. Choice (C) is too strong; she's *impatient*, not *enraged*. If you're down to (A) and (B), compare the answers and read carefully. Choice (B) might initially look good because the author is definitely lashing, but she isn't lashing out because the teacher is instructing her improperly. Choice (A) nicely paraphrases our prediction and is the right answer.

Vocabulary-in-Context Questions

Gone are the days of memorizing lists and lists of obscure five-syllable "SAT words," but the test will still use vocabulary to test your reading comprehension skills. In Vocabulary-in-Context (VIC) questions, you'll see familiar words, but they'll be used in less familiar ways. The key to these questions is to make sure you're going back to the text and reading carefully! Don't assume you know what the word means. Find clues in the text that allow you to replace the word with something else that has a similar meaning.

> I guessed vaguely from my mother's signs
> and from the hurrying to and fro in the house
> that something unusual was about to happen,
> *Line* so I went to the door and waited on the steps.
> 5 The afternoon sun penetrated the mass of
> honeysuckle that covered the porch, and fell
> on my upturned face. My fingers lingered
> almost unconsciously on the familiar leaves and
> blossoms which had just come forth to greet the
> 10 sweet southern spring. I did not know what the
> future held of marvel or surprise for me. Anger
> and bitterness had preyed upon me continually
> for weeks and a deep languor had succeeded
> this passionate struggle.

13

As used in line 13, the word "succeeded" most nearly means

A) accomplished

B) split

C) followed

D) broken

Find the word *succeeded* in line 13 (the final sentence) and mark it out. Carefully read your window and use context clues to come up with your own word for the sentence. In the text, you see that the author *waited on the steps* and turned her face to the sun, and her *fingers lingered*. She also mentions that *anger and bitterness had preyed* upon her for weeks but then there was a *deep languor*. Since we have evidence that she's currently in the deep languor, we could replace *succeeded* with something like *came after* or *ended*. Be sure to use your prediction to POE, not any prior knowledge you have about what *succeeded* means. Choice (A) is a convincing definition for *succeeded*, but it has nothing to do with our prediction. Choice (C) is closest to *came after*.

Best Evidence Questions

On every Reading passage, you will see a question or two that look like this:

> Which choice provides the best evidence for the
> answer to the previous question?

According to ETS, these questions will test your ability to "cite the textual evidence that best supports a given claim or point." If you are following the Basic Approach, some of these "best evidence" questions will be a literal two-for-one deal. Let's take a look.

15

The author's reference to "finger play" in line 36 emphasizes her

A) childish need to learn by playing games with dolls and toys

B) teacher's technique for teaching her grammar

C) initial inability to understand that she was spelling words with her hands

D) opinion that learning sign language was as easy as a child's game

---

16

Which choice provides the best evidence for the answer to the previous question?

A) Lines 33-35 ("When I . . . d-o-l-l")

B) Lines 40-42 ("I did . . . existed")

C) Lines 43-45 ("But my . . . name")

D) Lines 49-51 ("Earlier in . . . w-a-t-e-r")

When you see a set of a paired questions, the first thing you need to decide is if you can answer the first question by itself. It will look like any other specific question on the test. You'll have a line reference or lead word to use, or you can use chronology to find the location of the window.

This question gives us a line reference, so we can treat it just like any other specific question. Let's follow the steps of the Basic Approach.

Step 2: Read and Understand the Question

Turn the original question into an actual question. Let's ask it like this:

> Why does the author mention "finger play" in line 36?

Let's read the passage and find out.

Step 3: Read What You Need

This question comes right in the middle of a paragraph that's 11 lines, so we have a well-defined window provided for us. Find the phrase "finger play" in the window and underline it. Then carefully read your window and see if you can find anything that indicates why the author mentions "finger play."

> The morning after my teacher came she led
> me into her room and gave me a doll. When I had
> played with it a little while, Miss Sullivan slowly
> 35 spelled into my hand the word "d-o-l-l." I was at
> once interested in this finger play and tried to
> imitate it. When I finally succeeded in making the
> letters correctly I was flushed with childish pleasure
> and pride. Running downstairs to my mother I
> 40 held up my hand and made the letters for doll. I did
> not know that I was spelling a word or even that
> words existed; I was simply making my fingers go
> in monkeylike imitation. But my teacher had been
> with me several weeks before I understood that
> 45 everything has a name.

In the text, the author says she was *interested in this finger play* and *tried to imitate it*. This tells you *what* she was doing, but doesn't quite answer the *why* question. Make sure you read enough to answer the question that is asked. When you continue reading the window, the author further explains *I did not know that I was spelling a word or even that words existed*. There's your prediction! The author calls it "finger play" because it is a game to her, not a way to spell words.

15

The author's reference to "finger play" in line 36 emphasizes her

A) childish need to learn by playing games with dolls and toys.

B) teacher's technique for teaching her grammar.

C) initial inability to understand that she was spelling words with her hands.

D) opinion that learning sign language was as easy as a child's game.

Use your prediction to eliminate anything that is inconsistent with what you found in the text. Choices (B) and (D) have nothing to do with your prediction. Choice (A) has some words that look good initially (*childish, games, dolls*), but that answer doesn't match the prediction. Choice (C) is a direct paraphrase of your underlined prediction.

Once you've answered the first question in a specific paired set, you've got what you need for the "best evidence" question. Since you used evidence from the text to answer the question, you've already found the best evidence! Which line did you underline? That's your answer. (Note: the full lines have been written out for this question, but you'll normally be given only the first and last words.)

16

Which choice provides the best evidence for the answer to the previous question?

A) Lines 33-35 ("When I ... d-o-l-l")

B) Lines 40-42 ("I did ... existed")

C) Lines 43-45 ("But my ... name")

D) Lines 49-51 ("Earlier in ... w-a-t-e-r")

General Questions and the Golden Thread

Once you have answered the specific questions, underlined lead words, and bracketed windows for careful reading, you will have a solid idea of what's happening in the text and how the general structure fits together. More importantly, you will have an understanding of what the test writers think is important. This will make the general questions more approachable and much more efficient than they would have been if you'd started with them. Let's take a look at the entire passage, remembering what we've answered so far.

The following passage was excerpted from the autobiography of Helen Keller, who was stricken with an illness that left her deaf and blind as a young child. *The Story of My Life* by Helen Keller. Copyright 1902.

I guessed vaguely from my mother's signs and from the hurrying to and fro in the house that something unusual was about to happen,

Line

so I went to the door and waited on the steps.

5   The afternoon sun penetrated the mass of honeysuckle that covered the porch, and fell on my upturned face. My fingers lingered almost unconsciously on the familiar leaves and blossoms which had just come forth to greet the

10   sweet southern spring. I did not know what the future held of marvel or surprise for me. Anger and bitterness had preyed upon me continually for weeks and a deep languor had succeeded this passionate struggle.

15   Have you ever been at sea in a dense fog, when it seemed as if a tangible white darkness shut you in, and the great ship, tense and anxious, groped her way toward the shore with plummet and sounding-line, and you waited with beating

20   heart for something to happen? I was like that ship before my education began, only I was without compass or sounding-line, and had no way of knowing how near the harbour was. "Light! Give me light!" was the wordless cry of

25   my soul, and the light of love shone on me in that very hour.

I felt approaching footsteps, I stretched out my hand as I supposed to my mother. Someone took it, and I was caught up and held close in the

30   arms of her who had come to reveal all things to me, and, more than all things else, to love me.

The morning after my teacher came she led me into her room and gave me a doll. When I had played with it a little while, Miss Sullivan slowly

35   spelled into my hand the word "d-o-l-l." I was at once interested in this finger play and tried to imitate it. When I finally succeeded in making the letters correctly I was flushed with childish pleasure and pride. Running downstairs to my

40   mother I held up my hand and made the letters for doll. I did not know that I was spelling a word or even that words existed; I was simply making my fingers go in monkeylike imitation. But my teacher had been with me several weeks before I

45   understood that everything has a name.

One day, while I was playing with my new doll, Miss Sullivan put my big rag doll into my lap also, spelled "d-o-l-l" and tried to make me understand that "d-o-l-l" applied to both. Earlier

50   in the day we had a tussle over the words "m-u-g" and "w-a-t-e-r." Miss Sullivan had tried to impress it upon me that "m-u-g" is mug and that "w-a-t-e-r" is water, but I persisted in confounding the two. In despair she had dropped the subject for

55   the time, only to renew it at the first opportunity. I became impatient at her repeated attempts and, seizing the new doll, I dashed it upon the floor. I was keenly delighted when I felt the fragments of the broken doll at my feet. Neither sorrow

60   nor regret followed my passionate outburst. I had not loved the doll. In the still, dark world in which I lived there was no strong sentiment or tenderness.

We walked down the path to the well-house,

65   attracted by the fragrance of the honeysuckle with which it was covered. Someone was pumping water and my teacher placed my hand under the spout. As the cool stream gushed over one hand she spelled into the other the word

70   water, first slowly, then rapidly. I stood still, my whole attention fixed upon the motions of her fingers. Suddenly I felt a misty consciousness as of something forgotten—a thrill of returning thought; and somehow the mystery of language

75   was revealed to me. I knew then that "w-a-t-e-r" meant the wonderful cool something that was flowing over my hand. That living word awakened my soul, gave it light, hope, joy, set it free! There were barriers still, it is true, but barriers that

80   could in time be swept away.

I left the well-house eager to learn. Everything had a name, and each name gave birth to a new thought. As we returned to the house every object which I touched seemed to quiver with life. That

85   was because I saw everything with the strange, new sight that had come to me. On entering the door I remembered the doll I had broken. I felt my way to the hearth and picked up the pieces. I tried vainly to put them together. Then my eyes

90   filled with tears; for I realized what I had done, and for the first time I felt repentance and sorrow.

16

The author's attitude toward breaking the doll changes from

A) sorrow to understanding.

B) excitement to disgust.

C) anger to joy.

D) pleasure to regret.

This question doesn't tell you where to go in the passage, but you've got a useful lead word. We've already answered one question about the broken doll, so we know we're looking somewhere around lines 58-59.

Notice this question asks about the author's *change in attitude*. Let's see what's in the text. She says she was *keenly delighted* when she felt the fragments and *neither sorrow nor regret* followed the outburst. We don't have enough information to figure out the change, but we know how she felt at first. Using the context clues we can eliminate (A) and (C) simply by looking at the first words. Remember, if even one word is wrong, the whole answer choice is wrong.

Now we need to figure out the change. It'll have to come somewhere in the last two paragraphs, so skim through those to look for a reference to the *broken doll*. It's in line 87. She says *For the first time I felt repentance and sorrow*. This makes (D) the best answer.

Earlier we looked at a specific paired set. Those were a two-for-one deal, remember, as long as you consistently used the Basic Approach. Not all paired questions will be like that, though. There will be questions that ask about the passage as a whole or questions that don't have lead words or line references.

Take a look at the following paired set.

19

It can be inferred from the passage that the author would most likely agree with which of the following statements?

A) Without language, humans are destined to feel anger and bitterness.

B) People often destroy treasured objects without fully realizing the consequences of their actions.

C) Learning can free a person from the barriers they construct around themselves.

D) Children need positive role models to help shape their lives.

20

Which choice provides the best evidence for the answer to the previous question?

A) Lines 1-4 ("I guessed . . . steps")

B) Lines 58-60 ("I was . . . outburst")

C) Lines 68-70 ("As the . . . rapidly)

D) Lines 77-80 ("That living . . . away")

If you try to answer question 19 first and then find the answer to question 20, you'll be taking part in one of the worst scavenger hunts ever. There are no line references or lead words to tell you where to go in the passage, and the best evidence lines are scattered from the beginning to the end of the passage. Trying to answer these the same way you answered the earlier example—a specific paired set—will eat up your valuable time. Luckily, we have another strategy for you to use.

Parallel POE is a strategy you can use to answer paired sets when you can't easily answer the first question. Think for a moment about how paired questions must operate. The correct answer to the first question *must* be supported by an answer to the evidence question, and the correct answer to the evidence question *must* support an answer to the first question. In other words, if there is an evidence answer that doesn't support an answer to the first question, it is wrong. Period. Likewise, if there is an answer to the first question that isn't supported by an evidence answer, it is wrong. Period.

Let's use this to our advantage! Rather than worry about what the first question is asking and what the answer might be, just start making connections between the two answer sets. If an evidence answer supports a first question answer, literally draw a line connecting them. You should not expect to have four connections. If you are lucky, you will have only one connection: the correct answer pair. Otherwise, you might have two or three connections and will then (and only then) worry about the first question. The important thing to remember is that any answer choice in the first question that isn't physically connected to an evidence answer—and any evidence answer that isn't connected to an answer in the first question—must be eliminated.

Let's take a look at how this first Parallel POE pass would look. (The paired questions have been arranged in two columns to help understand this, and the lines have been written out for your convenience. This does not represent what you will see on the official test.)

19. It can be inferred from the passage that the author would most likely agree with which of the following statements?	20. Which choice provides the best evidence for the answer to the previous question?
A) Without language, humans are destined to feel anger and bitterness.	A) "I guessed vaguely from my mother's signs and from the hurrying to and fro in the house that something unusual was about to happen, so I went to the door and waited on the steps."
B) People often destroy treasured objects without fully realizing the consequences of their actions.	B) "I was keenly delighted when I felt the fragments of the broken doll at my feet. Neither sorrow nor regret followed my passionate outburst."
C) Learning can free a person from the barriers they construct around themselves.	C) "As the cool stream gushed over one hand she spelled into the other the word water, first slowly, then rapidly."
D) Children need positive role models to help shape their lives.	D) "That living word awakened my soul, gave it light, hope, joy, set it free! There were barriers still, it is true, but barriers that could in time be swept away."

Don't worry about the question itself yet. Go straight to the "best evidence" lines.

- 20 (A) says *"I guessed vaguely from my mother's signs and from the hurrying to and fro in the house that something unusual was about to happen, so I went to the door and waited on the steps."* Read through all four answers to Q19. Notice those lines don't support any of the answers from Q20, so you can eliminate 20 (A). It doesn't matter what the question asks: if the best evidence lines don't support any answers in the previous question, they cannot be the right answer.
- 20 (B) says *"I was keenly delighted when I felt the fragments of the broken doll at my feet. Neither sorrow nor regret followed my passionate outburst."* Now read through the answers to Q19. Notice any lines to support 20 (B)? Physically draw a line to connect 20 (B) and 19 (B). The lines don't support any other answers, so move on.
- 20 (C) says *"As the cool stream gushed over one hand she spelled into the other the word water, first slowly, then rapidly."* These lines don't support any Q19 answers, so you can eliminate 20 (C).
- 20 (D) says *"That living word awakened my soul, gave it light, hope, joy, set it free! There were barriers still, it is true, but barriers that could in time be swept away."* These lines support 19 (C), so draw a line connecting them.

At this point, 19 (A) and 19 (D) don't have lines that support them. If there is no evidence given to support those answers, they cannot be right either. Eliminate them. You should be left with something that looks like this:

19. It can be inferred from the passage that the author would most likely agree with which of the following statements?	20. Which choice provides the best evidence for the answer to the previous question?
A) ~~Without language, humans are destined to feel anger and bitterness.~~	A) ~~"I guessed vaguely from my mother's signs and from the hurrying to and fro in the house that something unusual was about to happen, so I went to the door and waited on the steps."~~
B) People often destroy treasured objects ~~without fully~~ realizing the consequences of their actions.	B) "I was keenly delighted when I felt the fragments of the broken doll at my feet. Neither sorrow nor regret followed my passionate outburst."
C) Learning can free a person from the barriers they construct around themselves.	C) ~~"As the cool stream gushed over one hand she spelled into the other the word water, first slowly, then rapidly."~~
D) ~~Children need positive role models to help shape their lives.~~	D) "That living word awakened my soul, gave it light, hope, joy, set it free! There were barriers still, it is true, but barriers that could in time be swept away."

You have a lovely 50/50 split now, and it's time to look back at the question. Question 19 asks which statement the author would agree with. While she did destroy a possession and later regret it, there is no evidence that the author would agree people *often* destroy treasured objects. She was speaking of a single incident that happened to her, not a generalization about all people. You can eliminate 19 (B), which also eliminates 20 (B). The correct answer is 19 (C)/20 (D).

Now let's go back to that first question we skipped at the beginning because we didn't want to read the entire passage. You still haven't read the entire passage, not every word from start to finish, but you'll see that it doesn't matter. You've read what you need.

The passage as a whole suggests the narrator views language as

A) a necessary but frustrating part of life.

B) the key to her appreciation of the world around her.

C) a phenomenon that remains mysterious.

D) the only method she can use to express her feelings.

Without going back to the text, see what you can eliminate! Choice (A) is gone; although you could argue the author sees language as necessary, her frustration happened before she began to learn language. Choice (B) looks pretty good, so we'll hang on to it. Choice (C) doesn't work. Choice (D) might initially look good, but think back to the passage. The author did a pretty good job expressing her frustration when she broke the doll, and that was before she had language. This is a good example of a Mostly Right/Slightly Wrong answer. It looks really good except for the word "only." Eliminate it. Choice (B) is the right answer, and you got there without having to read the passage in its entirety.

BASIC APPROACH EXERCISE

Questions 1-6 are based on the following passage.

The following passage, adapted from a 2005 article, discusses the common garden slug.

As a professional ecologist, I find one image held by amateur gardeners to be particularly irksome: the idea that a "pest-free" garden,
Line cleansed of any creatures that might threaten the
5 gardener's precious plants, is a healthy garden.

As an example, consider *Deroceras reticulatum*, otherwise known as the common garden slug. The average gardener believes that this creature is nothing more than an enemy to
10 be exterminated. In attempting to beautify their yards, gardeners utilize an impressive arsenal of chemical weapons designed to bombard the slugs from the air as well as attack them on the ground. Success is attained only when no trace of
15 slugs can be found, although the wary gardener must watch and wait for their return, since permanently ridding a garden of slugs can prove nearly impossible.

There are important consequences that result
20 from viewing the slug as mortal enemy. Repeated spraying of chemicals damages topsoil and saps it of essential nutrients. To compensate, gardeners frequently apply artificial fertilizers, which encourage plant growth in the short term, but
25 damage the soil in the long term. As a result, the weakened garden is left susceptible to invasion by all sorts of pests, requiring further application of chemical sprays. Thus, in attempting to attain the cherished ideal of a pristine, pest-free
30 garden, amateur gardeners create a vicious circle: contamination, followed by artificial regeneration and a slow depletion of natural resources, followed by more contamination.

It seems to me that a solution to this dilemma
35 starts with the recognition that a healthy garden is not one that has been emptied of every organism that we find objectionable. Even creatures as repulsive as slugs have a role to play in a properly functioning ecosystem. Instead of trying to rid
40 ourselves of slugs, wouldn't we be better off coming to some sort of accommodation with them?

The gardener who decides to coexist with the garden slug soon discovers that its nefarious reputation is at least partially unwarranted.
45 Although it is true that the slug can devour garden plants from the roots up with frightening efficiency, it also produces nutrients for the soil, helping other plants to grow. The diet of a slug consists not just of living plants, but also of plant
50 waste and mold, making this diminutive creature into a sort of natural recycling center. The unique structure of a slug's digestive system enables it to take these discarded products, transform them into the nutrients that plants need to thrive, and
55 then release these nutrients into the soil by means of viscous, slime-like excretions.

In order to reap the benefits that slugs provide while at the same time minimizing the slug's destructive effects, the gardener should focus
60 on two tasks: reducing the slug population to manageable proportions, and diverting the slug's efforts into activities that do the least harm. There are a number of ways to control the population of slugs without resorting to noxious chemicals,
65 but one of the easiest is to welcome a few of the slug's natural predators into the garden. Ground beetles, toads, and hedgehogs are all naturally predisposed to hunt slugs. Providing a habitat for these creatures will ensure that the slug
70 population is held to reasonable levels.

To limit the slug's destructive effects, the gardener should provide sacrificial plants for the slug to dine on. Lettuce, Zinnias, and Marigolds are all considered delicacies by slugs; the loss of
75 a few of these plants will not distress the typical gardener. At the same time, natural barriers of white ash or diatomaceous earth should be placed around plants that are held in higher esteem by the gardener. These barriers will naturally deter
80 slugs, especially if tastier and more accessible treats are available nearby.

It is true that these measures may seem cumbersome, but in the long run the benefits outweigh the temporary inconvenience to
85 the gardener. A garden should not be a place devoid of all creatures that the gardener finds troublesome; it should be a place in which

competing forces balance each other out. By
exchanging the ideal of a pest-free garden for
90 one in which pests are tolerated and managed,
the gardener ensures a healthier garden and
minimizes the hazards associated with chemical
pesticides.

1

The author would most likely describe the
"important consequences" (line 19) as

A) a decisive victory.

B) a complicated affair.

C) a superior result.

D) an unintended reaction.

2

The author would most probably characterize
the "cherished ideal" (line 29) as

A) carefully planned.

B) deeply insightful.

C) inconclusive.

D) misguided.

3

The primary purpose of lines 34-41 ("It seems . . .
with them") is to

A) explain people's responses to certain animals.

B) propose an alternative course of action.

C) offer evidence of environmental destruction.

D) praise the scope of a comprehensive effort.

4

In line 65, "welcome" most nearly means

A) acknowledge.

B) thank.

C) return.

D) introduce.

5

Lines 71-76 ("To limit . . . gardener") imply that

A) predators will inevitably destroy a garden
unless the gardener takes drastic action.

B) plants that appeal to slugs are not necessarily
considered valuable by gardeners.

C) slugs prefer Lettuce, Zinnias, and Marigolds
to all other types of plants.

D) gardeners should be sensitive to the needs of
other species.

6

The last paragraph chiefly serves to

A) restate the author's evidence.

B) suggest a direction for further study.

C) intensify an emotional effect.

D) underscore the author's position.

Summary

Let's revisit our list of challenges from the beginning of this chapter. We said the following things make SAT reading difficult:

○ There's not enough time to read the passage and work the questions.

○ Large parts of each passage don't seem to matter, so it's impossible to focus your reading.

○ You end up reading a ton of stuff you don't need.

○ The questions are written in a confusing way.

○ It often seems like more than one answer can work.

The Basic Approach addresses all of these difficulties in the following ways:

○ When we skip or skim the passage rather than reading it in its entirety, we save a tremendous amount of time.

○ When we are guided by the questions, we read only what we need to answer those questions.

○ When we are guided by the questions, we don't read the stuff we don't need.

○ When we rewrite the questions, we make them clearer and more answerable.

○ When we use the text to predict and defend the answer, we are much less likely to pick distracting answers.

Chapter 5
Reading Exercises:
Answers and
Explanations

CHAPTER 3: READING INTRODUCTION EXERCISE ANSWERS

1. **C** The question asks about the whole passage, but it also quotes a specific line, so begin there. The narrator's "complex about music" involves "hopes" that "crashed too low" (lines 1–3), and this led her to obsess negatively about the concert she performed in. If you stop there, (A) might seem like the correct answer, but instead, the narrator relates that while her poor performance at Town Hall made her doubt her ambition to be a singer, she eventually resolved to do it anyway. You can now eliminate (D), which is contradicted by the passage, and see that (C) offers the best summary. Choice (A) is incorrect because the passage doesn't tell us whether she changed careers, although it implies she did not. Choice (B) Could Be True, but it does not explain the complex.

2. **B** The question asks what "fortunate swimmers" means in this context. Read around the window for line 6, and it should be clear that this is an extended metaphor—"plunged" into "the mainstream of American musical life"—and that "fortunate swimmers" are those who performed at Town Hall. She had wanted, in other words, to be famous. Choice (B), "desire to be a popular singer," is basically saying that she wanted to be famous.

3. **A** The question asks what the quoted phrase is trying to convince readers of. By reading around line 8, you can see that the narrator's memories of the performance at Town Hall are either vivid or pushed (thrust) aside. The ones she remembers are negative, which eliminates (D), and the mood of panic is closest to (A), which essentially means "upset." There's nothing in the passage to suggest that the author resents anybody, (B), or is unstable, (C).

4. **B** The question asks which two contradictory statements or facts constitute the "misrepresentation." Reading the reference in context, we find that the narrator believes she might have performed better if she "had not been told the auditorium was full," and that a "misrepresentation like that can throw you off balance." Tying together these two statements, we can conclude that the misrepresentation refers to the number of people actually in attendance versus those the narrator expected to see. Choice (B) best expresses this relationship. Choice (A) is incorrect because the author's actual skill as a singer is not mentioned here. Choice (C) is incorrect because the reaction of the audience is never mentioned. Choice (D) is incorrect because the narrator's desire to please everyone is not mentioned in this paragraph.

5. **D** The question asks what happens in the third paragraph. Reading from there, after the Town Hall performance, the author "stopped going regularly to Mr. Boghetti's studio," because the "fiasco had shaken" her. In other words, the paragraph desecribes what happened to the author as a result of her Town Hall performance. Choice (D) matches this. While the passage implies that she attended rehearsals with Mr. Boghetti, their importance, (A), is not mentioned in the passage. Choices (B) and (C) are also misleading—the mother is kind in another passage, but is not a stranger, and while the passage concludes with a decision to return to singing as a potential career, it doesn't happen in the specified third paragraph.

6.   **A**   The question asks what the narrator means by saying she gave "critics the opportunity." According to the sentence, the author realizes that the "criticism was right" and that her performance had enabled them to write negative reviews. This suggests that the author knows that she had a role in earning the unfavorable criticism. This is best paraphrased by (A). Choice (C) contradicts this point and can be eliminated, as can (B), as there's nothing about "journalism" in this passage. Choice (D) Could Be True, but the passage doesn't actually say that this is something she recognized, and so it should be eliminated as well.

CHAPTER 4: BASIC APPROACH TO READING ANSWERS

1.   **D**   The question asks for another way to describe these "important consequences." The author describes them as a vicious circle: "contamination, followed by…a slow depletion…, followed by more contamination." Only (D), an unintended reaction, is a good match. The other answers are not supported by the passage.

2.   **D**   The question is asking how the author feels about this "cherished ideal." There's a contrast in the surrounding sentence, in which the "attempt" to pursue this ideal leads to its opposite, a "vicious circle." This implies that it's misguided, (D), and the other choices can be eliminated.

3.   **B**   The question is asking for the main idea of the paragraph. Reading the window shows that in the previous passage, the author was attempting to show how trying to wipe out slugs doesn't work, and in this paragraph, is proposing "an alternative course of action": learning to live with the slugs. Choice (B) matches that prediction, and is correct. Choice (A) Could Be True, in that it does explain how people are dealing with the slugs, but that's only a part of the passage, not the author's purpose. Choices (C) and (D) don't appear in this passage.

4.   **D**   Remember to use the context of the passage when considering the definition of a word, and not your own prior usage of "welcome." In this case, try coming up with your own synonym. Something like "bring" would work, because the author states that "providing a habitat for these creatures" would help to hold down the slug population. Choice (D) is the best fit for that prediction. Choice (C) is close, but we don't know that the natural predators had been in the garden before now, so there's no way of knowing if they are returning to the garden.

5.   **B**   The question is asking what the point of this selection is, which comes down to why the author bothers to tell us any of it. Since the author is trying to save the slugs, it should be clear that the author is trying to stress that the slugs can be appeased with plants that the gardeners don't care about protecting, which is closest to (B). Choices (A) and (C) are too extreme, while (D) is not mentioned.

6.   **D**   The question is asking for the purpose of the last paragraph. In general, and in this case, too, this is usually a restatement or summary of the author's main point, which makes (D) the best match. The other choices are all things that can be done in a conclusion, but none of them happen in this passage.

Chapter 6
Synthesis and
Reading Drill

We have one more question category to look at, and then it's time to put the Basic Approach, POE Criteria, and Parallel POE to the test! Over the next several pages you will find sample passages from Science, History/Social Studies, and World Literature. As you work through the passages, the main question you should have in mind is, "Where is the support in the text?" When you circle your answer, you should have concrete evidence either from the text or from earlier questions to back up that circle. After you finish each drill, check your answers in the next chapter.

SYNTHESIS QUESTIONS

While most of the questions in your Reading passages will be consistent with what we've seen up to this point, there will be two additional question types that will show up somewhere in the Science or History/Social Studies passages.

1. **Quantitative Information (charts, graphs, tables)**
   You may see some type of graphic, like a chart, table, or graph, that connects to the passage in some way. The graphic will be straightforward. Make sure you identify the variables and read the graphic carefully. When you get to the question, the key is making sure you can put your pencil on the data point that supports keeping or eliminating the answer.

2. **Dual Passages**
   One of your Science or History/Social Studies passages will be a dual passage set. There will be two shorter passages about one topic. You will have a few questions about the first passage, a few about the second passage, and the remaining questions will ask about both passages together.

Although the two passages will be about the same topic, there will also be differences that you'll need to pay attention to. Rather than attempting to read and understand both passages at the same time, just follow the Basic Approach and focus on one at a time.

The questions for Passage 1 will come before the questions for Passage 2, and the questions for each passage follow the order of the passage, just like single-passage questions. The questions about both passages will follow the questions for Passage 2.

For questions asking you to *compare* or *contrast* both passages, it's helpful to consider one passage at a time rather than trying to juggle both passages at the same time. First, find the answer for the first passage (or the second passage if that one is easier) and use POE to narrow down the answer choices. Then find the answer in the other passage and use POE to arrive at the correct answer. This will save time and keep you from confusing the two passages when you're evaluating the answer choices. Always keep in mind that the same POE criteria apply, no matter how two-passage questions are presented.

- If a question asks what is supported by both passages, make sure that you find specific support in both passages, and be wary of all the usual trap answers.
- If a question is about an issue on which the authors of the two passages disagree or on how the passages relate to one another, make sure you find support in each passage for the author's particular opinion.
- If the question asks how one author would respond to the other passage, find out what was said in that other passage, and then find out exactly what the author you are asked about said on that exact topic.

The bottom line is that if you are organized and remember your basic reading comprehension strategy, you'll see that two-passage questions are no harder than single-passage questions! In the following drill, you'll have a chance to try a set of dual passages.

QUANTITATIVE QUESTION

This drill contains questions that ask about graphs in the passage. Follow the Basic Approach through the rest of the questions. When you get to the graphs, make sure you can put your pencil on the data point you need to answer the question.

Reading Drill

Passage A

Adaptive Vaccination Strategies to Mitigate Pandemic Influenza: Mexico as a Case Study Gerardo Chowell, Cécile Viboud, Xiaohong Wang, Stefano M. Bertozzi, Mark A. Miller

Virological subtyping of a novel pandemic virus can provide an early clue to target vaccination efforts. While the elderly are

Line
5 normally at most risk for severe outcomes during seasonal influenza, warranting the targeting of vaccination for direct protection to that group, they may have residual protection during pandemics. By contrast, younger groups generally respond better to vaccine and provide a

10 greater reduction of transmission. Given residual protection in seniors in early pandemic waves, younger age groups become a clear priority group for pandemic vaccine allocation. In the current 2009 pandemic, those who were born between

15 1919 and around 1957 would have been first exposed to H1N1 during their childhood and may enjoy protection against S-OIV infection and death, as observed in the early wave of S-OIV in Mexico.

20 Several studies have assessed the effects of potential vaccination strategies against pandemic influenza in terms of reducing morbidity and mortality based on priority age groups, transmissibility, timing of vaccination efforts,

25 and number of years of life lost. A recent study has evaluated the influenza vaccine allocation problem considering a vaccination coverage of 35% at the pandemic onset or near the pandemic peak when the population is stratified by age

30 and low and high risks. Results suggest that vaccines should be allocated to individuals with high-risk complications whenever the vaccine becomes available late in the pandemic (close to the peak) while targeting high transmitter groups

35 (children) is more effective when the vaccine is available close to the start of the pandemic. Most studies of influenza vaccination strategies to date have assumed a given epidemiological profile based on past influenza epidemics and pandemics

40 but have not necessarily considered novel profiles

that could arise in future pandemics. Given high levels of uncertainty as to the epidemiology of the next outbreak of S-OIV or other novel influenza virus, unfortunately, no single strategy can fit

45 all scenarios. Our adaptive strategy is flexible enough to accommodate a range of possible scenarios illustrating our experience with past pandemics, and potentially new ones.

We note that other intervention strategies

50 have been proposed to mitigate the burden of pandemic influenza. Social distancing and facemasks have been suggested as mitigation strategies, but their efficacy against pandemics remains debated. Strategies involving antiviral

55 treatments are helpful to mitigate disease burden, but resources are limited and effectiveness assumes speedy delivery and susceptibility of circulating viruses. Any of these interventions could be used in combination with the adaptive

60 vaccine allocation strategy proposed here.

Mexico began vaccinating against seasonal influenza in 2004, and annual campaigns target children 6 to 23 months old, adults over 65 years, and those with chronic conditions. In the past,

65 Mexico has relied on other countries for influenza vaccine production, which in the setting of a pandemic is likely to be available in limited supplies. Although a preparedness and response plan against pandemic influenza for Mexico had

70 been drafted with the objective of optimizing resources and conducting a timely response, it lacks guidance on how to define priority groups in the scenario of a limited vaccine supply. Our study shows that even limited vaccine supplies, if

75 used optimally, can have an impact on mitigating disease burden in a middle-income country like Mexico.

There are many limitations to policy models with respect to choice of parameter

80 estimates and the incorporation of bio-medical, environmental, operational, political, economic features. No one model can claim to incorporate all assumptions and features given the limited data on the epidemiology of novel pandemic

85 viruses and paucity of data on contact rates, especially in Mexico. This model illustrates

a prioritization scheme based on age groups but does not further discriminate other sub-groups such as those persons with other medical conditions, including pregnancy. Models do not necessarily provide answers but help articulate the questions, assumptions and numerous uncertainties in rapidly evolving circumstances as a tool to formulate rational policy based on the best available evidence. Pandemics evolve rapidly relative to capabilities to enact policies; therefore, pre-formulated adaptive strategies can readily take into account new data. Knowledge of the specific sub-type circulating and real-time information on age-specific rates of severe outcomes are crucial to help policy makers infer who may be at most risk, and tailor intervention strategies accordingly. These adaptive pandemic strategies could be readily adopted by other countries.

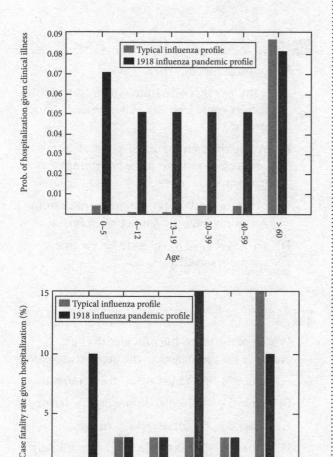

12

Based on the passage, the authors' statement "they may have residual protection during pandemics" (lines 7-8) implies that

A) younger people respond better to vaccines than older people do.

B) compared to younger people, elderly people aren't a priority during pandemics.

C) elderly people may be able to fight off pandemics better than younger people can.

D) younger people are less likely to get influenza.

13

The authors use the word "enjoy" in line 17 to indicate that children who are exposed to influenza

A) are unlikely to die from it as adults.

B) handle the effects of the illness well.

C) are happy to overcome it.

D) may have some immunity to it later in life.

14

A politician claims that Mexico is in dire need of more funds for creating its own vaccines, since, unless the majority of citizens are vaccinated, a pandemic could wipe out the population. Which of the following statements in the passage contradicts the politician's claim?

A) Lines 10-13 ("Given residual . . . vaccine allocation.")

B) Lines 41-45 ("Given high . . . all scenarios.")

C) Lines 73-77 ("Our study . . . like Mexico.")

D) Lines 82-86 ("No one model . . . in Mexico.")

The authors' main purpose of including the information about how "Mexico has relied on other countries for influenza vaccine production" (lines 65-66) is to

A) support the proposed Mexican vaccination strategy.

B) encourage Mexico to create more influenza vaccinations.

C) deter Mexico from seeking foreign vaccine producers.

D) discourage Mexico from venturing into a new industry.

Based on the figures, which choice gives the correct percentage of the case fatality rate given hospitalization percentage for the 1918 Influenza Pandemic Profile for ages 0-5?

A) 1%

B) 7%

C) 10%

D) 15%

Do the data in the tables support the authors' statement that elderly patients have some residual protection during pandemics?

A) Yes, the probability of hospitalization for age groups above 5 years and below 60 years is much higher for the 1918 pandemic than for the typical influenza profile.

B) Yes, the probability of hospitalization and the case fatality rate given hospitalization percentage for people older than 60 are higher for the typical influenza profile than for the 1918 pandemic.

C) No, the probability of hospitalization for age groups above 5 years and below 60 years is much higher for the 1918 pandemic than for the typical influenza profile.

D) No, the probability of hospitalization and the case fatality rate given hospitalization percentage for people older than 60 are lower for the typical influenza profile than for the 1918 pandemic.

According to the figures, which of the following pairs of percentages provides evidence in support of the answer to the previous question?

A) 15% and 10%

B) 15% and 5%

C) 15% and 2.5%

D) 10% and 7%

As it used in line 88, the word "discriminate" most nearly means

A) differentiate.

B) rank.

C) condescend.

D) victimize.

The passage suggests that

A) a strategy that takes into account a variety of factors could lead to a better disease control policy.

B) young children should be given all doses of vaccine available at the beginning of a pandemic.

C) other methods to prevent pandemics from spreading have proven to be helpful.

D) viruses change too quickly for vaccine producers to adapt.

Which of the following provides the best evidence for the answer to the previous question?

A) Lines 34-36 ("targeting . . . the pandemic.")

B) Lines 51-54 ("Social distancing . . . debated.")

C) Lines 54-58 ("Strategies . . . viruses.")

D) Lines 98-103 ("Knowledge . . . accordingly.")

DUAL PASSAGES

When you have two smaller passages at once, remember to do the questions about Passage 1 first, followed by the questions about Passage 2. As you're doing the questions for each, stick with the steps of the Basic Approach. Even though you'll be doing fewer questions about each passage, you can still do the specific questions followed by the general questions. Once you've done the questions for each individual passage, then work on the questions that ask about the two passages together.

Passage B

Passage 1 is adapted from *Easy Lessons in Einstein: A discussion of the more intelligible features of the theory of relativity*, by Edwin E. Slosson, M.S., Ph.D., published by Harcourt, Brace and Howe 1920. Passage 2 is adapted from *Einstein's Relativity: A criticism*, by D.J. McAdam, published by Richard G. Badger 1922. Both passages discuss Einstein's theories regarding relativity, which had recently been published.

Passage 1

All three of Newton's laws of motion are now questioned and the world is called upon to unlearn the lesson which Euclid taught it that
Line parallel lines never meet. According to Einstein
5 they may meet. According to Newton the action of gravitation is instantaneous throughout all space. According to Einstein no action can exceed the velocity of light. If the theory of relativity is right there can be no such thing as absolute time
10 or way of finding whether clocks in different places are synchronous. Our yardsticks may vary according to how we hold them and the weight of a body may depend upon its velocity. The shortest distance between two points may not be a straight
15 line. These are a few of the startling implications of Einstein's theory of relativity.

According to Einstein the size and shape of any body depends upon the rate and direction of its movement. For ordinary speeds the alteration
20 is very slight, but it becomes considerable at rates approaching the speed of light, 186,000 miles a second. If, for instance, you could shoot an arrow from a bow with a velocity of 160,000 miles a second, it would shrink to about half its
25 length, as measured by a man remaining still on earth. A man traveling along with the arrow could discover no change. No force could bring the arrow or even the smallest particle of matter to a motion greater than the speed of light, and
30 the nearer it comes to this limit the greater the force required to move it faster. This means that the mass of a body, instead of being absolute and unalterable as we have supposed, increases with the speed of its movement. Newton's laws
35 of dynamics are therefore valid only for a matter in motion at such moderate speeds as we have to deal with in our experiments on earth and in our observations of the heavenly bodies. When we come to consider velocities approximating that of
40 light the ordinary laws of physics are subject to an increasing correction.

Passage 2

If it does those alarming things claimed for it, distort our bodies, make our clocks unreliable, shorten our yard-sticks, we ought to study it to
45 see if we can invent some counter irritant.

Yet a glance through books that have been written from Slossen and Harlow at one end to Eddington, Cunningham and Einstein himself at the other, seems to discourage serious study. "In
50 the history of science, the year 1919 is not likely to be known as the year of the overthrow of the German Empire, but as the year of the overthrow of Newton's law of gravitation."

It is scarcely an exaggeration to say that
55 Einstein hitched the earth to space or the moon and jerked it up to hit Newton's apple. (Though he speaks of a stone falling.)

To any who may be disposed to question his claim, he can say you are not one of the eleven.
60 He is reported to have said that "not *twelve* men in the world can read and understand fully his book." This, probably, is a surer way to protect his device than even an international patent. Also it is a good way to thwart the critic. The eleven
65 men who break in will not give it away, and those outside dare not criticize what they cannot read. Besides, *eleven* apostles is the standard, even another one might be dangerous.

Maybe this astronomer would honestly tell
70 him that his yard-stick would contract one-hundredth of the thickness of a cat's hair, and if the cloth did not change and the yard-stick did, when he had measured two million yards of cloth he would gain an inch.

75 It is a little provoking that not alone sensational writers, whom we could disregard, but men of learning and who seem to speak with authority, speak of our bodies, yard-sticks and clocks as if they had found something seriously
80 wrong affecting them.

22

The author of Passage 1 takes a position that he would most likely describe as

A) critical of the stated implications of Einstein's theory.

B) sensational and unworthy of serious study.

C) analogous description to provide a frame of reference.

D) dismissive of Newton's laws.

23

Which choice provides the best evidence for the answer to the previous question?

A) Lines 1-4 ("All three of . . . meet.")

B) Lines 22-26 ("If, for instance . . . earth.")

C) Lines 46-49 ("Yet a glance . . . study.")

D) Lines 75-80 ("It is a . . . them.")

24

The primary purpose of the first paragraph of Passage 1 (lines 1-16) is to

A) introduce the basic elements of Newton's laws of motion.

B) rebuff arguments against the new ideas mentioned in the paragraph.

C) contrast familiar assumptions with abnormal concepts.

D) qualify an assertion into an appropriate context.

25

Which of the following hypothetical situations most nearly matches the analogy in the second paragraph (lines 26-34) of Passage 1?

A) An archer shoots an arrow at 200 miles per hour in a competition and the arrow appears much smaller to a watching crowd.

B) A comet travelling at 170,000 miles a second appears the same size to both an observer on the comet and one on a nearby planet.

C) A speck of dust travels at 190,000 miles a second, and appears as different sizes from different frames of reference.

D) A grain of sand travelling at 175,000 miles a second appears as different sizes from different frames of reference.

26

As used in line 45, "irritant" most nearly means

A) problem.

B) itch.

C) devastation.

D) salve.

27

The rhetorical effect of the sentence in lines 67-68 ("Besides, *eleven* apostles . . . dangerous") is to

A) imply that if more than eleven people worked with Einstein there would be an unacceptable margin of error in the calculations.

B) demonstrate the fervor with which Einstein promotes and protects his theories.

C) suggest, through a religious reference, that those who attempt to refute Einstein's theories are betraying the progress of science.

D) evoke memory of a reference which serves to emphasize the author's stance that trusting Einstein's theories requires faith.

Which choice provides the best evidence for the answer to the previous question?

A) Lines 58-59 ("To any who . . . eleven.")

B) Lines 62-63 ("This, probably, is . . . patent.")

C) Lines 64-66 ("The eleven men . . . read.")

D) Lines 75-80 ("It is a . . . them.")

29

The author of Passage 1 would most likely respond to the claim in lines 75-80 ("It is a . . . them.") of Passage 2 by

A) countering that relatable examples do more to educate than to harm.

B) agreeing that there is nothing wrong with our yard-sticks and clocks.

C) arguing that the discrepancies in yard-sticks and clocks change aspects of everyday life.

D) adding that more study should be done before accepting any new theories.

30

The opinions of the author of Passage 1 and the author of Passage 2 differ in that the author of Passage 2

A) disagrees with Einstein's theories and supports Newton's laws, while the author of Passage 1 discards Newton's laws for Einstein's theories.

B) disagrees with those who use mundane analogies to describe Einstein's theories, while the author of Passage 1 utilizes such methods.

C) acknowledges limits to his argument, while the author of Passage 1 does not.

D) believes that Einstein's theories have no application, while the author of Passage 1 believes those theories apply to sports and travel on earth.

31

Both authors would most likely agree that

A) Einstein's theories are unsound.

B) Einstein's theories are of significant value.

C) application of Einstein's theories is not always necessary.

D) exaggerations of Einstein's theories should be restricted.

Here are two more passages for you to try. Remember to focus on the text!

Passage C

The following passage was adapted from *Up from Slavery: An Autobiography*, by Booker T. Washington (1856–1915), published in 1901.

I was born a slave on a plantation in Franklin County, Virginia. I am not quite sure of the exact place or exact date of my birth, but at any rate I suspect I must have been born somewhere and
5 at some time. As nearly as I have been able to learn, I was born near a cross-roads post-office called Hale's Ford, and the year was 1858 or 1859. I do not know the month or the day. The earliest impressions I can now recall are of the plantation
10 and the slave quarters—the latter being the part of the plantation where the slaves had their cabins.

The first pair of shoes that I recall wearing were wooden ones. They had rough leather on
15 the top, but the bottoms, which were about an inch thick, were of wood. When I walked they made a fearful noise, and besides this they were very inconvenient since there was no yielding to the natural pressure of the foot. In wearing
20 them one presented an exceedingly awkward appearance. The most trying ordeal that I was forced to endure as a slave boy, however, was the wearing of a flax shirt. In the portion of Virginia where I lived it was common to use flax as part
25 of the clothing for the slaves. That part of the flax from which our clothing was made was largely the refuse, which of course was the cheapest and roughest part. I can scarcely imagine any torture, except, perhaps, the pulling of a tooth,
30 that is equal to that caused by putting on a new flax shirt for the first time. It is almost equal to the feeling that one would experience if he had a dozen or more chestnut burrs, or a hundred small pin-points, in contact with his flesh. Even
35 to this day I can recall accurately the tortures that I underwent when putting on one of these garments. The fact that my flesh was soft and tender added to the pain. But I had no choice. I had to wear the flax shirt or none; and had it been
40 left to me to choose, I should have chosen to wear no covering. In connection with the flax shirt, my brother John, who is several years older than I am, performed one of the most generous acts that I ever heard of one slave relative doing for
45 another. On several occasions when I was being forced to wear a new flax shirt, he generously agreed to put it on in my stead and wear it for several days, till it was "broken in." Until I had grown to be quite a youth this single garment was
50 all that I wore.

I pity from the bottom of my heart any nation or body of people that is so unfortunate as to get entangled in the net of slavery. I have long since ceased to cherish any spirit of bitterness
55 against the Southern white people on account of the enslavement of my race. No one section of our country was wholly responsible for its introduction, and, besides, it was recognized and protected for years by the General Government.
60 Having once got its tentacles fastened on to the economic and social life of the Republic, it was no easy matter for the country to relieve itself of the institution. When persons ask me in these days how, in the midst of what sometimes seem
65 hopelessly discouraging conditions, I can have such faith in the future of my race in this country, I remind them of the wilderness through which and out of which, a good Providence has already led us.

1

The author's attitude can be best described as

A) amused.

B) bitter.

C) determined.

D) tempered.

2

The primary purpose of the passage is to

A) detail the author's life and current situation.

B) illustrate an optimism gained through trials.

C) describe a particular suffering endured by the author.

D) seek sympathy for a group of people.

3

Which choice provides the best evidence for the answer to the previous question?

A) Lines 1-2 ("I was born . . . Virginia.")

B) Lines 21-23 ("The most trying . . . shirt.")

C) Lines 51-53 ("I pity from . . . slavery.")

D) Lines 63-69 ("When persons ask . . . us.")

4

In the context of the passage as a whole, the principal rhetorical effect of the first paragraph, lines 1-12, is to

A) demonstrate, through a commonplace illustration, that the author has a sense of humor within a serious subject.

B) engage the reader with a universal uncertainty, shared by all people, about the exact circumstances of a person's birth.

C) hint at the author's main point through an extended analogy that relates "birth" with a deeper concept.

D) make a point, through distinguishing features of an otherwise shared experience, that stylistically continues in other parts of the passage.

5

The author uses the word "accurately," line 35, primarily in order to

A) emphasize the intensity of an experience.

B) provide evidence for the clarity of the author's memory.

C) give support for the following sentence.

D) show the author's gratitude towards his brother.

6

The sentence in lines 38-41, ("I had to . . . covering") most directly suggests

A) the author had been ordered by the plantation owners to wear a shirt.

B) no other forms of clothing were available.

C) some choices were not left to the author's discretion.

D) the author would have enjoyed not wearing clothing.

7

As used in line 54, "cherish" most nearly means to

A) prefer.

B) keep secret.

C) love.

D) hold resolutely.

8

Based on the passage, which of the following best describes the author's position regarding responsibility for the institution of slavery?

A) The slave owners bear full responsibility for their actions.

B) No one is responsible for the institution of slavery.

C) The responsibility rests most strongly on the government.

D) Responsibility is shared among many parties.

Which choice provides the best evidence for the answer to the previous question?

A) Lines 51-53 ("I pity from . . . slavery.")

B) Lines 53-56 ("I have long . . . race.")

C) Lines 56-59 ("No one section . . . Government.")

D) Lines 65-69 ("I can have . . . us.")

As used in line 67, "wilderness" most nearly means

A) an uncultivated terrain.

B) a difficult journey.

C) a desert.

D) slavery.

Passage D

This passage is adapted from *A Short History of the World*, by H.G. Wells, published in 1922, and discusses the rise and fall of Napoleon. This excerpt begins with the aftermath of the French Revolution (1792).

For some time the French thrust towards Italy was hung up, and it was only in 1796 that a new general, Napoleon Bonaparte, led the ragged and hungry republican armies in triumph across Piedmont to Mantua and Verona. Says C. F. Atkinson, "What astonished the Allies most of all was the number and the velocity of the Republicans. These improvised armies had in fact nothing to delay them. Tents were unprocurable for want of money, untransportable for want of the enormous number of wagons that would have been required, and also unnecessary, for the discomfort that would have caused wholesale desertion in professional armies was cheerfully borne by the men of 1793–94. Supplies for armies of then unheard-of size could not be carried in convoys, and the French soon became familiar with 'living on the country.' Thus 1793 saw the birth of the modern system of war—rapidity of movement, full development of national strength, bivouacs, requisitions and force as against cautious manœuvring, small professional armies, tents and full rations, and chicane. The first represented the decision-compelling spirit, the second the spirit of risking little to gain a little."

And while these ragged hosts of enthusiasts were chanting the Marseillaise and fighting for *la France,* manifestly never quite clear in their minds whether they were looting or liberating the countries into which they poured, the republican enthusiasm in Paris was spending itself in a far less glorious fashion.

Unhappily for France and the world a man arose who embodied in its intensest form this national egotism of the French. He gave that country ten years of glory and the humiliation of a final defeat. This was that same Napoleon Bonaparte who had led the armies of the Directory to victory in Italy.

Throughout the five years of the Directorate he had been scheming and working for self-advancement. Gradually he clambered to supreme power. He was a man of severely limited understanding but of ruthless directness and great energy. He had begun life as an extremist of the school of Robespierre; he owed his first promotion to that side; but he had no real grasp of the new forces that were working in Europe. His utmost political imagination carried him to a belated and tawdry attempt to restore the Western Empire. He tried to destroy the remains of the old Holy Roman Empire, intending to replace it by a new one centring upon Paris. The Emperor in Vienna ceased to be the Holy Roman Emperor and became simply Emperor of Austria. Napoleon divorced his French wife in order to marry an Austrian princess.

He became practically monarch of France as First Consul in 1799, and he made himself Emperor of France in 1804 in direct imitation of Charlemagne. He was crowned by the Pope in Paris, taking the crown from the Pope and putting it upon his own head himself as Charlemagne had directed. His son was crowned King of Rome.

For some years Napoleon's reign was a career of victory. He conquered most of Italy and Spain, defeated Prussia and Austria, and dominated all Europe west of Russia. But he never won the command of the sea from the British and his fleets sustained a conclusive defeat inflicted by the British Admiral Nelson at Trafalgar (1805). Spain rose against him in 1808 and a British army under Wellington thrust the French armies slowly northward out of the peninsula. In 1811 Napoleon came into conflict with the Tsar Alexander I, and in 1812 he invaded Russia with a great conglomerate army of 600,000 men, that was defeated and largely destroyed by the Russians and the Russian winter. Germany rose against him, Sweden turned against him. The French armies were beaten back and at Fontainebleau Napoleon abdicated (1814). He was exiled to Elba, returned to France for one last effort in 1815 and was defeated by the allied British, Belgians and Prussians at Waterloo. He died a British prisoner at St. Helena in 1821.

The forces released by the French revolution were wasted and finished. A great Congress of the victorious allies met at Vienna to restore as far as possible the state of affairs that the great storm had rent to pieces. For nearly forty years a sort of peace, a peace of exhausted effort, was maintained in Europe.

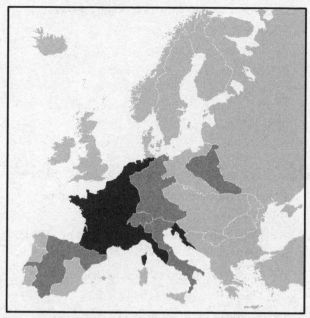

Map of Napoleon's French Empire and satellite states, in 1811

■ French Empire, including parts of Belgium and Italy
■ Satellite states of the French Empire
■ Non-French Empire

32

The author's rhetorical style can be described as

A) a meticulously detailed examination of minute facets.

B) rapid overview interspersed with specific detail.

C) reverential regard for objective depictions of historical events.

D) callous nonchalance towards all depicted parties.

33

Which choice provides the best evidence for the answer to the previous question?

A) Lines 18-23 ("Thus 1793 saw . . . chicane.")

B) Lines 37-39 ("This was that . . . Italy.")

C) Lines 83-86 ("He was exiled . . . Waterloo.")

D) Lines 89-92 ("A great Congress . . . pieces.")

34

The author's attitude towards the French armies is best characterized as

A) contemptuous.

B) divided.

C) approving.

D) neutral.

35

As used in line 10, "want" most nearly means to

A) lack.

B) desire.

C) require.

D) gain.

36

The author supports his description of Napoleon as "a man of severely limited understanding" primarily by

A) providing an example in which Napoleon made a decision that alienated his French compatriots.

B) indirectly referencing a state of affairs that is implied to have had an impact on Napoleon's success.

C) refuting claims that Napoleon had no real grasp of matters beyond his own extremist background.

D) demonstrating Napoleon's lack of response to overtures from other heads of state which could have altered the course of events.

37

Which choice provides the best evidence for the answer to the previous question?

A) Lines 33-35 ("Unhappily for France . . . French.")

B) Lines 35-37 ("He gave that . . . defeat.")

C) Lines 47-48 ("but he had . . . Europe.")

D) Lines 56-57 ("Napoleon divorced his . . . princess.")

38

In the sixth paragraph, lines 66-87, the author primarily contrasts

A) Napoleon's defeat of Austria with his last effort to return to power.

B) types of victories won by Napoleon.

C) the responses of different nations.

D) multiple outcomes of a larger endeavor.

39

As used in line 89, "wasted" most nearly means

A) spoiled

B) lost

C) used up

D) thrown away

40

The passage suggests that Napoleon did not have significant success in which of the following regions?

A) Russia

B) Belgium

C) Prussia

D) Spain

41

Based on the map and the passage, it can be inferred that

A) Napoleon's armies were separated by hostile territory.

B) Napoleon had no interest in Britain or Portugal.

C) Napoleon never attacked Greece.

D) Napoleon held some influence in areas he did not directly rule.

Chapter 7
Reading Drill:
Answers and
Explanations

READING DRILL ANSWERS AND EXPLANATIONS

Passage A

12. **C** The question specifically asks what the authors mean by "they will have residual protection during pandemics." The "they" is referring to the elderly and the "protection" is immunity acquired during previous outbreaks. So, while the passage discusses the younger groups, those answers don't address the concept of residual protection. This makes (A) and (D) incorrect, since they are true, but don't answer the question. Choice (B) is incorrect because while the authors do state that younger people should get vaccines before the elderly, the answer choice doesn't address the reason, which is that older people may have some immunity due to previous exposure.

13. **D** The question asks what the authors are trying to indicate by using the word "enjoy". Choices (B) and (C) assume that "enjoy" means to take pleasure in something. While the word does have a positive meaning in context, it simply means "to have." In this case, children who might have been exposed to influenza in the past may grow up to have some form of immunity to it that prevents it from becoming fatal. Choice (A) is too strong, since people can still die from it later in life, even if they were exposed as children, as is clear from the charts. Choice (D) is based on the statement in the first paragraph: "While the elderly are normally at most risk for severe outcomes during seasonal influenza, warranting the targeting of vaccination for direct protection to that group, they may have residual protection during pandemics."

14. **C** The question asks which statement contradicts the politician's statement. Choices (B) and (D) somewhat support the idea that there's no simple way to protect against a pandemic, so they do not contradict it. Choice (A) discusses which age group should be a priority for vaccination, but doesn't support the idea that Mexico needs vaccines for a majority of the population. Only (C) contradicts the politician by stating that it's possible to protect the population with a limited supply of vaccines.

15. **A** The question asks why certain information about Mexico's vaccine production was included. Because the passage states that Mexico relies on foreign producers and thus could face a shortage if the world suffers a pandemic, it could be assumed that the authors are suggesting that Mexico create more of its own vaccines. However, this is a trap to get you to choose (B), which talks about vaccinations as opposed to vaccines and doesn't meet the overall intent of the authors. Instead, note that the authors' mention of the potential shortage is to point out that their strategy can work even with a limited supply, which matches (A). Choices (C) and (D) also address the idea of Mexico producing its own vaccines, but in a negative way, so they are wrong.

16. **C** Quantitative questions like this are fairly straightforward if you work carefully. Make sure you identify exactly what the question wants, find the graph for fatality rate given hospitalization (Figure 2), and then look for the number that corresponds to the 1918 profile and the ages 0–5.

17.   **B**   The question is asking for evidence that elderly people have some sort of immunity or protection against pandemics. If this were true, it would mean that fewer get sick and die, so that's the information you are looking for in the figures. Choice (B) agrees with the information in the figures and supports the authors' contention that the elderly "may have residual protection during pandemics," since fewer elderly people get sick and die from a pandemic than from typical Influenza.

18.   **A**   Remember to keep an eye out for questions that are related to one another. In this case, you should already have the answer from the previous question: Figure 2 shows the percentages for people over 60 as 15% for the typical influenza outbreak and 10% for the 1918 pandemic, which suggests that elderly people have protection against pandemics.

19.   **A**   Remember to read for the word in context, and not just to leap to a conclusion based on your prior knowledge. The passage says, "This model illustrates a prioritization scheme based on age groups but does not further discriminate other sub-groups such as those persons with other medical conditions including pregnancy." The use of the term "sub-groups" means breaking up the sample into smaller groups, which means to differentiate them.

20.   **A**   This question asks for the main idea of the passage. The authors suggest that creating a flexible strategy that takes into account several factors such as age will help policy makers prepare for a pandemic. Choice (A) best reflects that. Choice (B) is too strong, since the passage doesn't say children should have *all* of the vaccine. The passage says that the other methods have "debatable efficacy," which means it's unclear how much they help. They definitely aren't "proven" to help, so (C) is incorrect. The passage does imply that viruses may not be susceptible to vaccines but it's unclear whether producers can't adapt or whether it's a matter of getting the vaccines delivered to people who need them, so (D) is incorrect.

21.   **D**   This question asks for the evidence you used to answer the previous question, so if you can't find something to support your answer to Question 20, take a moment to reassess. In this case, only (D) supports the idea that creating a flexible strategy that takes into account several factors such as age will help policy makers prepare for a pandemic.

Passage B

22.   **C**   This is a General Paired question, so see the explanation for Question 23.

23.   **B**   This is a General Paired question, so approach Questions 22 and 23 together. Choice (A) for Question 23 could match (D) for Question 22. Choice (B) for Question 23 could match (C) for Question 22. Choice (C) for Question 2 could match (B) for Question 23. Choice (D) for Question 23 could match (B) for Question 22. Choice (A) for Question 22 does not match any line reference for Question 23, so it is not the best answer. Now, look closely at Question 22, which asks how the author of Passage 1 would describe his own position. Because (B) for Question 22 is supported only by references from Passage 2, it does not represent how the author of Passage 1 would "most likely describe his own position," and both 22 (B) and 23 (D) can be eliminated. Look more closely

at Passage 1: "Newton's laws of dynamics are therefore valid only for…our experiments on earth and in our observations of the heavenly bodies." Because the author of Passage 1 states situations in which Newton's laws are valid, he is not "dismissive" of those laws, eliminating (D) for Question 22 as well as (A) for Question 23. The best answers are (C) for Question 22 and (B) for Question 23.

24.   **C**   This question asks why the author of Passage 1 wrote the first paragraph, so look there. "These are a few of the startling implications of Einstein's theory of relativity" provides a contrast between *Newton's laws* and *Einstein*['s theories] in order to describe some of the "startling" elements of Einstein's theories. Underline the last sentence of the first paragraph of Passage 1, which matches (C). Choice (A) does not match the prediction. The confusing language of (B) resolves to mean that the author of Passage 1 disagrees with Einstein's theories, which does not match the prediction, so (B) is not the best answer. The word *abnormal* means "different from average," which matches the author's use of the word *startling*. Choice (D)'s confusing language means that the author of Passage 1 is stating the limits of an *assertion*, which does not match the prediction, and is therefore not the best answer.

25.   **D**   This question asks what hypothetical situation most nearly matches the analogy in the second paragraph of Passage 1. Begin by summing up the analogy: an object at ordinary speed has a slight alteration whereas one that approaches the speed of light undergoes a major alteration. Underline the analogy and its description in the first through fifth sentences of the second paragraph of Passage 1. Choice (A) is not the best answer because it describes an arrow shot only at a speed of 200 miles per hour, which does not approach the speed of light, and which would therefore not appear much smaller. Choice (B) is not the best answer because while the comet matches the considerable alteration of rates, it is contradictorily described as remaining the same size. Choice (C) is not the best answer because it describes an object going faster than the speed of light, which the article asserts is impossible. Choice (D) is therefore the best answer, as it describes an object "approaching the speed of light" and "appearing as different sizes," which matches the information in Passage 1.

26.   **A**   This question asks what the word "irritant" means. According to Passage 2, "if [relativity] does those alarming things claimed for it, distort our bodies, make our clocks unreliable, shorten our yard-sticks, we ought to study it to see if we can invent some counter irritant." The word "counter" indicates that the "irritant" refers to the "alarming things." Underline the first sentence of Passage 2. Choices (B) and (D) are not the best answer because they do not match the prediction. Choice (C) Could Be True, but "devastation" is more extreme than anything supported by Passage 2. The best answer is (A).

27.   **D**   This question asks what the rhetorical effect of the last sentence of the fourth paragraph of Passage 2 is. According to Passage 2, if you "question [Einstein's] claim, he can say you are not one of the eleven…men in the world [who] can read and understand fully his book." The sentence itself suggests that Einstein's theories are difficult to criticize because few can understand those theories, and those who don't may feel that they have to agree. Rhetorically, the use of "apostles" and "eleven" is a reference to the 12 *apostles* in the Christian faith, one of whom is commonly

known as a traitor. Even without direct knowledge of the reference, the word *apostle* means a believer. Therefore, this sentence suggests that the answer will have something to do with faith. Choice (A) is not the best answer because it does not match the prediction. The confusing language of (C) resolves to mean the opposite of what the author states, so it is not the best answer. Choice (B) may seem to match the prediction at first glance, but its Deceptive Language does not directly address that *those outside dare not criticize what they cannot read*, and so it is not the best answer. Choose (D) because it matches the prediction: *trusting Einstein's theories requires faith*.

28. **C** This is a Specific Paired question, so look at what was underlined as support for Question 27. The sentence underlined for Question 27 is the second-to-last sentence of the fourth paragraph of Passage 2, so (C) is the best answer.

29. **A** This question asks what the author of Passage 1 would most likely give as a response to the claim in the last paragraph of Passage 2. Begin by paraphrasing that claim: even men of learning and authority alter facts in order stick to their claims against relativity. Given that the author of the first passage uses the analogy of the arrow in order to describe an event which could not literally happen to an arrow, it can be shown that he disagrees with the author of Passage 2, and is willing to use a relatable example in order to educate. The best answer is therefore (A). Choices (B) and (D) do not match the prediction, and while (C) Could Be True, the author of Passage 1 suggests the opposite by stating that Newton's laws apply only to his earth-bound experiments, which means it is not the best answer.

30. **B** This question asks what is different between the two authors' opinions. There are many potential differences, so evaluate the answer choices. According to Passage 1, "if...you could shoot an arrow from a bow with a velocity of 160,000 miles a second, it would shrink to about half its length." According to Passage 2, "it is a little provoking that...writers...speak of our bodies, yard-sticks and clocks as if they had found something seriously wrong affecting them." These references support (B), which is the best answer. Choice (A) is Mostly Right/Slightly Wrong because the author of Passage 1 seems to support Einstein's theories but states that Newton's laws are valid for experiments on earth. Choice (C) Could Be True about Passage 2, but does not match Passage 1, which acknowledges that Newton's laws are sometimes valid. Choice (D) also Could Be True about Passage 2, but does not match Passage 1, and it uses Deceptive Language by referring to sports and travel. Passage 1 states that Newton's laws are valid for "experiments on earth," so (D) is not the best answer.

31. **C** This question asks what both authors would most likely agree about. According to Passage 1, "Newton's laws...are...valid...for...our experiments on earth and in our observations of the heavenly bodies, and when we come to consider velocities approximating that of light the ordinary laws...are subject to...correction." The author of Passage 2 writes that "men of learning...speak of our...yard-sticks...as if they had found something seriously wrong affecting them," which implies that the contraction of "one-hundredth of the thickness of a cat's hair" isn't alarming, and thus

is not something that we necessarily ought to study. Both authors acknowledge that Einstein's theories do not significantly change some calculations, so (C) is the best answer. Choice (A) Could Be True for Passage 2, but is not the best answer because it does not match Passage 1. Choice (B) Could Be True for Passage 1, but is not the best answer because it does not have support from Passage 2. Choice (D) is supported by Passage 2, and Could Be True for Passage 1, but the author of Passage 1 uses an analogy of having a man travel along with an arrow moving with a velocity of 160,000 miles a second, which implies that the author of Passage 1 is willing to utilize hypothetical situations which are unlikely to be literally true in order to explain elements of Einstein's theories. This means that (D) can be eliminated, as the author of Passage 1 doesn't agree with it.

Passage C

1. **D** This question is asking for the author's attitude, or tone. While this can often be challenging to discern, this passage provides direct evidence: "when persons ask me how...I can have such faith... I remind them of the wilderness through which and out of which, a good Providence has already led us." This suggests that the author has a faith that is strengthened by living through hard circumstances. Choice (A) is not the best answer, because it does not match the prediction. Choice (B) is not the best answer because it does not match the prediction, and the author states "I have long since ceased...any spirit of bitterness." Choice (C) is not the best answer because it does not match the prediction. Moreover, the author uses artistic phrases, such as "I suspect I must have been born somewhere and at some time," and the discussion about the author's first pair of shoes demonstrates that the author's attitude goes beyond simple determination. Choice (D) matches the prediction, and is the correct answer, because *tempered* means strengthened through hardship.

2. **B** This is a General Paired question, so see the explanation for Question 3.

3. **D** Choice (A) for Question 3 could match Choice (A) for Question 2. Choice (B) for Question 3 could match Choice (C) for Question 2. Choice (C) for Question 3 could match Choice (D) for Question 2. Choice (D) for Question 3 could match Choice (B) for Question 2. Because all the answer choices for Question 3 could match a choice for Question 2, nothing can be eliminated yet. Look more closely at what exactly the choices for Question 3 support to eliminate weak matches. Choice (A) for Question 2 contains the phrase *current situation*, which is not supported by the matching (A) for Question 3, so both choices can be ruled out. Now, look closely at Question 2, which asks for the *primary purpose of the passage*, and consider why the author wrote the passage. Choice (C) for Question 2, and (B) for Question 3 suggest that the author wrote the passage in order to *describe* [the] *particular suffering* of *wearing...a flax shirt*. Because the final paragraph of the passage broadens the scope of the passage to talk about *slavery* in general, and *the future of my race in this country*, the author did not write the passage in order to discuss *wearing...a flax shirt*, so (C) for Question 2 and (B) for Question 3 can be eliminated. Now, determine whether the author wrote the passage to *seek sympathy* or *illustrate an optimism gained through trials*. The best evidence to answer the question is (D) for Question 3, which states that the author has *such faith in the*

future of [his] *race in this country* due to *the wilderness through which and out of which* his race has been *led*. The hopeful tone with which the author ends the passage will help to eliminate (D) for Question 2 and (C) for Question 3, and supports (B) for Question 2 and (D) for Question 3.

4. **D** This question is asking what the "rhetorical effect" is, so you're looking for unusual elements included in the passage. For instance, the first paragraph details the author's birth (a thing that we all have in common), but adds that he is "not quite sure of the exact place or…date," and that "I must have been born somewhere and at some time." This might suggest (B) or (C), but remember that the question specifies that the answer must be "in the context of the passage as a whole," so consider other elements. In the second paragraph, the author again discusses a universal thing (clothing) with some unusual specifics: "I can scarcely imagine any torture…equal to that caused by putting on a new flax shirt." Choices (B) and (C) can now be eliminated as too specific, and (A) can be ruled out, as there's little funny about these descriptions. Choice (D) is the best answer because it matches both the *shared experience* and *distinguishing features* of the prediction.

5. **A** This question asks why the author uses a specific word. According to the passage, the author "can scarcely imagine any torture…that is equal to that caused by putting on a new flax shirt." The author continues to emphasize the painful nature of the experience with analogies about "chestnut burrs" and "a hundred small pin-points." Because memories are known to fade over time, the author uses the word "accurately" in order to continue emphasizing the painful nature of putting on a new flax shirt. This matches (A) and eliminates (B) which does not match the context. Choice (C) is not the best answer, because "the following sentence" describes another element that "added to the pain," which means that both sentences are support. Choice (D) Could Be True, in that John does the author the favor of breaking in a new shirt for him, but it doesn't have anything to do with the use of the word "accurately."

6. **C** This question asks what is most directly suggested by the sentence. Begin by underlining it, and then focus on which answer choices are supported by the text. Choice (A) is not the best answer, because although the passage states that the author was forced to wear a shirt on at least "several occasions," it is not directly stated in the text that the planation owners forced this upon him. Choice (B) is not the best answer, because the author states that "it was common to use flax as part of the clothing," not that flax was the only available option, which means that it can be eliminated as Mostly Right, Slightly Wrong. Choice (D) is not the best answer, because the author "would have chosen to wear no covering" instead of the flax shirt, and while it Could Be True, it is not directly supported by the text. Choice (C) is the best answer, because the author wore the shirt, and states that "had it been left to me to choose," he would not have worn the shirt, which directly suggests that he was not given a choice.

7. **D** This question asks what "*cherish*" most nearly means in context. According to the passage, the author has "long ceased to cherish any spirit of bitterness" towards a group of people. Because the author follows that statement by adding that "no one section of our country was wholly responsible," the author means that he does not feel bitter, so he must have "long ceased to have any spirit

of bitterness." Underline the second and third sentences of the last paragraph. Only (D) matches this prediction.

8. **D** This question asks for the author's position on slavery. According to the passage, "no one section of our country was wholly responsible for [slavery's] introduction," so the author feels that responsibility is shared, (D). This directly contradicts (A), so eliminate it. Choice (B) is Mostly Right, Slightly Wrong because "no one section...was wholly responsible" does not mean that "no one is responsible at all," so (B) is not the best answer. Choice (C) Could Be True, because the author states that slavery "was recognized and protected for years by the...Government," but the author does not directly state that the government has *most* of the responsibility, so this is not the best answer.

9. **C** This is a Specific Paired question, so look at what was used as support for Question 8, which makes (C) the best answer.

10. **B** This question asks what *wilderness* means in the context of the passage, so look at the sentence in which it is used. "Already" indicates that the author relates the "hopelessly discouraging conditions" to the wilderness, so "wilderness" refers to those kinds of conditions, (B). Choices (A) and (C) may make for a difficult journey, but they're not specific enough and can be eliminated. Choice (D) may seem tempting, but it is not the best answer. While the wilderness through which he has been led may refer to slavery, questions about meanings in context are about the word itself, and replacing the word *wilderness* with the word *slavery* does not keep the meaning of the sentence, because the author is referring to how a journey through one type of difficulty gives him hope that his *race* can handle another difficult journey.

Passage D

32. **B** This is a General Paired question, so refer to the explanation for Question 33.

33. **C** This is a General Paired question, so approach Questions 32 and 33 together. Choice (A) for Question 33 could match (A) for Question 32. Choice (B) for Question 33 can be eliminated, because it does not match any choice for Question 32. Choice (C) for Question 33 could match (B) for Question 32. Choice (D) for Question 33 can be eliminated, because it does not match any choice for Question 32. Now, look closely at Question 32, which asks for "the author's rhetorical style." Because (A) for Question 32 and (A) for Question 33 represent a quote from C.F. Atkinson, and not the author, this pair can be eliminated, which leaves the correct answer as (B) for Question 32 and (C) for Question 33.

34. **B** This question asks what the best characterization is of "the author's attitude towards the French armies." According to the passage, the French armies are described in a variety of positive and negative ways, ranging from "enthusiasts" who are "cheerfully" accepting of "discomfort" to "ragged and hungry." This suggests that the author has both positive and negative feelings about the French armies, or (B). Underline the last sentence of the first paragraph, and the sentence that makes up

the entire second paragraph, and then eliminate (A), (C), and (D), which do not match that prediction or fully account for the author's feelings.

35.   **A**   The question asks what *want* most nearly means in the context of the passage: "tents were unprocurable for want of money." Because *unprocurable* means "could not be obtained," *want* must mean something like "lack," or (A). Underline the fourth sentence of the first paragraph. Choices (B) and (D) can now be eliminated. While it's true that buying *tents* may *require* money, *want* is used in the sentence to show the current state of money, not what would be needed, so (C) can also be eliminated.

36.   **B**   This question asks what the author uses to support his description of Napoleon as "a man of severely limited understanding." Read the sentences immediately following that quote until you get to a list of Napoleon's actions, which is where the window cuts off. Underline the portion that states "he had no real grasp of the new forces that were working Europe," as this demonstrates that there were things he did not understand. This should lead to (B), as it implies that Napoleon failed due to his poor comprehension of the political state of affairs—"new forces that were working in Europe." Choice (A) Could Be True, because Napoleon "divorced his French wife," but that doesn't mean that the French felt alienated. Choice (C) uses Deceptive Language, in that Napoleon is called an "extremist," but that doesn't show a lack of understanding. And (D) can be eliminated, for while it Could Be True that he received "overtures from other heads of state," there's no proof to support this.

37.   **C**   This is a Specific Paired question, so look at what was underlined as support for Question 36. The sentence underlined for Question 36 is the fourth sentence of the fourth paragraph, so choice (C) is the best answer.

38.   **D**   This question asks what ideas the author is contrasting in the sixth paragraph, so begin there. The author provides examples of various victories, but then continues by noting that "he never won the command of the sea" and suffered a series of defeats and losses that eventually led to his death. This is a contrast, then, of Napoleon's victories and defeats, which is another way of describing "multiple outcomes" of a "larger endeavor," Napoleon's full career. Underline the first and third sentences of the sixth paragraph, which matches (D). Choice (A) uses Deceptive Language, because while it does contrast a victory with a defeat, it's too specific. Likewise, (B) only illustrates part of the scope of the paragraph, and can be eliminated. Choice (C) doesn't offer any contrast or match the prediction.

39.   **C**   The question asks what "wasted" most nearly means in the context of the passage: "the forces released by the French Revolution were wasted and finished," and a group "met…to restore…the state of affairs" that had existed before the armies of the French Revolution had moved through Europe. Therefore, *wasted* and *finished* are used for the same meaning, and *wasted* means "finished," (C). Choice (A) doesn't fit the context, and (B) and (D) hint at a meaning that isn't present in the context.

40. **A** This question asks in what region "Napoleon did not have significant success." According to the passage, Napoleon's army "was defeated and largely destroyed by the Russians and Russian winter." Additionally, the passage states that Napoleon "dominated all Europe west of Russia." Underline that phrase, and note that (A) best matches it. Be careful of the trap answer at (B): while Belgium is later mentioned as part of the allied group that defeated Napoleon, "all Europe west of Russia" includes Belgium, as indicated by the map.

41. **D** This question asks what can be inferred based on the map and the passage. According to the passage, Napoleon "dominated all Europe west of Russia," but the map shows a large portion of "Europe west of Russia" that is neither part of the French Empire nor a satellite state. It can be inferred that Napoleon dominated areas that were not part of the French Empire or a satellite state, which matches (D). Choice (A) Could Be True, because the map shows a gap between the eastern-most satellite state and the bulk of the territory controlled by Napoleon, but there's no support to show that this territory was hostile. Choice (B) contradicts the passage, for if Napoleon *never won the command of the sea from the British*, then he must have fought them at sea. Choice (C) Could Be True, in that Napoleon does not control Greece on the map, but there's no mention of it on the passage, which means that we cannot assume he didn't attack (and fail to capture) it.

Part III
Writing &
Language

Chapter 8
Introduction to SAT Writing and Language Strategy

The Writing and Language section of the SAT takes 35 minutes and consists of 44 questions. In this chapter, we will talk about the unique format of some of these questions and a strategy that will help you to tackle any Writing and Language question you see.

CAN YOU REALLY TEST WRITING ON A MULTIPLE-CHOICE TEST?

We'd say no, but the SAT (and a heck of a lot of other tests) seems to think the answer is yes. To that end, the SAT is giving you 35 minutes to answer 44 multiple-choice questions that ask about a variety of grammatical and stylistic topics. If you like to read and/or write, this test may frustrate you a bit because it may seem to boil writing down to a couple of dull rules. But as you will see, we will use the next few chapters to suggest a method that keeps things simple for pro- and anti-grammarians alike.

WHERE DID ALL THE QUESTIONS GO?

One thing that can seem a little strange about the Writing and Language section of the SAT is that many of the questions don't have, well, questions. Instead, most look something like this:

The history of **1** language although it may sound like a boring subject, is a treasure trove of historical, cultural, and psychological insights.

1

A) NO CHANGE

B) language, although it may sound like a boring subject

C) language, although it may sound, like a boring subject,

D) language, although it may sound like a boring subject,

This may seem a little odd. How are you supposed to pick an answer when there's no question? It might seem as if the SAT is not giving you enough information.

Well, actually, as we'll discuss throughout the next few chapters, the SAT gives you a *lot* of information—it's just hidden in the answer choices.

Look at these pairs, and you'll see just what we mean. As you read through these pairs of answer choices, think about what each question is probably testing.

i. A) could of
    B) could have

ii. A) tall, dark, and handsome
    B) tall, dark and handsome

iii. A) let them in
     B) let Sister Susie and Brother John in

iv. A) We arrived in Paris on a Sunday. Then we took the train to Nantes. Then we took the train to Bordeaux.

B) We arrived in Paris on a Sunday. Then we took the train to Bordeaux. Then we took the train to Nantes.

If you were able to see the differences in these answer choices, you're already more than halfway there. Now, notice how the differences in these answers can reveal the question that is lurking in the heart of each list of answer choices.

i. The difference between the word "of" and "have" means that this question is asking, *Is the correct form "could of" or "could have"?*

ii. The difference between having a comma after the word "dark" and not having one there means that this question is asking, *How many commas does this sentence need, and where do they belong?*

iii. The difference between "them" and "Sister and Susie and Brother John" means that this question is asking, *Is "them" adequately specific, or do you need to refer to people by name?*

iv. The difference between the order of these sentences asks, *What order should the sentences be in?*

Therefore, what we have noticed in these pairs of answer choices is something that may seem fairly simple but is essential to success on the SAT.

THE ANSWER CHOICES ASK THE QUESTIONS

At some point, you've almost certainly had to do the English-class exercise called "peer editing." In this exercise, you are tasked with "editing" the work of one of your fellow students. But this can be really tough, because what exactly does it mean to "edit" an entire essay or paper when you aren't given any directions? It's *especially* tough when you start getting into the subtleties between whether things are *wrong* or whether they could merely be improved.

Look, for example, at these two sentences:

It was a beautiful day outside birds were singing cheerful songs.

It was a beautiful day outside; birds were singing cheerful songs.

You'd have to pick the second one in this case because the first has a grammatical error: it's a run-on sentence.

Now, look at these two sentences:

The weather was just right, so I decided to play soccer.

Just right was how I would describe the weather, so a decision of soccer-playing was made by me.

In this case, the first sentence is obviously better than the second, but the second technically doesn't have any grammatical errors in it. The first may be *better*, but the second isn't exactly *wrong*.

What made each of these pairs of sentences relatively easy to deal with, though, was the fact that you could compare the sentences to one another. In doing so, you noted the differences between those sentences, and you picked the *better* answer accordingly.

Let's see how this looks in a real SAT situation.

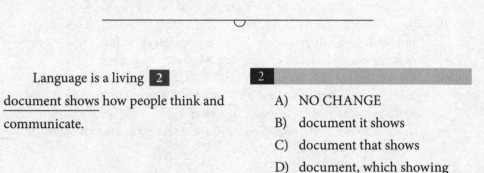

Language is a living [2] document shows how people think and communicate.

2

A) NO CHANGE
B) document it shows
C) document that shows
D) document, which showing

Here's How to Crack It

First, look at what's changing in the answer choices. The word "document" remains the same in each, but the subsequent word or words change each time. This question, then, seems to be asking, *Which words will best link the two ideas in the sentence?*

Choices (A) and (D) create sentence fragments, so those should be eliminated. Choice (B) creates a run-on sentence, so that should also be eliminated. It looks like only (C) appropriately links the ideas without adding new errors.

Notice how that entire process started by asking, "What's changing in the answer choices?" With that question, we figured out what was being tested, and we used POE to do the rest.

Let's try another.

A community's very soul, we might say, is communicated through **3** their language.

3

A) NO CHANGE

B) they're language.

C) their languages.

D) its language.

Here's How to Crack It

As always, start with what is changing in the answer choices. It looks like the main change is between the words "their," "they're," and "its," with a minor change between the words "language" and "languages." As such, this question seems to be asking, *What is the appropriate pronoun to use in this context, and just how many "languages" are we talking about?*

Start wherever is easiest. In this case, it can be a bit difficult to say for sure whether we are talking about one language or about a bunch of languages. Instead, let's work with the pronoun. What does it refer back to? In this sentence, it seems that the pronoun refers back to "a community," which is a singular noun (even though it describes a lot of people). Therefore, the only possible answer that could work is (D), which contains the singular pronoun "its."

Notice that the ambiguity between one language and many languages became irrelevant. Sometimes fixing one problem takes care of others!

LEARN FROM THE ANSWER CHOICES

Let's think about the previous question a bit more. If someone said to you, *A community's very soul, we might say, is communicated through their language*, you might not necessarily hear that as wrong. That's because the way we speak is often very different from the way we write. Bear in mind that you are taking the SAT Writing and Language test: in this section, the SAT is therefore more concerned with how we write and with the stricter set of rules that go along with writing.

As such, the answer choices can not only tell us what a particular question is testing, they can also reveal mistakes that we might not have otherwise seen (in the original sentence) or heard (in our heads). In the previous question, we might not have noted the mistake at all if we hadn't looked at what was changing in the answer choices.

Let's look at another.

---

4 For all intensive purposes, any social, cultural, or historical study *must* start with an analysis of language.

4

A) NO CHANGE
B) For all intents and purposes,
C) For all intent's and purpose's,
D) For all intensive purpose's,

Here's How to Crack It

First, as always, check what's changing in the answer choices. In this case, that step is especially important because you can't really hear the error. People misuse this idiom all the time because they so rarely see it written, and all four of the answer choices sound basically the same. So, having checked the answer choices in this case *reveals* an error that you might not have otherwise seen or heard.

Then, start the process of elimination. There's no good reason to have apostrophes anywhere (there are neither contractions nor possessions), so eliminate (C) and (D). Then, if you're not sure, take a guess. The correct form of the saying here is (B).

Notice, though, that looking at the answer choices revealed the problem that you might not have otherwise been able to see or hear. POE got you the rest of the way.

POE DOES THE BIG WORK

Once you have a sense of what the question is testing, POE can get you closer and closer to the answer. POE is especially helpful when you're dealing with sentences that have lots of issues, like the following one:

It may seem that how people speak is distinct from how [5] they are acting; however, there's something that most historians will tell you is wrong.

5

A) NO CHANGE

B) they act, however, there's something

C) they are acting, however, that's something

D) they act; however, that's something

Here's How to Crack It

First, as always, check what's changing in the answer choices. In this case, there are three things changing: the difference between *act* and *are acting*, the difference between *that's* and *there's*, and the difference between a period and a semicolon. While this may seem like a lot, this is actually a huge POE opportunity! Start with the one you find easiest, and work backward from there.

Because the semicolon is not commonly used, let's save the punctuation part for last. Hopefully we can get the right answer without having to deal with the punctuation at all. Let's start with the difference between *that's* and *there's*. The sentence doesn't contain any mention of place, so the sentence can't contain *there's*, eliminating (A) and (B). Then, to choose between the last two, *they act* is more concise and more consistent with the rest of the sentence than is *they are acting*, which makes (D) better than (C). In this instance, we got to the correct answer without having to deal with all the messiness in the question!

ALL OF THE QUESTIONS CAN'T BE WRONG ALL OF THE TIME

Now that our strategy is basically set, let's look at one more tough one.

———————○———————

6 Your knowledge of grammar and vocabulary may be shaky, but you can learn a lot from some basic tenets of linguistics.

6

A) NO CHANGE

B) You're knowledge of grammar or vocabulary might be shaky,

C) Your knowledge of grammar and vocabulary might be shakily,

D) You're knowledge of grammar and vocabulary might be shaky,

Here's How to Crack It

As always, check the answers first. In this case, here's what's changing: the answers are switching between *your* and *you're*, between *and* and *or*, and between *shaky* and *shakily*. Let's do the easy parts first!

First of all, there's no reason to insert the word *shakily* here. You can't say that someone has *shakily knowledge* of something, so eliminate (C). Then, the *knowledge* belongs to *you*, so it is *your knowledge*, not *you are knowledge*, thus eliminating (B) and (D). This leaves us with (A).

Remember, NO CHANGE is right sometimes! Some people pick it too often. Some people don't pick it enough, but if you've done the other steps in the process and have eliminated all the other choices, go ahead and pick (A)!

———————○———————

> **How to Ace the Writing and Language Section: A Strategy**
>
> - Check what's changing in the answer choices.
> - Figure out what the question is testing and let the differences reveal potential errors.
> - Use Process of Elimination.
> - If you haven't eliminated three answers, pick the shortest one that is most consistent with the rest of the sentence.

A Note for the High-Scorer

Whatever your scoring level, the strategy we've outlined in this chapter will help you. In fact, it may help you more the higher you score. If you do well in your English classes, or if you've got a pretty good grasp of grammar, you might rely a little too much on your ability to intuit mistakes. The SAT's got some tricks up its sleeve, however, and they know that even the best grammarians out there will make some mistakes by going with some vaguely defined intuition.

If you check what's changing in the answer choices, you don't have to go on sense alone. You can use your knowledge of grammar in conjunction with a good strategy. For instance, we recently saw this sentence in an e-mail subject line.

Can you score more points than us?

Sounds fine, right? How about if we ask you to choose between these sentences?

Can you score more points than us?

Can you score more points than we?

It still seems like the first sounds better, but now at least you know that there *might* be a problem because you see the two sentences next to each other. Now you might see that, in fact, the better choice is the second one because the sentence could be extended to say, *Can you score more points than we can?*

This is a pretty simple example, but it shows that you can't always trust your ear even if you do speak (for the most part) correctly. The changes in the answer choices reveal mistakes that you might not have been able to see or hear initially.

In the next few chapters, we'll get into some of the more technical issues in Writing and Language, but we'll be using this strategy throughout. Try the exercises on the next page to get some of the basics down.

Quick Quiz: Answer Choices

Instructions: The object of this drill is to get a basic idea of what each question is testing from only the answer choices. Check your answers on page 97.

1

A) NO CHANGE

B) babies' favorite bottles

C) baby's favorite bottle's

D) babies' favorite bottles'

What's changing in the answer choices?

_____

What is this question testing?

_____

2

A) NO CHANGE

B) did

C) does

D) have done

What's changing in the answer choices?

_____

What is this question testing?

_____

3

A) NO CHANGE

B) Although

C) While

D) Because

What's changing in the answer choices?

_____

What is this question testing?

_____

4

A) NO CHANGE

B) was notable for their

C) were notable for its

D) were notable for their

What's changing in the answer choices?

_____

What is this question testing?

_____

5

A) NO CHANGE

B) beautiful, as in super pretty.

C) beautiful, like easy on the eyes.

D) beautiful.

What's changing in the answer choices?

_____

What is this question testing?

_____

ANSWER KEY
1. Apostrophes; apostrophes and where they go
2. Verbs; verb tense and number
3. Words; transition words (direction)
4. Was/were and their/its; verb number and pronoun number
5. Number of words; conciseness

Summary

○ The Writing and Language Test on the SAT is 35 minutes long and contains 44 questions.

○ Many of the "questions" on the W&L Test aren't exactly questions; instead, you'll be presented with a series of passages with different portions of it underlined.

○ **Check what's changing in the answer choices.** The answer choices not only tell you what a particular question is testing, but also reveal mistakes that you might not have otherwise seen.

○ Use POE to get rid of the incorrect choices. If you can't eliminate three choices, pick the shortest one that is most consistent with the rest of the sentence.

Chapter 9
Punctuation

Punctuation will be the focus of many questions on the Writing and Language Test. But how do you know when to use the different punctuation marks that are being tested? This chapter will answer that question, as well as highlight some of the SAT's rules for using punctuation and the strategies you can use to outsmart the test writers.

WAIT, THE SAT WANTS ME TO KNOW HOW TO USE A SEMICOLON?

Kurt Vonnegut once wrote, "Here is a lesson in creative writing. First rule: Do not use semicolons…. All they do is show you've been to college." Unfortunately, SAT doesn't quite agree. SAT wants you to know how to use the semicolon and a few other types of infrequent punctuation. In this chapter, we're going to talk about the varieties of punctuation that SAT wants you to know how to use. Learn these few simple rules, and you'll be all set on the punctuation questions.

First and foremost, remember how you can spot a question that's asking about punctuation.

> Start by asking, "What's changing in the answer choices?"

As If That's Not Enough

Mind you, just because a question is testing punctuation doesn't mean that it's only testing punctuation. As we discussed in the previous chapter, this actually works out to your advantage, because you can then pick the grammar rule that you feel most comfortable with and begin by eliminating any answers that violate it. To that end, if you can master the punctuation in this chapter, it'll be much easier for you to rule out wrong choices that might otherwise have tricked you.

If you see punctuation marks—commas, periods, apostrophes, semicolons, colons—changing, then the question is testing punctuation. As you work the problem, make sure to ask the big question:

> Does this punctuation need to be here?

The particular punctuation mark you are using—no matter what it is—must have a specific role within the sentence. You wouldn't use a question mark without a question, would you? Nope! Well, all punctuation works that way, and in the following section, we'll give you seven basic instances in which you would use some type of punctuation. Otherwise, let the words do their thing unobstructed!

Think about it this way. Punctuation is tough to use because we don't really use it as we speak. A spoken language is really just a combination of words and inflections and therefore doesn't seem to have quite as many rules. Written language *wants* to be as free as spoken language, so let it be free! Use punctuation only where there's a specific reason to do so.

STOP, GO, AND THE VERTICAL LINE TEST

Let's get the weird ones out of the way first. Everyone knows that a period ends a sentence, but once things get more complicated, even a particularly nerdy grammarian can get lost. Because of this confusion, we've come up with a basic chart that summarizes the different times you might use what SAT calls "end-of-sentence" and "middle-of-sentence" punctuation.

Keep the following list in mind when you are linking ideas.

STOP
- Period
- Semicolon
- Comma + FANBOYS
- Question mark
- Exclamation Mark

HALF-STOP
- Colon
- Long dash

GO
- Comma
- No punctuation

> STOP punctuation can link ONLY complete ideas.
>
> HALF-STOP punctuation must be *preceded* by a complete idea.
>
> GO punctuation can link anything EXCEPT two complete ideas.

Let's see how these work. Here is a complete idea:

> *Samantha studied for the SAT.*

Notice that we've already used one form of STOP punctuation at the end of this sentence: a period.

Now, if we want to add a second complete idea, we'll keep the period.

> *Samantha studied for the SAT. She ended up doing really well on the test.*

In this case, the period is linking these two complete ideas. But the nice thing about STOP punctuation is that you can really use any of the punctuation in the list to do the same thing, so we could also say this:

> *Samantha studied for the SAT; she ended up doing really well on the test.*

Fans of FANBOYS
You might not care much for any of the individual components of FANBOYS, but this pop group of grammar can do a lot more to save you on a test than your average musical idol. Just remember the members: For, And, Nor, But, Or, Yet, and So.

What the list of STOP punctuation shows us is that, essentially, a period and a semicolon are the same thing. We could say the same for the use of a comma plus one of the FANBOYS.

Samantha studied for the SAT, and she ended up doing really well on the test.

You can also use HALF-STOP punctuation to separate two complete ideas, so you could say

Samantha studied for the SAT: she ended up doing really well on the test.

Or

Samantha studied for the SAT—she ended up doing really well on the test.

There's a subtle difference, however, between STOP and HALF-STOP punctuation: for STOP, both ideas have to be complete, but for HALF-STOP, only the first one does.

Let's see what this looks like. If we want to link a complete idea and an incomplete idea, we can use HALF-STOP punctuation as long as the complete idea is first. For example,

Samantha studied for the SAT: all three sections of it.

Or

Samantha studied for the SAT: the silliest test in all the land.

When you use HALF-STOP, there has to be a complete idea before the punctuation, so these examples wouldn't be correct:

Samantha studied for: the SAT, the ACT, and every AP test in between.

The SAT—Samantha studied for it and was glad she did.

When you are not linking two complete ideas, you can use GO punctuation. So you could say, for instance,

Samantha studied for the SAT, the ACT, and every AP test in between.

Or

Samantha studied for the SAT, all three sections of it.

These are the three types of mid-sentence or end-of-sentence punctuation: STOP, HALF-STOP, and GO. You'll notice that there is a bit of overlap between the concepts, but for all its technicalities, even the SAT wouldn't make you get into the minutia of choosing between, say, a period and a semicolon. All you need to be able to do is figure out which of the big three (Stop, Half-Stop, and Go) categories you need.

Let's see what this looks like in context.

Jonah studied every day for the big **1** test he was taking the SAT that Saturday.

1

A) NO CHANGE
B) test, he was taking
C) test, he was taking,
D) test; he was taking

Here's How to Crack It

As always, check what's changing in the answer choices. In this case, the words all stay the same. All that changes is the punctuation, and notice the types of punctuation that are changing: STOP and GO.

Now, when you see STOP punctuation changing in the answer choices, you can do a little something we like to call the Vertical Line Test.

Draw a line where you see the punctuation changing—in this case, between the words *test* and *he*. Then, read up to the vertical line: *Jonah studied every day for the big test*. That's complete. Now, read after the vertical line: *he was taking the SAT that Saturday*. That's also complete.

So let's think: we've got two complete ideas here. What kind of punctuation do we need? STOP or HALF-STOP. It looks like STOP is the only one available, so let's choose (D).

Let's try another.

---○---

It was very important for him to do [2] well. High scores in all the subjects.

2

A) NO CHANGE

B) well; high

C) well: high

D) well, he wanted high

Here's How to Crack It

Check the answer choices. What's changing? It looks like the punctuation is changing, and some of that punctuation is STOP. Let's use the Vertical Line Test. Draw a vertical line where you see the punctuation: between *well* and *high* or *well* and *he*.

What's before the vertical line? *It was very important for him to do well* is complete. Then, *high scores in all the subjects* is not. Therefore, because we have one complete idea (the first) and one incomplete idea (the second), we can't use STOP punctuation, thus eliminating (A) and (B).

Now, what's different between the last two? Choice (C) contains Half-Stop punctuation, which can work, so we'll keep that. Choice (D) adds some words, with which the second idea becomes *he wanted high scores in all the subjects*, which is complete. That makes two complete ideas separated by a comma, but what do we need when we're separating two complete ideas? STOP punctuation! Eliminate (D)! Only (C) is left.

---○---

Let's see one more.

---○---

Whenever Jonah had a free [3] moment—he was studying.

3

A) NO CHANGE

B) moment; he

C) moment, he,

D) moment, he

Here's How to Crack It

The punctuation is changing in the answer choices, and there's some STOP punctuation, so let's use the Vertical Line Test. Put the line between *moment* and *he*. The first idea, *Whenever Jonah had a free moment*, is incomplete, and the second idea, *he was studying*, is complete. Therefore, we can't use STOP (which needs two complete ideas) or HALF-STOP (which needs a complete idea before the punctuation), thus eliminating (A) and (B). Then, because there is no good reason to put a comma after the word *he*, the best answer must be choice (D).

A SLIGHT PAUSE FOR COMMAS

Commas can be a little tricky. In the last question (#3), we got down to two answers, (C) and (D), after completing the Vertical Line Test. So how do you decide whether to keep a comma in or not? It seems a little arbitrary to say that you use a comma "every time you want to pause," so let's reverse that and make it a little more concrete.

> If you can't cite a reason to use a comma, *don't use one.*
>
> On the SAT, there are only 4 reasons to use a comma.
> - In STOP punctuation, with one of the FANBOYS
> - In GO punctuation, to separate incomplete ideas from other ideas
> - In a list of three or more things
> - In a sentence containing unnecessary information

We've already seen the first two concepts, so let's look at the other two.

Try this one.

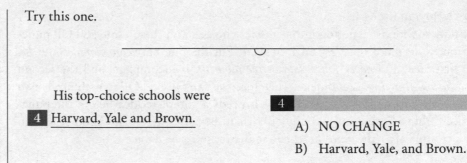

His top-choice schools were
4 Harvard, Yale and Brown.

4

A) NO CHANGE

B) Harvard, Yale, and Brown.

C) Harvard, Yale, and, Brown.

D) Harvard Yale and Brown.

Here's How to Crack It

First, check what's changing in the answer choices. It looks like the commas in this list are changing. Because there's not any obvious STOP or HALF-STOP punctuation, the Vertical Line Test won't do us much good.

Instead, it will help to know that that SAT wants a comma after every item in a series. Think of it this way. There's a potential misunderstanding in this sentence:

I went to the park with my parents, my cat Violet and my dog Stuart.

Without a comma, it sure sounds like this guy has some interesting parents. If there's no comma, how do we know that this sentence isn't supposed to say his parents are *my cat Violet and my dog Stuart.* The only way to remove the ambiguity would be to add a comma:

I went to the park with my parents, my cat Violet, and my dog Stuart.

Keep that in mind as we try to crack number 4. In this problem, *Harvard, Yale, and Brown* form a list, so they should be set off by commas as they are in (B).

Let's try another.

---

5 Jonah, everyone seemed fairly certain, was going to get into one of those schools.

5

A) NO CHANGE
B) Jonah everyone seemed fairly certain
C) Jonah, everyone seemed fairly certain
D) Jonah everyone seemed fairly certain,

Here's How to Crack It

First, check what's changing in the answer choices. Just commas. And those commas seem to be circling around the words *everyone seemed fairly certain*. When you've got a few commas circling around a word, phrase, or clause like this, the question is usually testing necessary vs. unnecessary information.

A good way to test whether the idea is necessary to the meaning of the sentence is to take it out. Read the original sentence again. Now read this one: *Jonah was going to get into one of those schools*.

Is the sentence still complete? Yes. Has the meaning of the sentence changed? No, we just lost a little extra information. Therefore, the idea is *unnecessary* to the meaning of the sentence and should be set off with commas as it is in (A).

Quick Quiz: Punctuation

Let's try a few more. Try to figure out whether the word or idea in italics is necessary to the meaning of the sentence.

    i.   The student *with the best GPA* will be admitted to the best college.
   ii.   Edward wants to go to Pomona College *which is a really good school.*
  iii.   The car *that was painted red* drove off at a hundred miles an hour.
  iv.   Charles Chesnutt *who wrote a lot of great stories* was also a lawyer.
   v.   Philadelphia Flyers goalie *Steve Mason* is an underappreciated player.

    i.   NECESSARY to the meaning of the sentence (no commas). If you remove the italicized part, the sentence is not adequately specific.
   ii.   UNNECESSARY to the meaning of the sentence (commas). If you remove the italicized part, the sentence is still complete and does not change meaning.
  iii.   NECESSARY to the meaning of the sentence (no commas). If you remove the italicized part, the sentence is not adequately specific.
  iv.   UNNECESSARY to the meaning of the sentence (commas). If you remove the italicized part, the sentence is still complete and does not change meaning.
   v.   NECESSARY to the meaning of the sentence (no commas). If you remove the italicized part, the sentence is no longer complete.

Let's put it all together in this question.

Everyone [6] hoped, he would get in, after his brother and two sisters had gone to their first-choice schools.

6

A) NO CHANGE

B) hoped, he would get in, after his brother, and two sisters had

C) hoped, he would get in after his brother, and, two sisters had

D) hoped he would get in after his brother and two sisters had

Here's How to Crack It

Check what's changing in the answer choices. There are varying numbers of commas in varying places. Remember, the rule of thumb with commas is that if you can't cite a reason to use a comma, *don't use one.*

It looks like *he would get in* is being set off by commas. Let's see whether it's necessary or unnecessary information. Read the original sentence; then read the sentence again without that piece of information: *Everyone hoped after his brother and two sisters had gone to their first-choice schools.* It looks like the sentence has changed meaning and is not really complete anymore. Therefore, that bit of information is necessary to the meaning of the sentence, so it doesn't need commas. Then, there are no good reasons to put commas around or in the phrase *after his brother and two sisters.*

In the end, there aren't reasons to put commas anywhere in this sentence. The best answer is (D). Sometimes SAT will test "unnecessary punctuation" explicitly, so make sure you have a good reason to use commas when you use them!

YOUR GOING TO BE TESTED ON APOSTROPHE'S (AND INTERNET SPELLING IS A TERRIBLE GUIDE!)

As with commas, apostrophes have only a very limited set of applications. Apostrophes are a little trickier, though, because you can't really hear them in speech, so people misuse them all the time. Think about the header of this section. The apostrophes are wrong there. Here's the correct way of punctuating it: *You're going to be tested on apostrophes.* Can you hear the difference? Neither can we.

Therefore, as with commas, if you can't cite a reason to use an apostrophe, don't use one. There are only two reasons to use apostrophes on the SAT.

If you can't cite a reason to use an apostrophe, *don't use one.*

On the SAT, there are only two reasons to use an apostrophe.
- Possessive nouns (NOT pronouns)
- Contractions

Let's see some examples.

———————◯———————

Some of those very [7] selective schools' require really high score's.

7

A) NO CHANGE

B) selective school's require really high scores'.

C) selective schools require really high score's.

D) selective schools require really high scores.

Here's How to Crack It

Check what's changing in the answer choices. In this case, the words are all staying the same, but the apostrophes are changing. Remember! We don't want to use apostrophes at all if we can't cite a good reason to do so.

Does anything belong to *schools* or *score*? No! Are they forming contractions like *school is* or *score is*? No! Therefore, there's no reason to use apostrophes, and the only possible answer is (D), which dispenses with the apostrophes altogether.

As in the previous question, there's no need for any punctuation, and in a question like this, SAT is testing whether you can spot unnecessary punctuation.

———————◯———————

But sometimes the apostrophes will be necessary. Let's have a look at another.

———————◯———————

[8] It's tough to get into you're top-choice schools.

8

A) NO CHANGE

B) Its tough to get into your

C) Its tough to get into you're

D) It's tough to get into your

Here's How to Crack It

Check what's changing in the answer choices. The main changes have to do with apostrophes, particularly on the words *its/it's* and *your/you're*.

The first word, *its/it's*, needs an apostrophe: it creates the contraction *it is*. Therefore, because this one needs an apostrophe, get rid of (B) and (C). As for the other, this word is possessive (as in, the *top-choice schools* belonging to *you*), but remember! Possessive *nouns* need an apostrophe, but possessive *pronouns* don't. Therefore, because *you* is a pronoun, this word should be spelled *your*, as it is in (D).

Phew! These apostrophes can get a little tricky, so let's try a few more. On these (as on many parts of the SAT), you'll find that using your ear to sound things out doesn't really help all that much.

Quick Quiz: Apostrophes

Circle the option that works. The big question is as follows: apostrophes or no apostrophes?

i. *Tinas/Tina's* boss said *shes/she's* allowed to take the next few *days/day's* off.
ii. If *your/you're* not coming to my party, *its/it's* really fine with me.
iii. *There/they're* are really no good *reasons/reason's* for *your/you're* bad attitude.
iv. *Well/we'll* get back to you as soon as *your/you're* application is received.
v. *Its/it's his/his'* guacamole, and he said we *cant/can't* have any because *its/it's* not *ours/our's*.

A NOTE ON GRANULARITY

Sorry for the weird word in the title of this section, but it's one that, we think, is worth knowing. We'd like to be able to give you a little extra "Elite" set of tips, but so far as punctuation is concerned, there's nothing more to say. That's because the SAT couldn't be quite so *granular* as to ask you to know the difference between a period and semicolon. They want to see that you have a basic knowledge of grammar, not that you understand that words like *however* are conjunctive adverbs whereas words like *whereas* are subordinating conjunctions.

Apostrophes: Answer key
i. Tina's, she's, days
ii. You're, it's
iii. There, reasons, your
iv. We'll, your
v. It's, his, can't, it's, ours

As a result, these rules about Stop, Go, Commas, and Apostrophes can be more useful to you than you may think. First of all, they can remind you that SAT couldn't possibly make you choose between a semicolon and a period. If you get a list of answer choices that looks like the following, you can reason your way into the correct answer:

A) NO CHANGE

B) choose. The following

C) choose; the following

D) choose the following

In this instance, you know that the answer can't be (B) or (C) because both of those answers contain basically identical punctuation. Even if the idea of Stop and Go punctuation may seem a little simplistic, you can apply the concepts in more complex ways.

It can also help to remember that a lot of grammatical stuff is basically beyond consensus, and that stuff therefore can't be tested. For instance, let's say you're talking about a novel by Henry James. Would you call it *Henry James' novel* or *Henry James's novel*? SAT wouldn't make you choose because there's not enough consensus around which one is right. Some style guides say only the apostrophe after any noun that ends in *s*; some say *'s* after any singular noun.

The same goes for subordinating conjunctions—words like *because, although, if, since,* and *when.* When you use one to link two ideas, do you need a comma or not? For instance, which one of these is correct?

> *It's tough to say whether a comma is necessary because grammar experts don't agree.*

> *It's tough to say whether a comma is necessary, because grammar experts don't agree.*

So which one is it? Tough call, and even grammarians disagree with one another. A comma before a subordinating conjunction is a *style choice,* so SAT couldn't make you pick between these answers:

A) necessary, because grammar

B) necessary because grammar

Those two answers are separated by nothing more than a stylistic choice, so how could you be expected to pick between them as if one were correct and the other incorrect?

In short, once you've mastered all the punctuation and techniques in this chapter, take the next step by looking to apply this knowledge on the meta-level. If you're stuck between two answers, at least give some consideration to the fact that if the answers are really that similar, there's probably something else wrong.

CONCLUSION

In sum, we've looked at all the punctuation you'd ever need on the SAT. It's really not so much, and you probably knew a lot of it already. In general, checking what's changing in the answer choices can help reveal mistakes that you may not have heard, and POE can help you narrow those answers down.

Punctuation rules are easy to learn, as is the biggest rule of all about punctuation.

> Know why you are using punctuation, whether that punctuation is Stop, Half-Stop, Go, commas, or apostrophes. If you can't cite reasons to use these punctuation marks, don't use them!

In the last few pages of this chapter, try out these skills on a drill.

PUNCTUATION EXERCISES

Time: 5-6 minutes

More and more of our lives are mechanized, and at some point, we have to start wondering, what's the limit of that mechanization? Many factory workers in the 19th century thought their jobs [1] were safe but we know now that they were wrong. Many people [2] in today's world believe there jobs are safe, but how safe are those jobs really?

Studies abound that ask whether man or machine is better at particular tasks, and the results are not always so obvious. Sure, a machine is obviously [3] better at say, welding huge pieces of steel together, but what would you say if someone told you people are more likely to open up to a machine than to a psychologist? Or that a machine could write a quicker, more efficient news story than an experienced reporter?

[1]

A) NO CHANGE
B) were safe, but we know
C) were safe but we know,
D) were safe. But, we know

[2]

A) NO CHANGE
B) in todays world believe their jobs
C) in todays world believe they're jobs
D) in today's world believe their jobs

[3]

A) NO CHANGE
B) better at, say welding
C) better at, say, welding
D) better at say welding

These questions may seem overly pessimistic (or overly optimistic depending on [4] your point of view); however, some recent studies have been truly remarkable. Take Ellie, a computer program used primarily to diagnose patients with [5] depression, PTSD and other mood disorders. Many patients found it easier to talk to "Ellie" than [6] to a real person: she didn't react in some of those seemingly judgmental ways that a person would, and her voice [7] never broke on top of that she could help psychologists to diagnose mental illnesses better than human observation could. She could detect facial movements or voice tones that a person might have heard or ignored.

4

A) NO CHANGE
B) your point of view), however,
C) you're point of view), however,
D) you're point of view); however,

5

A) NO CHANGE
B) depression, PTSD, and other
C) depression, PTSD, and, other
D) depression, PTSD, and other,

6

A) NO CHANGE
B) to a real person, she
C) to, a real person, she
D) to a real person she

7

A) NO CHANGE
B) never broke, on top of that,
C) never broke. On top of that,
D) never broke; on top, of that,

Whether Ellie is the way of the future is yet to be determined. We can't know right now, but there is no doubt that she raises some interesting questions, not only about **8** the work of psychologists' but about all of what we think are definitively human activities.

On the other side of the discussion, however, there's some evidence that humans may have the upper hand. In some of the more basic **9** tasks those learned before the age of about 10 humans have a huge upper hand. Computers can do the complex thinking, but one thing with which they have a lot of trouble is, paradoxically, simplicity. Sure, a computer **10** can tell your washer's and dryer's what a perfect washing and drying cycle is, but can it fold your laundry? Your GPS can tell you the fastest route to the next state, but can it tell you the prettiest way to go or the best restaurants along the way? Not without humans!

While the battle of man against machine rages **11** on. The questions will persist. No matter who wins, though, humans will almost assuredly find ways to adapt: that's something we've been doing for thousands of years, which is something that no computer can say.

8
A) NO CHANGE
B) psychologists work
C) the work of psychologists
D) the work of psychologist's

9
A) NO CHANGE
B) tasks those learned before the age of about 10, humans
C) tasks, those learned before the age of about 10 humans
D) tasks, those learned before the age of about 10, humans

10
A) NO CHANGE
B) can tell your washer and dryer what
C) can tell you're washers and dryers
D) can tell you're washer and dryer

11
A) NO CHANGE
B) on; the
C) on—the
D) on, the

For further practice, go online to your Student Tools and complete the Chapter 9 Punctuation Drill.

Summary

○ Remember STOP, HALF-STOP, and GO punctuation.
  • STOP punctuation can link only complete ideas.
  • HALF-STOP punctuation must be preceded by a complete idea.
  • GO punctuation can link anything except two complete ideas.

○ When you see STOP punctuation changing in the answer choices, use the Vertical Line Test.

○ On the SAT, there are only four reasons to use a comma:
  • STOP punctuation (with one of the FANBOYS)
  • GO punctuation
  • after every item in a list
  • to set off unnecessary information

○ On the SAT, there are only two reasons to use an apostrophe:
  • possessive nouns (NOT pronouns)
  • contractions

○ Know why you are using punctuation, whether that punctuation is STOP, HALF-STOP, GO, commas, or apostrophes. If you can't cite reasons to use these punctuation marks, don't use them!

Chapter 10
Words

The Writing and Language Test will also focus on words—mainly nouns, pronouns, and verbs. While we will discuss a few of these grammatical concepts along the way, this chapter will boil these many concepts down to three main terms: Consistency, Precision, Concision. With fewer minutiae to remember, you will be able to work through Words questions with confidence and ease.

THE WORDS CHANGE, BUT THE SONG REMAINS THE SAME

In the last chapter, we looked at what to do when SAT is testing punctuation. In this chapter, we're going to look at what to do when SAT is testing words—mainly verbs, nouns, and pronouns.

Our basic strategy, however, has remained the same. As we saw in the previous two chapters, when faced with an SAT Writing and Language question, we should always do the following:

> Check what's changing in the answer choices and use POE.

Throughout this chapter, we talk a lot about certain parts of speech, but we don't really use a lot of grammar terms. That's because we find that on the SAT, the best answers across a lot of different parts of speech can be summed up most succinctly with three basic terms: Consistency, Precision, and Concision. You will be most prepared if you remember these three basic rules.

> **CONSISTENCY:** Correct answers are consistent with the rest of the sentence and the passage.
>
> **PRECISION:** Correct answers are as precise as possible.
>
> **CONCISION:** Barring other errors, correct answers are as concise as possible.

Let's look at some examples of each.

CONSISTENCY

The speakers of what has come to be known as **1** Appalachian English has used a form of English that few can explain.

1

A) NO CHANGE

B) Appalachian English uses

C) Appalachian English use

D) Appalachian English using

Here's How to Crack It

First, as always, check what's changing in the answer choices. In this case, *Appalachian English* stays the same, but the forms of the verb *to use* change. Therefore, because the verbs change, we know that the question is testing verbs.

When you see verbs changing in the answer choices, the first thing to check is the subject of the sentence. Is the verb consistent with the subject? In this case, it's not. The subject of this sentence is *speakers*, which is plural. Therefore, (A) and (B) have to be eliminated, and (D) creates an incomplete idea. Only (C) can work in the context.

Thus, when you see verbs changing in the answer choices, check the subject first. Subjects and verbs need to be consistent with each other.

Let's have a look at another question.

Many scholars believe Appalachian pronunciation comes from Scots-Irish immigration, but **2** some theorizes that this dialect of English may be closer to what Londoners spoke in Elizabethan times.

2

A) NO CHANGE

B) some theorized

C) some have theorized

D) some theorize

Here's How to Crack It

Check what's changing in the answer choices. The word *some* remains consistent, but the verbs are changing. Remember from the first question that whenever you see verbs changing, you should make sure the verb is consistent with the subject. Because the subject of this sentence is *some*, you can eliminate (A), which isn't consistent.

Then, because all the others are consistent with the subject, make sure they are consistent with the other verbs. It looks like all the other verbs in this sentence—*believe, comes, may be*—are in the present tense, so the underlined verb should be as well, as it is in (D). Choices (B) and (C) could work in some contexts, but not this one!

As you can see, verbs are all about consistency.

> When you see verbs changing in the answer choices, make sure those verbs are
>
> - CONSISTENT with their subjects.
> - CONSISTENT with other verbs in the sentence and surrounding sentences.

Let's try one that has a little bit of everything.

Trying to understand these changes **3** demonstrate that although we all technically speak English, we speak very different languages indeed.

3

A) NO CHANGE

B) demonstrate that although we all technically spoke English, we speak

C) demonstrates that although we all technically speak English, we might have been speaking

D) demonstrates that although we all technically speak English, we speak

Here's How to Crack It
Check what's changing in the answer choices. It looks like lots of verbs!

Let's start with the first. See which one, *demonstrate* or *demonstrates*, is consistent with the subject. That subject is *Trying*, which is singular, thus eliminating (A) and (B).

Then, we have to choose between *speak* and *might have been speaking*. Since both of these are consistent with the subject *we*, let's try to pick the one that is most consistent with other verbs. The only other verbs are *demonstrates* and *speak*, both of which are in the present tense and don't use the odd *might have been* form. Therefore, if we have to choose between (C) and (D), (D) is definitely better.

———————○———————

Consistency applies across the test. Let's see another question where the idea of Consistency might help us.

———————○———————

Appalachian-English speakers and **4** their family communicate in a way that shows just how influential diversity can be on the language we speak.

4

A) NO CHANGE
B) they're families communicate
C) their families communicate
D) their family communicates

Here's How to Crack It
Check the answer choices first. It looks like pretty much everything is changing here: *they're/their*, *families/family*, and *communicate/communicates*. Let's look at the ones we have done already.

We can't cite a good reason to use an apostrophe, so let's get rid of (B). Then, the verb changes, so let's check the subject. That subject is *Appalachian-English speakers and their family/families*, which is plural regardless of the word *family* or *families*. Keep the verb consistent with the plural subject and eliminate (D).

Then, we have to choose between *family* and *families*, two nouns. As with verbs, nouns are all about consistency. When you see nouns changing in the answer choices, make sure they are consistent with the other nouns in the sentence. In this case, we are talking about *Appalachian-English speakers*, all of them, so we must be talking about all of their *families* as well. Many speakers must mean many families, as (C) suggests.

———————○———————

Noun consistency can show up in other ways as well. Let's have a look at #5.

———————◯———————

The language of the West Virginians in Appalachia is almost nothing like **5** New Yorkers or even other West Virginians.

5

A) NO CHANGE

B) the language of New Yorker's or even other West Virginian's.

C) that of New Yorkers or even other West Virginians.

D) people from New York or from West Virginia.

Here's How to Crack It

Look at what's changing in the answer choices. It looks like the main change is between the nouns—*New Yorkers or even other West Virginians* and *the language.* We saw in the last problem that when nouns are changing in the answer choices, we want to make sure those nouns are consistent with other nouns in the sentence.

In this case, the nouns are being compared. The language of Appalachia is being compared with the language of New Yorkers and West Virginians. Choices (A) and (D) suggest that the *language* is being compared with the *people*, so those are inconsistent. Then, (B) contains some unnecessary apostrophes, so only (C) is left.

SAT calls this concept "faulty comparison," but we don't have to know that name. Instead, we can just remember that *nouns have to be consistent with other nouns.* When the answer choices show a change in nouns, look for the sentence's other nouns. They'll provide the clue!

———————◯———————

———————◯———————

Scholars today are not sure whether to call it a purely European dialect or **6** a uniquely American one.

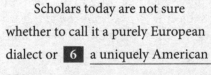

6

A) NO CHANGE

B) uniquely American.

C) a unique one.

D) American.

Here's How to Crack It

Check what's changing in the answer choices. There's a fairly significant change between *American* and *American one*. As in the previous sentence, let's make sure this is consistent. The part of the sentence right before the underlined portion refers to a *European dialect*, so we should make our part of the sentence consistent: an *American dialect*, not merely *American*, as in (B) and (D).

Then, we are down to (A) and (C). The difference here comes between the words *unique* and *uniquely American*. While we do want to be concise when possible, we need to make sure first and foremost that we are being *precise*. Choice (A) is more precise than choice (C) in that it has a clearer relation to the *European dialect* with which it is being contrasted. Therefore, (A) is the best answer because it is the most *consistent* with the rest of the sentence and the most *precise* of the remaining possible answers.

CONSISTENCY

- When the verbs are changing in the answer choices, make sure those verbs are consistent with their subjects and with other verbs.
- When the nouns are changing in the answer choices, make sure those nouns are consistent with the other nouns in the sentence and the paragraph.

GRAMMAR BY ANY OTHER NAME WOULD SMELL AS SWEET

Although it may seem like we've only talked about this thing called "Consistency," there's actually a ton of grammar buried in that term. When we say that verbs need to be consistent with their subjects and other verbs, we're really referring to what the SAT calls "Subject-verb agreement" and "Verb tense, mood, and voice." When we talk about noun consistency, we're talking about "Noun agreement" and "Logical comparison." Consistency can also describe some grammatical concepts like "parallelism."

Really, though, these are all about consistency, and the SAT is not testing your knowledge of grammar terms so much as your ability to *apply* your knowledge of grammar. To that end, we think that the word "Consistency" is the way to go, because it describes the five concepts just mentioned and a bunch of others besides, is the way to go. After all, the SAT can test you on 40 different topics in 44 questions, so it's not likely that you'll get a lot of mileage out of learning all 40 grammar terms when just a few will suffice.

That said, some concepts are tougher than others. Since we're trying to maximize our score potential, it's worth talking a bit more about certain grammar topics than can show up on the SAT. One difficult and tough-to-spot concept from the batch of Consistency topics that sometimes shows up is called "logical comparison."

The main idea here is that like things need to be compared. We actually gave an example of this in Chapter 8. Remember the e-mail subject line we cited? It went like this:

> *Can you score more points than us?*

The error here is one of logical comparison. What's being compared? Is it *you* and *us*? Or *points* and *us*? It's obviously the former: you can't score *us*. In situations like this one, it can help to extend the sentence to make the comparison as specific as possible. In this case, *us* would have to change to *we* because the sentence would extend to say,

> *Can you score more points than we [can score]?*

Have a look at these three sentences and try to pick the best answer for each.

> *Paul is better at singing than (I/me).*
> *I ended up with more points than (he/him).*
> *I like Jacob more than (she/her).*

In the first instance, you would expand the sentence to say that *Paul is better at singing than I [am].* In the second sentence, you'd expand the sentence to say that *I ended up with more points than he [had/did].*

The third one is a little ambiguous, and it actually could mean two different things. The first is this:

> *I like Jacob more than **she [likes Jacob].***

The other wouldn't be wrong; it would just mean something different.

> *I like Jacob more than **[I like] her.***

Comparisons are all about consistency. You want to make sure that you're keeping the pronouns consistent with the meaning. As the last example shows, you also want to make sure that those comparisons are as precise as possible.

Comparisons, however, are not just about pronouns. Nouns need to be consistent and logical in comparisons as well. Have a look at this one:

> *I think the Phillies' bullpen is better than the Braves.*

What's actually being compared here? We know what the writer means, probably, but what he says here is that one team's *bullpen* is better than another *team*. In order to fix the comparison, then, we'd have to make sure to compare like things, so a clearer version of this sentence would be

> *I think the Phillies' bullpen is better than **that of** the Braves.*

Or

> *I think the Phillies' bullpen is better than the Braves' bullpen.*

Try these next few and see if you can rewrite each sentence to make it more logical.

> *James Joyce's novels are more concerned with the geography of Ireland than Samuel Beckett.*
>
> *The tacos at Juan's are better than Jorge's.*
>
> *Poems by amateur writers can sometimes be as good as professionals.*

In the first instance, you want to compare the *novels* of Joyce with the *novels* of Beckett: right now the *novels* of Joyce are being compared with *Beckett* himself. Rewrite the sentence to say *James Joyce's novels are more concerned with the geography of Ireland than **are those of** Samuel Beckett.*

The second sentence should compare *tacos* to *tacos*, not *tacos* to *Jorge's*. Fix the sentence this way: *The tacos at Juan's are better than **those at** Jorge's.*

The third sentence should compare *poems* to *poems*, not *poems* to *professionals*. Fix the sentence this way: *Poems by amateur writers can sometimes be as good as **those written by** professionals.*

All of these fixes make good logical sense when they are pointed out, but faulty comparisons can be tough to spot because we misuse them so frequently in our day-to-day speech. First and foremost, when you see nouns changing in the answer choices, make sure that those nouns are consistent. If the bad comparison doesn't jump out at you, look out for words like *more*, *better*, or *as much as*. Make sure your sentences are as internally consistent and precise as possible.

FOR WHEN YOU'RE NOT JUST TALKING ABOUT ANYTHING: PRECISION

Consistency is probably the most important thing on the SAT, but precision is a close second. Once you've made sure that the underlined portion is consistent with the rest of the sentence, then make sure that the underlined portion is as consistent as possible. Perfect grammar is one thing, but it won't matter much if no one knows what the writer is talking about!

Let's hear that one more time.

> Once you are sure that a word or phrase is consistent with the non-underlined portion of the sentence, make that word or phrase as precise as you can.

Really, [7] most are collections of many influences, but the Appalachian dialect seems unique.

7
A) NO CHANGE
B) most of them
C) most Americans
D) most American dialects

Here's How to Crack It

Check what's changing in the answer choices. The changes could be summed up with the question "*most* what?" We've got four different options, so let's use our main guiding principles of consistency and precision.

First of all, there's a comparison in this sentence between different kinds of *dialects*, so (C) can be eliminated because it changes the comparison to something else inconsistent.

Then, let's be as precise as possible. Choices (A) and (B) are very similar in that they say *most*, but they don't specify *what* that *most* refers to. Even though these are grammatically consistent with the rest of the sentence, they're not quite precise enough, which makes (D) a lot better.

As question #7 shows, pronouns can be a bit of a challenge. They can appear in otherwise grammatically correct sentences. Still, precision is key when you're dealing with pronouns. See what you can do with these sentences. Circle the potentially imprecise pronouns and rewrite the sentences.

Quick Quiz: Precise Pronouns

i. Certain dialects have obvious sources, but that doesn't make it any easier to understand.

ii. Each of us speaks with an accent because of where they are from.

iii. Whether word choice or pronunciation, it's usually easy to hear in someone's accent.

iv. Everyone uses some kind of dialect words in their everyday speech.

v. Movies, TV, the Internet: it may be destroying differentiated dialects in the modern world.

Precision can show up in some other ways as well. Have a look at this question.

The Appalachian region's **8** <u>isolation has led to some hypotheses from major urban centers that its dialect has remained intact</u> from the days of its earliest settlers.

8

A) NO CHANGE

B) isolation has led to some hypotheses that its dialect from major urban centers has remained intact

C) isolation from major urban centers has led to some hypotheses that its dialect has remained intact

D) isolation has led to some hypotheses that its dialect has remained intact from major urban centers

Here's How to Crack It

Check what's changing in the answer choices. This step is crucial because there are no obvious grammatical errors, so the answer choices are essential to figuring out exactly what the question is asking you to do.

In the end, the only difference among the answer choices is that the phrase *from major urban centers* is in different places. In the end, we will just need to put that phrase in the most precise place, hopefully right next to whatever it is modifying.

In this case, we can choose from among *hypotheses*, *dialect*, *isolation*, and *intact*. Which of these would have the most precise need for the phrase *from major urban centers*? Because *urban centers* seems to have something to do with place, we should eliminate (A), *hypotheses*, and (D), *intact*, which don't have anything to do with place. Then, because the passage as a whole has talked about the remoteness of the Appalachian dialect, we can say for sure that it is not a *dialect from major urban centers*, eliminating (B). All that remains, then, is (C), which completes the phrase *isolation from major urban centers*, which is the most precise answer possible.

Pronouns: Answer Key

i. *it* is the problem. *Certain dialects have obvious sources, but that doesn't make them any easier to understand.*

ii. *they* is the problem. *Each of us speaks with an accent because of where he or she is from.*

iii. *it* is the problem. Take it out and rearrange the sentence accordingly. *Word-choice and pronunciation are usually easy to hear in someone's accent.*

iv. *their* is the problem. *Everyone uses some kind of dialect words in his or her everyday speech.*

v. *it* is the problem. *Movies, TV, the Internet: all three may be destroying differentiated dialects in the modern world.*

Let's have a look at some more of these modifiers. As with faulty comparisons, modifiers can easily go undetected. That's because a lot of the time you end up supplying information for the speaker. For example, the following sentence has a problem:

> *Looking through the chapter, faulty comparisons are the toughest grammar concept.*

If someone said this to you, you'd know they meant that *we* or *you* are *looking through the chapter*, but the sentence doesn't actually say that. Instead, the modifier *looking through the chapter* doesn't modify anything at all. This is a classic case of what's called a "dangling" modifier because it just dangles there without being attached to anything.

Modifiers can be tough, so try a few more. Rewrite each sentence so the modifier makes the *precise* sense that it should.

Quick Quiz: Dangling Modifiers
i. With all its ins and outs, many people find language a tough thing to study.
ii. Dialects are really fascinating to anyone who wants to study them of a particular language.
iii. Once opened up, you can find endless mysteries in the study of language.
iv. I first learned about the Appalachian dialect from a professor in college at age 19.
v. Frankly pretty boring, Donald didn't pay much attention in his linguistics class.

Modifiers Answer Key
i. Many people find language a tough thing to study because of all its ins and outs.
ii. Dialects of a particular language are really fascinating to anyone who wants to study them.
iii. Once opened up, the mysteries of a language can be endless.
iv. I first learned about the Appalachian dialect from a college professor when I was 19 years old.
v. Donald didn't pay much attention in his linguistics class, which he found frankly pretty boring.

CONCISION. PERIOD.
This is not to say, however, that more words always mean more precision. In fact, a lot of the time less is more. If you were to ask for directions, which answer would you rather receive?

> *Turn right at Main Street and walk four blocks.*

Or

> *Since this street, Elm Street, is facing in a northerly direction, and your destination is due northeast, go east when you arrive at the intersection of Elm and Main. Going east will entail making a right turn in quite that easterly direction. After having made this turn and arriving on the perpendicular street...*

The first one. Obviously.

And that's because concision is key when you want to communicate meaning. Really, as long as everything else is in order—as long as the grammar and punctuation are good to go—the best answer will almost always be the shortest.

Let's see an example.

It is precisely this isolation that has led many scholars to believe that Appalachian English is **9** alike and similar to the English spoken in Shakespeare's time.

9

A) NO CHANGE

B) similar

C) likely similar

D) similarly alike

Here's How to Crack It

Check what's changing in the answer choices. In this case, the word *similar* appears in all the answer choices, and in some, it is paired with the word *alike*. Typically, if you see a list of answer choices wherein one answer is short and the rest mean the same thing but are longer, the question is testing conciseness.

What, after all, is the difference between the words *similar* and *alike*? There really isn't one, so there's no use in saying both of them, as in (A), or pairing them awkwardly, as in (D). In fact, the shortest answer, (B), does everything the other answers do, but it does so in the fewest words. Choice (B) is therefore the best answer.

Let's see one more.

10 Whatever the case may be, Appalachian is a fascinating dialect, and we can only hope that it persists against the onslaught of mass media.

10

A) NO CHANGE

B) In any case, Appalachian

C) All things considered, Appalachian

D) Appalachian

Here's How to Crack It

As always, check what's changing in the answer choices. The changes could be summed up like this: there's a bunch of stuff before the word *Appalachian*. Does any of that stuff contribute in a significant way to the sentence? No. Does the word *Appalachian* alone help the sentence to fulfill its basic purpose? Yes. Therefore, the best answer is choice (D).

As we have seen in this chapter, when SAT is testing *words* (which they are any time the words are changing in the answer choices), make sure that those words are

- **Consistent.** Verbs, nouns, and pronouns should agree within sentences and passages.
- **Precise.** The writing should communicate specific ideas and events.
- **Concise.** When everything else is correct, the shortest answer is the best.

WORDS EXERCISE
Time: 7-8 minutes

War and Peace (1869) is **1** well-known and famous mainly for its length. Not many readers, especially in the modern day, **2** has the time or the patience to work through Leo Tolstoy's 1400 pages and countless characters and plot twists. **3** They are missing a major opportunity, not only because the novel is more fun than its page count suggests but also because it marks the end of a particular moment in history.

1
A) NO CHANGE
B) famous and well-known
C) famously well-known
D) well-known

2
A) NO CHANGE
B) have
C) are having
D) do have

3
A) NO CHANGE
B) Those readers
C) Many of them
D) Some

Czech novelist Milan Kundera cited Tolstoy as the last novelist who could [4] be possessing the sum of his era's human knowledge. This may seem like an odd claim. Some people may be very intelligent, others may be know-it-alls, but is it really possible to know everything? A book like *War and Peace* makes the case that it is possible to know it all, or at least that it *was* possible, [5] alongside Tolstoy's other great novels and non-fiction writings. Shakespeare [6] seemed to have an emotional vocabulary that was advanced for his age, but Tolstoy lived in [7] an era of facts and discoveries, and his novels show the fruits of his vast study. It is frankly conceivable that a man with Tolstoy's leisure, intelligence, and curiosity [8] learns about his age's most current findings in literature, politics, religion, and science.

4

A) NO CHANGE

B) of had

C) possess

D) possessed

5

If the punctuation were adjusted accordingly, the best placement for the underlined portion would be

A) where it is now.

B) after the word *Peace*.

C) after the word *that*.

D) after the word *least*.

6

A) NO CHANGE

B) seems having

C) has

D) seemingly has

7

A) NO CHANGE

B) an era,

C) a historical time period,

D) one,

8

A) NO CHANGE

B) had been learning

C) could have learned

D) are learning

The very fact that such an achievement is impossible now shows us just how much things have changed since Tolstoy's death in 1910. [9] This was the year, in fact, that Virginia Woolf cited in her oft-quoted remark, "On or about 1910 human character changed." If we at least entertain the idea that she is correct, we can begin to see why she would be willing to make such a grandiose remark. After 1910, the twentieth century started in earnest. Knowledge became more complex as it became more specialized, and although airplanes seemed to make the world a smaller place, the differences among all the places in that small world truly emerged.

War and Peace is the great document of that pre-1910 era, of a moment when the great scientists were also [10] into philosophy and when the great mathematicians were also the great theologians. A great discovery in one field could also be [11] another. Although it was certainly remarkable, it was also possible for a man like Tolstoy to have a fundamental grasp of all that united the many branches of knowledge. Tolstoy's achievement is impossible today, but it is a wonderful reminder of the value of intellectual curiosity and cosmopolitanism. No matter how brilliant and refined we may become, we can always stand to be reminded that there is a world outside of our immediate circle.

9

The writer is considering deleting the phrase *since Tolstoy's death in 1910* and ending the sentence with a period after the word *changed*. Should the phrase be kept or deleted?

A) Kept, because it contributes to the essay's biographical sketch of the author of *War and Peace*.

B) Kept, because it introduces a topic of discussion that is continued throughout the paragraph.

C) Deleted, because the remainder of the paragraph describes the insignificance of Tolstoy's death.

D) Deleted, because the paragraph as a whole is focused on the achievements of another author.

10

A) NO CHANGE

B) fascinated with philosophical inquiry

C) interested in philosophy

D) the great philosophers

11

A) NO CHANGE

B) another field.

C) a great discovery in another.

D) the same thing elsewhere.

For further practice, go online to your Student Tools and complete the Chapter 10 Words Drill.

Summary

- When faced with an SAT Writing and Language question, always check what's changing in the answer choices and use POE.

- When you see verbs changing in the answer choices, make sure those verbs are consistent with their subjects as well as with other verbs in the sentence and surrounding sentences.

- When the nouns are changing in the answer choices, make sure those nouns are consistent with the other nouns in the sentence and the paragraph.

- Once you are sure that a word or phrase is consistent with the non-underlined portion of the sentence, make that word or phrase as precise as you can.

- Concision is key when you want to communicate meaning. As long as the grammar and punctuation are good to go, the best answer will almost always be the shortest.

Chapter 11
Questions

In the previous chapters, we've seen "questions" that don't have questions at all. In this chapter, we will deal with those questions that actually do contain questions and some of the strategies that can help to simplify them.

ANSWERING QUESTIONS ABOUT QUESTIONS

In the previous two chapters, we saw most of the concepts that SAT will test. In this chapter, we're not going to learn a lot of new stuff in the way of grammar. Instead, we'll look at some of the questions that SAT asks.

As we've seen, a lot of the questions don't have questions at all. They're just lists of answer choices, and we start the process of answering them by asking a question of our own: "What's changing in the answer choices?"

Because you need to move quickly through this test, you may fall into the habit of not checking for questions. Even when you do read the questions, you may read them hastily or vaguely. Well, we are here to tell you that neither of these approaches will work.

> The most important thing about Writing and Language questions is that you *notice* those questions and then *answer* those questions.

This may seem like just about the most obvious advice you've ever been given, but you'd be surprised how much less precise your brain is when you're working quickly.

Here's an example. Do these next 10 questions as quickly as you can.

1. $2 + 1 =$
2. $1 + 2 =$
3. $3 + 1 =$
4. $3 + 2 \neq$
5. $1 + 2 =$
6. $2 - 1 <$
7. $2 \pm 2 =$
8. $3 + 1 =$
9. $3 + 2 =$
10. $3 + 3 \neq$

Now check your answers.

1. 3
2. 3
3. 4
4. Anything but 5
5. 3
6. Any number greater than 1 (but not 1!)
7. 0 or 4
8. 4
9. 5
10. Anything but 6

Now, it's very possible that you got at least one of those questions wrong. What happened? It's not that the questions are hard. In fact, the questions are about as easy as can be. So why did you get some of them wrong? You were probably moving too quickly to notice that the signs changed a few times.

This is a lot like the Writing and Language section. You might miss some of the easiest points on the whole test by not reading carefully enough.

As we will see throughout this chapter, most of the questions will test concepts with which we are already familiar.

WORDS AND PUNCTUATION IN REVERSE

Many of the concepts we saw in the Punctuation and Words chapters show up explicitly with questions, but usually there's some kind of twist.

Here's an example.

Most people are familiar with the idea of a gender pay **1** gap. What most people don't realize is just how persistent that pay gap has been.

1

Which of the following alternatives to the underlined portion would NOT be acceptable?

A) gap; what

B) gap: what

C) gap, however, what

D) gap, but what

Here's How to Crack It

First and foremost, it's important to notice the question. This one is asking for the alternative that would NOT be acceptable, so we'll need to find an answer that doesn't work.

In the meantime, let's go through the steps. What's changing in the answer choices? STOP, HALF-STOP, and GO punctuation. Use the Vertical Line Test between the words *gap* and *what*. The idea before the line, *Most people are familiar with the idea of a gender pay gap*, is complete. The idea after the line, *what most people don't realize is just how persistent that pay gap has been*, is also complete. Therefore, we need either STOP or HALF-STOP punctuation.

Choices (A) and (B) definitely provide the punctuation we want. Choice (D) doesn't look like it does, but remember! *But* is one of the FANBOYS, and comma + FANBOYS is one of the forms of STOP punctuation! The only one, therefore, that doesn't work in the context is (C), so it is the alternative that would NOT be acceptable.

Notice how important the word NOT was in this question. If you missed it, you might have thought the question had three correct answers!

———————⊙———————

Let's try another.

———————⊙———————

The 2 size of the gap may have narrowed, but we still have a long way to go.

2

Which of the following substitutions would be LEAST acceptable?

A) magnitude

B) proportion

C) vastness

D) immensity

Here's How to Crack It

Again, the question asks for the LEAST acceptable, so find and eliminate answers that work. In this case, we need something similar in meaning to the word *size* as it is used in this sentence. All four words mean something similar to *size* in different contexts, but we want something that refers to just how *large* the gap is, so (A), (C), and (D) would work.

Choice (B) does give a synonym for the word *size*, but it means something more like *dimensions* than *largeness*, so it is the LEAST acceptable of the substitutions.

———————⊙———————

Let's look at another one that deals with some of the topics we've seen earlier.

———————————◯———————————

The problem has certainly gained a good deal of traction in public debates. The fact that it has gained such traction makes us wonder why there isn't more significant action to combat the gender pay gap. **3**

3

Which of the following gives the best way to combine these two sentences?

A) The problem has certainly gained a good deal of traction in public debates; the fact that it has gained such traction makes us wonder why there isn't more significant action to combat the gender pay gap.

B) The problem has certainly gained a good deal of traction in public debates, which raises the question of why more isn't being done to combat the gap.

C) The problem has certainly gained a good deal of traction in public debates: this fact of more public attention raises a serious question of why more isn't being done to close that gap.

D) The problem has certainly gained a good deal of traction in public debates. Why isn't more being done to combat the gap?

Here's How to Crack It

The question asks us to combine the two sentences. Your eyes were probably drawn immediately to (D), which is the most concise of the choices. There's just one problem: (D) doesn't answer the question! The question asks to *combine* the sentences, and while (D) shortens them, it doesn't combine them.

Choice (B) is therefore the best option. It combines the sentences and shortens them a bit, unlike (A) and (C), which combine the sentences, but don't really do much beyond changing the punctuation.

———————————◯———————————

Questions like #3 are why…

> The most important thing about Writing and Language questions is that you *notice* those questions and then *answer* those questions.

PRECISION QUESTIONS

Not all questions will just be applications of punctuation and parts of speech. Some questions will ask you to do more specific things. Remember the three terms we kept repeating in the Words chapter: Consistency, Precision, and Concision. We'll start with the Precision-related questions. Even in those in which Precision is not asked about directly, or is mixed with Consistency or Concision, remember:

> Answer the question in the most precise way possible. Read literally!

Let's try one.

The question of unequal pay for women draws on many other broader social issues. **4**

4

The writer is considering deleting the phrase *of unequal pay for women* from the preceding sentence. Should this phrase be kept or deleted?

A) Kept, because removing it would remove a crucial piece of information from this part of the sentence.

B) Kept, because it reminds the reader of social injustice in the modern world.

C) Deleted, because it wrongly implies that there is a disparity between what women and men are paid.

D) Deleted, because it gives information that has no bearing on this particular text.

Here's How to Crack It

This question asks whether we should keep or delete the phrase *of unequal pay for women*. Without that phrase, the sentence reads, *The question draws on many other broader social issues*. Because nothing in this sentence or any of the previous ones specifies what this *question* might be, we should keep the phrase. We want to be as precise as possible!

And, as (A) says, we want to keep the phrase because it is crucial to clarifying precisely what *the question* is. Choice (B) is a little too grandiose a reason to keep the phrase, especially when the whole passage is about the particular injustice of the gender pay gap. Choice (A) is therefore the best answer.

———————◯———————

Let's try another.

———————◯———————

The gender disparities persist in other areas than pay. It is a kind of open secret, for instance, that women have had the right to vote in the United States for less than a century. **5** There is a long history of misogyny written into the very cultural and social fabric of the United States.

5

At this point, the writer is considering adding the following true statement:

> The year that women's suffrage became legal in the United States was also the year that the American Football League was formed under the leadership of Jim Thorpe.

Should the writer make this addition here?

A) Yes, because it gives a broader context to the achievement of women's suffrage.

B) Yes, because it helps to ease some of the political rhetoric in the rest of the passage.

C) No, because it does not contribute in a significant way to the discussion of the gender pay gap.

D) No, because the question of gender pay is irrelevant when all football players are men.

Here's How to Crack It

The proposed sentence does contain an interesting bit of information, but that piece of information has no clear place either in these few sentences or in the passage as a whole. Therefore, it should not be added, thus eliminating (A) and (B).

Then, because it does not play a significant role in the passage, the sentence should not be added for the reason stated in (C). While (D) may be true in a way, it does not reflect anything clearly relating to the role the sentence might play in the passage as a whole. Read literally, and answer as literally and precisely as you can.

CONSISTENCY QUESTIONS

Just as questions should be answered as *precisely* as possible, they should also be answered with information that is *consistent* with what's in the passage.

When answering consistency questions, keep this general rule in mind:

> Writing and Language passages should be judged on what they *do* say, not on what they *could* say. When dealing with Style, Tone, and Focus, be sure to work with the words and phrases the passage has already used.

Let's look at two questions that deal with the idea of consistency.

[1] One need look no further than to the idea of the "traditional" family. [2] The shift, however, has yet to produce a substantive increase in how women, who are now nearly as likely to work as men, are paid. [3] In this idea, the father of the family earns the family wage <u>**6** and gives the children their last names.</u> [4] With such an idea bolstering what many consider to be the goal inherent in the "American dream," it is no wonder that women in the workplace should have a somewhat degraded position. [5] Shifting social and economic roles, however, have begun to change how people think about gender roles within the family. **7**

6

Which of the following choices would best complete the distinction described in this sentence and the paragraph as a whole?

A) NO CHANGE

B) while the mother tends to the children and the home.

C) though his interest in masculine things like sports may vary.

D) but will only be able to achieve a wage commensurate with his skills and education.

7

The best placement for sentence 2 would be

A) where it is now.

B) before sentence 1.

C) after sentence 4.

D) after sentence 5.

Here's How to Crack Them

Let's look at Question 6 first. In this case, the question tells us exactly what to look for: something that would *complete the distinction* in the sentence, a distinction made between what is expected of a man and a woman in a "traditional" family. Choices (A), (C), and (D) may be true in some definitions of what that a "traditional" family is, but none of those answers fulfills the basic demands of the question. Only (B) does so by describing what is expected of a *mother* in contrast to what is expected of a *father*, as described earlier in the sentence.

Now, as for Question 7, we need to find some very literal way to make sentence 2 consistent with the rest of the paragraph. Look for words and phrases that will link sentence 2 to other sentences. Remember, it's not what the passage *could* say, it's what the passage *does* say. Sentence 2, we should note, starts with *the shift*, thus clearly referring to a shift that has been mentioned before it. As such, sentence 2 belongs definitively after sentence 5, which discusses *shifting social and economic roles*.

As we have seen, these questions are not difficult, but they do require very specific actions. Make sure you read the questions carefully and that you answer those questions as precisely and consistently as you can.

The same goes for Charts and Graphs on the Writing and Language section. Don't let the strangeness of the charts throw you off! Just read the graphs with as much precision as you can and choose the most precise answers possible.

Let's have a look at one.

Even as women's roles in high-level positions, such as Congress, have increased almost four-fold since 1981, **8** the pay that women receive relative to men has increased by less than 20%.

8

Which of the following choices gives information consistent with the graph?

A) NO CHANGE

B) women's wages have increased by over 80%.

C) the wages of women in Congress have decreased.

D) the efforts of women in Congress to raise wages have failed.

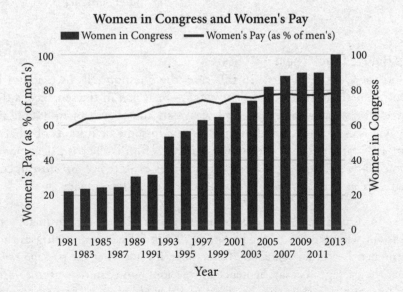

Here's How to Crack It

This question is asking for what agrees with the graph. From what we have seen, these questions are usually pretty straightforward. You don't have to do anything overly complex with the graphs.

It looks like "Women in Congress" goes up significantly whereas "Women's Pay" remains relatively consistent. The only choice that reflects that trend is (A). Choice (B) misreads the graph, and (C) and (D) can't be supported one way or the other. Choice (A) is therefore the best answer.

In general, graphs on the SAT Reading and Writing and Language sections are very straightforward, and the fundamental question they ask is, "Can you read a graph?" These are easy points as long as you read the graphs carefully and use POE.

CONCLUSION

As we have seen in this chapter, SAT can ask a lot of different kinds of questions, but they're not going to throw anything really crazy at you. The biggest things to remember, aside from the punctuation rules, are *CONSISTENCY* and *PRECISION*. If you pick answers that are precise and consistent with other information in the passage, you should be good to go. Just be sure to answer the question!

QUESTIONS EXERCISE
Time: 10 minutes

[1]

1 Genre in Hollywood movies is a constant but inconstant thing. Horror, Western, Sci-Fi: all of these are staples of Hollywood production, but the amount varies widely. For example, as the number of Westerns has stayed at or below about 25 per year since the 1960s, the number of Horror films, especially Zombie and Vampire films, **2** has risen dramatically between 1950 and 2000, during which time the production of Vampire films has increased nearly tenfold.

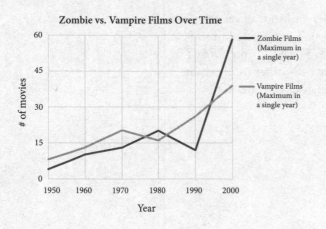

Zombie vs. Vampire Films Over Time

[2]

While the saying goes that there's "no accounting for the public's taste," **3** lots of people like lots of different things. Why should the number of Westerns have remained relatively low while the number of Zombie films has skyrocketed? Maybe we should ask the question another way: what do people today get from Zombie films that they don't from Westerns?

1

Which of the following choices would best introduce the essay by pointing to the potential confusion in how to understand the role of genre in Hollywood films?

A) NO CHANGE

B) You don't have to be a "geek" to love a good science-fiction movie.

C) Everyone knows that the highest form of Hollywood film is the drama.

D) There's a lot that you may not know about how films are made in Hollywood.

2

Which of the following gives information consistent with the graph?

A) NO CHANGE

B) has risen dramatically between 1950 and 2000, during which time the production of Zombie films has increased nearly tenfold.

C) has declined sharply between 1950 and 2000, during which time the production of Zombie films has decreased to almost a tenth.

D) has declined sharply between 1950 and 2000, during which time the production of Zombie films has increased nearly tenfold.

3

Which of the following choices would offer the most effective transition between the paragraph and the current one?

A) NO CHANGE

B) these trends nonetheless invite us to try.

C) a lot of people don't even care about Zombie movies.

D) science has not yet shown that zombies exist.

[3]

Westerns dominated the 1920s. Zombie films have dominated the 1990s and 2010s. Beginning with these facts alone, we can start to see why these films might have been popular in different eras. [4] The 1920s, for instance, spoke to a particular American moment of crusades. [5] Only a tough sheriff, the kind one might get in an old-west town, could find the perfect balance between justice and [6] brutality. Thus, if America could not be contained by law and order, at least its citizens could turn to the imaginary version of the West being offered by films.

4

The writer is considering deleting the phrase *in different eras* and ending the sentence with a period after the word *popular.* Should the phrase be kept or deleted?

A) Kept, because the meaning of the sentence changes without the phrase.

B) Kept, because it is interesting to think about history and film together.

C) Deleted, because the essay is more concerned with the genres' popularity across time periods.

D) Deleted, because the essay is already dull and could stand to have some words removed.

5

At this point, the writer wants to insert an idea that will support the idea given in the previous sentence ("The 1920s . . . crusades"). Which of the following true statements would offer that support?

A) These were crusades altogether distinct from those conducted by the Catholic Church starting in 1095.

B) The U.S. is still interested in crusades today, so it's hard to see why they don't make as many Westerns anymore.

C) Motivated by Woodrow Wilson's plan for a U.S.-led League of Nations, the world, reeling from World War I, wanted justice among the outlaws.

D) The stock market wouldn't crash for another nine years, at which point people would really freak out.

6

Which of the following alternatives to the underlined portion would NOT be acceptable?

A) brutality, and if

B) brutality: if

C) brutality; thus, if

D) brutality, thus, if

[4]

It may seem that genre conventions never change. Because they never change, it probably seems like a Western today follows the same set of rules as a Western from 100 years ago. **7** What the rise in Zombie films shows, however, is that the genres themselves change, and they provide different things to different eras. **8** This is not to say that one is better than the other—that it's better, for instance, to watch a tough cowboy fight off a gang of cattle rustlers –, but it is to say that these genres hold a lot more than their mere entertainment value.

7

Which of the following gives the most effective way to combine the previous two sentences, reproduced below?

It may seem that genre conventions never change. Because they never change, it probably seems like a Western today follows the same set of rules as a Western from 100 years ago.

A) (keep the sentences as they are)

B) It may seem that genre conventions never change; because of it, it could be argued that a Western today follows the same set of rules as a Western from 100 years ago.

C) It may seem that genre conventions never change, that a Western today follows the same set of rules as a Western from 100 years ago.

D) Because Westerns today follow the same set of rules as they did 100 years ago, it seems to most outside observers that genre conventions never change.

8

At this point, the author is considering adding the following true statement

For what it's worth, my personal favorite is Jacques Tourneur's *I Married a Zombie*, which is based loosely on *Jane Eyre*.

Should the writer make this addition here?

A) Yes, because the essay as a whole is filled with these kinds of examples and personal preferences.

B) Yes, because the author's quirky choice shows that he has an off-beat perspective.

C) No, because the author's strange choice disqualifies him from discussing popular taste.

D) No, because the essay as a whole is not primarily focused on the author's personal preferences.

[5]

The 1990s and 2010s, dominated as they are by Zombie films, show that contemporary conflicts are not so far away. Although we now have the world at the click of a button, Zombie films show that we are not all that interested in that world. Instead, we are interested in and suspicious of the people around us. Whether co-workers or fellow students, the people around us, especially when **9** viewed as a mass, can seem almost "dead." And the reasons for this are fairly obvious: our private or online personalities have become so robust **10** that the "real world" outside cannot help but seem dull or claustrophobic by comparison. **11**

9

Which of the following alternatives to the underlined portion would be LEAST acceptable?

A) taken

B) espied

C) seen

D) regarded

10

The writer is considering replacing the word *robust* with the word *healthy*. Should the writer make the change or keep the sentence as it is?

A) Make the change, because the word *robust* is not familiar to many readers.

B) Make the change, because the word *healthy* provides a more accurate representation of people's medical conditions.

C) Keep the sentence as it is, because the word *healthy* changes the meaning in a way inconsistent with the passage as a whole.

D) Keep the sentence as it is, because the word *robust* keeps the level of vocabulary within the passage at an appropriately high level.

11

The best placement for paragraph 5 would be

A) where it is now.

B) before paragraph 1.

C) after paragraph 2.

D) after paragraph 3.

For further practice, go online to your Student Tools and complete the Chapter 11 Questions Drill.

Summary

○ The most important thing about Writing and Language questions is that you notice those questions and then answer those questions. Don't miss out on some of the easiest points on the whole test by not reading carefully enough.

○ When answering consistency questions, keep this general rule in mind: Writing and Language passages should be judged on what they do say, not on what they could say. When dealing with Style, Tone, and Focus, make sure to work with the words and phrases the passage has already used. As in the Words chapter, answer questions in the most precise way possible.

○ There will be charts or graphs on the Writing and Language Test, but don't let that throw you off. Just read the graphs with the same focus that you'd use for a passage and choose the most precise answers possible.

Chapter 12
Writing &
Language Exercises:
Answers and
Explanations

CHAPTER 9: PUNCTUATION EXERCISE ANSWERS

1. **B** Notice the punctuation is changing in the answer choices. Since (B) contains a comma + FANBOY, and (D) contains a period, check to see if both parts of the sentence are complete ideas. In this case, both parts are complete, so (A) and (C) can be eliminated because STOP punctuation is needed. Choice (D) looks good, but between it and (B), it is less concise, with an unnecessary comma after "but." Note: sentences *can* start with conjunctions, so don't assume that to be an error. Also try to use Process of Elimination to narrow down your options.

2. **D** Notice that apostrophes are changing in the answer choice. *Today* needs to be a possessive noun to show its relationship to *world*, so an apostrophe is needed. Eliminate (B) and (C). The spelling of *there* is also changing. Context requires a possessive pronoun rather than a statement of location, so *their* is the correct usage. Choice (D) is correct.

3. **C** Notice that commas are changing in the answer choices. The word *say* should be surrounded by commas since this information is unnecessary, which makes (C) the correct answer.

4. **A** Notice the punctuation is changing in the answer choices. Since (A) and (D) contain semicolons, check to see if both parts of the sentence are complete ideas. Since they are both complete, (B) and (C) can be eliminated. The remaining answers vary in their spelling of the word *your*. Since a possessive pronoun is needed in this case rather than a contraction, (A) is correct.

5. **B** Notice that commas are changing in the answer choices. The sentence includes a list of items, so a comma needs to follow each item in this list: *depression, PTSD, and other mood disorders.* Choice (A) is missing the comma after *PTSD* while (C) and (D) have unnecessary commas after *and* and *other*, respectively. Choice (B) is correct.

6. **A** Notice that the punctuation is changing in the answer choices. Since (A) contains a colon, check to see if both parts of the sentence are complete ideas. Since they are both complete, you need to combine them with STOP or HALF-STOP punctuation. You cannot combine them with a comma, as in (B) and (C), or nothing, as in (D). Choice (A) is correct.

7. **C** Notice that the punctuation is changing in the answer choices. Since (C) contains a period and (D) has a semicolon, check to see if both parts of the sentence are complete ideas. Both are complete, so eliminate (A) and (B). Choice (D) has an unnecessary comma, leaving (C) as the correct answer.

8. **C** Notice that the apostrophes are changing in the answer choices. In the sentence, the *psychologists* possess the *work* so a possessive is needed. Eliminate (B). The *of* in the phrase *the work of psychologists'* already indicates possession and does not require an apostrophe. Eliminate (A) and (D). Choice (C) is correct.

9. **D** Notice that commas are changing in the answer choices. The phrase *those learned before the age of about 10* should be surrounded by commas since this information is unnecessary, which makes (D) the correct answer.

10. **B** Notice that apostrophes are changing in the answer choices. Since *washer* and *dryer* do not possess anything in the sentence, they do not have to be possessives. Eliminate (A). Expand out the contractions in (C) and (D). The phrase *can tell you are washer and dryer* does not make sense in context, so a contraction is not needed. Eliminate (C) and (D). Choice (B) is correct.

11. **D** Notice that the punctuation is changing in the answer choices. Since (A) contains a period and (B) contains a semicolon, check to see if both parts of the sentence are complete ideas. The first part (*While…on*) is incomplete, so (A) and (C) can be eliminated. Additionally, (B) can be eliminated because the use of a colon requires that the first part be complete. Choice (D) is correct.

CHAPTER 10: WORDS EXERCISE ANSWERS

1. **D** Check what's changing in the answer choices. In this case, the word *well-known* appears in all the answer choices, and in some it is paired with the word *famous*. *Well-known* and *famous* have the same meaning in this context, so there's no need to use both of them, as in (A) and (B), or to turn *famous* into an adverb describing *well-known,* as in (C). Choice (D) is the most concise answer.

2. **B** The verb is changing in the answer choices so check the subject. The subject is *readers,* so a plural verb is required. Eliminate (A). Both (C) and (D) are unnecessarily long, so eliminate them. Choice (B) is the best and most concise answer.

3. **B** Notice that both pronouns and nouns are among the answer choices. The *they* in the original sentence could refer to the *readers, pages, characters,* or *twists* from the previous sentence. So, a pronoun is not the most precise choice in this case. Eliminate (A), (C), and (D). Choice (B) clarifies the subject with a noun, so it is the best and most precise choice.

4. **C** Notice that the verb is changing in the answer choices. All the options match the subject (*Tolstoy*) in number but (A) and (D) are incorrect in tense and thus can be eliminated. Choice (B) introduces an incorrect idiom: the phrase is *could have,* not *could of.* Choice (B) can be eliminated. Choice (C) is correct.

5. **B** Notice the question. It is asking us to find the most logical placement for the underlined portion. The underlined portion references *Tolstoy's other great novels and non-fiction writings.* The *other* suggests that this portion follows a reference to a particular Tolstoy novel or non-fiction writing. Choice (B) places the portion directly after a reference to Tolstoy's *War and Peace,* and so it is the correct answer.

6. **A** Notice that the verbs are changing in this sentence. All the options match the subject (*Shakespeare*) in number, but (B), (C), and (D) are in the wrong tense. They are in the present tense while the context of the sentence requires the past tense. Choice (A) is correct.

7. **A** Notice that the wording and length of the answer choices is changing. Look at the context of the sentence to see which answer choice is the most precise. The sentence is contrasting Tolstoy's and Shakespeare's relationships with their respective eras. Therefore, the most precise answer has to give information about Tolstoy's era to distinguish it from Shakespeare's era. Choice (A) is the correct answer.

8. **C** Notice that the verbs are changing in this sentence, so check for the subject. The subject is *man,* so a singular verb is required; (D) can be eliminated. Next check for the tense required by the context of the sentence. A conditional verb is required, so (C) is correct.

9. **B** Notice what the question is asking. It is asking us to determine whether or not a specific portion of the sentence should be kept. The phrase *since Tolstoy's death in 1910* is necessary for the beginning of the next sentence (*This was the year*) to make sense, so eliminate (C) and (D). This essay is not a biographical sketch of Tolstoy, so (A) can be eliminated. Choice (B) is the correct answer.

10. **D** Notice what is changing in the answer choices. The words and phrasing are changing, so we need to look at the context of the sentence for the most precise answer. In the original sentence, the phrase *into philosophy* is held in relation to the phrase *the great theologians* later in the sentence. Therefore, the correct answer will match *the great theologians* in form. Choice (D) is correct.

11. **C** Notice what is changing in the answer choices. The words and phrasing are changing, so we need to look at the context of the sentence for the most precise answer. Choices (A) and (D) are unclear in what they're referencing, so they can be eliminated. Choice (B) is incorrect, because the sentence is referring to a *discovery* in another field. Choice (C) is the most precise and best answer.

CHAPTER 11: QUESTIONS EXERCISE ANSWERS

1. **A** Notice the question. It is asking us to identify which answer choice addresses *the potential confusion in how to understand the role of genre in Hollywood films.* Choice (D) doesn't refer specifically to the *role of genre* in Hollywood films, so it can be eliminated. Neither (B) nor (C) refers to any *potential confusion,* so they can be eliminated. Choice (A) is the correct answer.

2. **B** Notice the question. It is asking us to identify the answer choice that is consistent with the graph. The graph shows that the number of Zombie and Vampire films increased over time, so (C) and (D) can be eliminated. The graph shows that Vampire movies increased from approximately 9 movies to 39 movies over the 50-year period, while Zombie movies increased from approximately 6 movies to nearly 60 movies. Therefore Zombie movies increased tenfold over that period, which is consistent with (B).

3. **B**   Notice the question. It is asking us to find the most effective transition between the two paragraphs. The first paragraph discusses variance in genre popularity, while the second paragraph suggests that there might be a pattern in the genre choices audiences make. Choice (B) best captures this shift by introducing the idea that there might be a reason for why people go to certain kinds of movies.

4. **A**   Notice the question. It asks us to decide whether or not the phrase *in different eras* should be kept or deleted. If we take the phrase out of the sentence, it shifts the sentence away from the focus of the paragraph, which is to compare the popularity of different genres in different time periods. Choices (C) and (D) can be eliminated. Since the phrase's removal affects the meaning of the sentence, (A) is correct.

5. **C**   Notice the question. It asks us to find which answer best supports the idea of the previous sentence: *The 1920s, for instance, spoke to a particular American moment of crusades.* The supporting sentence should refer in some way to the specific time period and circumstances of the 1920s. Choices (A), (B), and (D) all discuss incidents outside of that time period. Choice (C) is correct.

6. **D**   Notice the question. It asks us to look for the answer that would NOT be acceptable, which means that the sentence, as written, is correct. STOP punctuation occurs in several of the answer choices, so check to see if both parts of the sentence are complete. Since both parts are complete, STOP or HALF-STOP punctuation is required. Choice (D) uses GO punctuation, so it is not acceptable and is therefore the correct answer.

7. **C**   Notice the question. It asks us for the most effective, or *concise*, combination of the sentences. To that end, it can't be (A), because the two sentences are not currently combined. Likewise, (B) isn't particularly concise, and it also misuses a pronoun ("it" instead of "that"). Choice (D) isn't all that concise either, and worse, it changes the meaning, so that instead of unchanging genre conventions having an effect on Westerns, it's unchanging Westerns that influence genre conventions. Choose (C).

8. **D**   Notice the question. It asks us to decide whether or not the sentence "For what it's worth, my personal favorite is Jacques Tourneur's *I Married a Zombie*, which is based loosely on *Jane Eyre*" should be added. The paragraph and passage as a whole are about the shifting role of genres in different time periods. This sentence about the author's personal preference would not add anything to this discussion. Therefore, eliminate (A) and (B). As previously stated, the sentence doesn't fit with the main idea of the passage, so (D) is correct.

9. **B**   Notice the question. It asks us to decide which answer would be LEAST acceptable, so the sentence is correct as written. The underlined portion is the word *viewed,* which in this context means to *regard in a particular light or with a particular attitude.* Choices (A), (C), and (D) all match this meaning, and so can be eliminated. *Espied,* (B), means to *catch sight of* and so is not an acceptable alternative. It is therefore the correct answer.

10. **C** Notice the question. It is asking us whether the author should replace *robust* with *healthy*. In context, *robust* must mean the opposite of *dull or claustrophobic,* so you could define it as *vigorous and expansive.* The word *healthy* does not match this meaning, so the author should not make this change. Choices (A) and (B) can be eliminated. Choice (C) is the best answer because it identifies the meaning shift that would occur should the change take place.

11. **D** Notice the question. It is asking us to find the correct placement for the fifth paragraph. The fifth paragraph discusses the reasons behind the popularity of Zombie films in the 1990s and 2010s. This discussion of a specific genre and a specific era of time should not conclude the piece, so (A) can be eliminated. The idea that Zombie films peaked in popularity in the 1990s and 2010s is first introduced in paragraph 3, so this paragraph must follow it. Therefore, (B) and (C) would be too early for this paragraph. Choice (D) is correct.

Chapter 13
Writing &
Language Drill

Writing & Language Drill

Questions 1–11 are based on the following passage.

A Little Pygmy Up

"When I last saw you, you were this tall," say aunts and grandmothers everywhere, as kids grow taller and taller. If you've ever thought that kids seem to be getting taller every generation, you may be right. Data from 1820 forward show that men from a large swath of [1] countries, with no exceptions, have grown in height, some by as much as 25 centimeters. The human species has, on the whole, grown taller since the earliest days of the species, whether from natural selection, improved health, or increased access to good food.

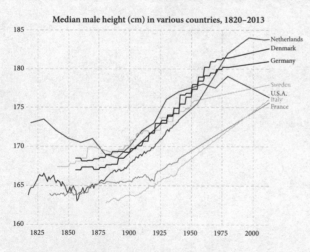

Median male height (cm) in various countries, 1820–2013

Netherlands
Denmark
Germany
Sweden
U.S.A.
Italy
France

Source/Olson, Randy (2014): Historical median heights for various countries, 1818-2013. figshare. http://dx.doi.org/10.6084/m9.figshare.1066523

1

Which choice offers an accurate interpretation of information in the graph?

A) NO CHANGE

B) countries, particularly Italy and France, have grown in median height, while many others have shrunk by as much as 20 centimeters.

C) countries have all seen a growth in median height of over 15 centimeters.

D) countries, with the exception of U.S.A., have grown in median height, some by as many as 20 centimeters.

In the discussion of human height, the pygmy populations of the equatorial rain-forest regions of Africa have always been considered a curious outlier. In one pygmy population in Cameroon, the average male **2** gets up to only 150 cm, well below the averages for the European and American nations shown in the graph. A recent study from University of Pennsylvania professor Sarah Tishkoff, a leading **3** scholar, on African genetics, may have revealed the reason and raised some interesting questions besides.

2
A) NO CHANGE
B) scales the mountain to
C) climbs up to
D) reaches a height of

3
A) NO CHANGE
B) scholar, on African genetics
C) scholar; on African genetics
D) scholar on African genetics,

(1) The study documents the early-life factors that limit the height of the pygmy populations. (2) In children from the pygmy group Baka, infants are the same size as infants from other populations. **4** (3) A variety of environmental and genetic factors in each produced the slow growth, with a particular genetic variation in CISH. (4) This gene is linked to **5** resistances, to some equatorial diseases but may also account for the height particularities of these groups. **6**

At this point, the writer is considering adding the following information and adjusting the punctuation accordingly:

> but they grow at a slower rate than other infants, particularly during the first two years of life.

Should the writer make this addition here?

A) Yes, because it explains the pygmy data that is shown on the graph.

B) Yes, because it explains the distinction indicated in the first sentence of the paragraph.

C) No, because it suggests that pygmy mothers are not as caring as European mothers.

D) No, because it contradicts data in the previous paragraph that suggests human populations always grow taller.

A) NO CHANGE

B) resistances to

C) resistances to,

D) resistances: to

Where is the most logical place in this paragraph to add the following sentence?

> In a group like the Sua, however, the slowed growth is mainly prenatal—it occurs before the children are born.

A) After sentence 1

B) After sentence 2

C) After sentence 3

D) After sentence 4

The truly fascinating questions [7] that have emerged from this study and have related to intra-species evolution. It is well known in the scientific community that humans and baboons evolved from a common ancestor, but [8] it's less known that evolutionary factors may be at play within the relatively "young" human species as well. The study presents [9] findings that suggest that the Baka broke off from the Efé and Sua approximately 20,000 years ago, showing very significant evolutionary adaptation in the recent past. Africa is a particularly notable place because it has more genetic [10] distinction than any other continent. It is home to the pygmies, yes; [11] in this sense, it is also home to the Maasai and the Dinka, who are tall by any standard, and to the mixed populations that have resulted from many years of border crossing and European colonization.

Now we just need to figure out whether this information tells us that it's a small world after all, or if we're all little snowflakes.

7

A) NO CHANGE

B) that have emerged from this study, in which they relate

C) to emerge from this study relate

D) to emerge from this study, they relate

8

A) NO CHANGE

B) its

C) they're

D) their

9

A) NO CHANGE

B) findings that suggest that it

C) findings that suggest that they

D) findings that are suggestive of its

10

A) NO CHANGE

B) relation

C) boundedness

D) diversity

11

A) NO CHANGE

B) nonetheless,

C) thus,

D) heretofore,

Questions 12–22 are based on the following passage.

B & O Cool Story

Because the people who would eventually found the United States were European, it should [12] be no surprise that the earliest population growth in the country took place on the Atlantic Coast. Some of the major population centers in the early [13] republic make obvious sense; Philadelphia and Boston, famed as the cities of Independence, and New York, renowned as the city of business and just about everything else. What may surprise us, however, is that in 1860, on the eve of the Civil War, the third-largest city in the United States was not Boston, Chicago, Los Angeles, Atlanta, or Houston. The third-largest city in the United States at that time was [14] Baltimore, Maryland, though Baltimore today ranks 26th. In fact, even by 1880, Baltimore had slipped considerably, from third to sixth. In the meantime, three other cities—Boston, St. Louis, and Chicago—had assumed the third, fourth, and fifth spots, respectively. [15]

Populations of Major Cities in the United States, 1860–1900			
City	1860	1880	1900
New York	1,174,800	1,912,000	3,437,000
Philadelphia	565,500	847,000	1,294,000
Boston	177,800	363,000	561,000
Baltimore	212,400	332,000	509,000
Cincinnati	161,000	255,000	326,000
St. Louis	160,800	350,000	575,000
Chicago	109,300	503,000	1,698,000

Source/Bureau of the Census and Schatz, Phil: U.S. History. http://philschatz.com/us-history-book/contents/m50109.html

[12]

The writer wants to maintain an informative tone in the passage and avoid the appearance of mockery. Which choice best accomplishes this goal?

A) NO CHANGE

B) not blow your minds

C) not send us for a loop

D) be no big whoop

[13]

A) NO CHANGE

B) republic make obvious sense:

C) republic make obvious sense

D) republic—make obvious sense,

[14]

A) NO CHANGE

B) Baltimore, Maryland, which

C) Baltimore, Maryland. Baltimore

D) Baltimore, Maryland, and this city of Baltimore

[15]

The writer wants the information in the passage to reflect the information in the chart as accurately as possible. Given that goal and assuming that no other part of the sentence would not change, in what sequence should the three cities be named?

A) NO CHANGE

B) St. Louis, Chicago, Boston

C) Chicago, Boston, St. Louis

D) Chicago, St. Louis, Boston

(1) In some ways, Baltimore's relatively small population size today seems unremarkable. (2) For most people alive today, Baltimore **16** has been the home of a storied baseball team, and the fact that Chicago and St. Louis grew as much as they did in the late 1800s can be explained by a more general population shift to the west. (3) The more interesting question should point us in another direction: why did Baltimore have such a relatively large population in the second half of the nineteenth century? (4) Baltimore has always been ideally positioned for a robust shipping industry and **17** holy capable of handling lots of freight. (5) Located as it is near the Atlantic Ocean and directly on the Chesapeake Bay, Baltimore was a perfect channel for goods coming from Europe and moving to the interior of the country. **18**

16

Which choice most effectively completes the idea presented in this sentence and is consistent with the rest of the passage?

A) NO CHANGE

B) is a mere forty-five miles north of Washington, D.C.,

C) was reintroduced to the American public through a series of media portrayals,

D) has "always" been a relatively small city,

17

A) NO CHANGE

B) holy capable for

C) holey capable for

D) wholly capable of

18

To improve the organization and clarity of this paragraph, the writer wants to add the following sentence.

> The answer is relatively simple and comes down to something fundamental: shipping.

The sentence would most logically be placed after

A) sentence 1.

B) sentence 2.

C) sentence 3.

D) sentence 4.

19 Fore it to come to the for in population, however, Baltimore also had to do something pioneering, and that something came with the growth of railroads. By the 1820s, Baltimore's prominence as a port was starting to decline after the opening and success of the Erie Canal, which enabled cargo **20** to travel by water from New York City to the Great Lakes, thus enabling easier delivery to the Midwest. In response, Baltimore officials pushed the development of a new and unknown technology, railroading, as a way to move goods through Baltimore to cities in the west, whether those cities had waterways or not.

The result of citizens' petitions and politicians' grand plans **21** have been the Baltimore and Ohio, or B&O, Railroad, which began operations in the late 1820s. While the B&O did have its share of struggles, it was nonetheless be one of the most powerful rail lines in the country for much of the nineteenth century. And it helped Baltimore to maintain its prominence at a time when the size of a city was largely a function of **22** how connected that city was to other places.

19

A) NO CHANGE

B) For it to come to the four

C) For it to come to the for

D) For it to come to the fore

20

A) NO CHANGE

B) traveling by

C) to travel in

D) traveling through

21

A) NO CHANGE

B) were

C) was

D) is

22

Which choice most effectively concludes the sentence and paragraph?

A) NO CHANGE

B) how many railroad lines and canals it had.

C) the number of people who thought of it as a large city.

D) a strong connection to both diversity and European roots.

Chapter 14
Writing &
Language Drill:
Answers and
Explanations

A LITTLE PYGMY UP: ANSWERS AND EXPLANATIONS

1. **D**   Use POE and the graph provided. Choice (A) can be disproven by the graph since no country has seen a growth of 25 cm in median male height. Choice (B) is not supported by the graph. Other countries (like the Netherlands) have experienced more growth in male height than Italy and France have. Furthermore, *many others* have not *shrunk* by as much as 20 cm. Choice (C) should be eliminated because not all countries saw a growth in median height of *over 15 cm* (in particular, the U.S. actually decreased) Therefore, by POE, the correct answer is (D), which is supported by the graph.

2. **D**   This sentence is about average male height, not the act of actually climbing up a mountain or another object. Eliminate (B) and (C). Choice (A) is not as precise as (D). Therefore, (D) is the best option since it best expresses the intended meaning of the sentence.

3. **D**   Notice the punctuation is changing in the answer choices. Since (C) contains a semicolon, check to see if both parts of the sentence are complete ideas. In this case, the first part (*A recent...scholar*) is incomplete, so a semicolon would be incorrect. Eliminate (C). The remaining answer choices vary the number and placement of the comma(s). The phrase *a leading scholar on African genetics* should be surrounded by commas since this information is unnecessary, which makes (D) the correct answer.

4. **B**   The suggested addition is necessary since it would add relevant details to the sentence. Eliminate (C) and (D). The graph does not contain data on the pygmy populations, so (A) is incorrect. The first sentence of this paragraph mentions that the study indicates that *early-life factors...limit the height of pygmy populations*. Thus, the additional information helps to explain the claim made in the beginning of this paragraph. Choice (B) provides the best reason for the writer to make this addition.

5. **B**   Notice the punctuation is changing in the answer choices. Since (D) contains a colon, check to see if the first part of the sentence is a complete idea. Technically, it is, but this represents an exception to the rule—you need to make sure that the rest of the sentence still makes sense. In this case, because the split occurs across an idiomatic phrase (*resistances to*), punctuation should be avoided in order to ensure that the flow of the sentence is not interrupted. This eliminates (A), (C), and (D) and makes (B) the correct answer.

6. **B**   Notice the question. It is asking us to determine the most logical place for the sentence "In a group like the Sua, however, the slowed growth is mainly prenatal—it occurs before the children are born." The "however" signals that this sentence provides a contrast to a previous sentence regarding the concept of "slowed growth." Sentence 2 sets up this contrast by stating that the infants from the pygmy group Baka are the same size as normal infants. The new sentence, therefore, follows logically after Sentence 2, so (B) is the correct answer.

7. **C** As written, this sentence is not a complete thought. There is no main verb in this sentence. Choices (B) and (D) do not fix this error. This makes (C) the only option. If you have trouble seeing the original error, try eliminating the filler-phrase *that have emerged from this study* to more easily identify the subject (*questions*) in order to see that a main verb (*relate*) is needed.

8. **A** Notice that the pronouns are changing in the answer choices. Since a possessive pronoun is not needed, (B) and (D) are incorrect. To see if the pronoun and verb should be singular or plural, look at the non-underlined portion. The sentence begins with *It is common knowledge....* In order to make the second part of the sentence consistent with the first, the correct answer is (A)—no change is necessary.

9. **A** Notice that the pronouns are changing in the answer choices. Since a possessive pronoun is not needed, (D) is incorrect. Of the remaining answer choices, only (A) provides clarity to the sentence. The *it* used in (B) could refer back to *the study* while the word *they* in (C) could refer back to *findings*. Neither of those is what broke off from the Efé and Sua. Thus, the correct answer is (A).

10. **D** Since all the answer choices mean essentially the same thing, choose the one that expresses the intended meaning of the sentence. In this case, the writer is conveying the idea that Africa has more genetic differences than any other continent. The only choice that would work in this context is (D). The remaining options do not mean "differences" in this context and, therefore, are not as precise as *diversity*.

11. **B** Notice that the transition word is changing in each answer choice. Since (A) and (C) have the same meaning, both can be eliminated since there can't be two right answers. Choice (D) means "before now," which is not appropriate in context. The writer is trying to set up a contrast—that the continent of Africa is home not only to the pygmies but also to many other populations as well. The only option that provides a contrast is (B).

B&O COOL STORY: ANSWERS AND EXPLANATIONS

12. **A** The question signals that you are looking for the answer choice that has a *sense of general interest* and will *avoid the appearance of mockery*. Choice (A) conveys that the location of population growth should be unsurprising given the context. It is informative and neutral in tone, so keep it. Choice (B) could seem to be mocking the reader, as it suggests the reader might be surprised but shouldn't be. Eliminate it. Choices (C) and (D) are both pretty informal; their casual tone is inconsistent with the neutral, informative tone of the passage. Eliminate them and choose (A).

13. **B**   Choice (A) contains STOP punctuation, so check to see whether there are complete ideas on both sides of the semicolon. What follows the semicolon is not a complete idea, so eliminate (A). Choice (B) features a colon, which can be used to connect a complete idea to an incomplete idea that provides an example or illustration of the complete idea it follows. Keep (B). Choice (C) removes the colon, when some punctuation is needed to connect the ideas. Choice (D) adds an unnecessary dash. Eliminate (C) and (D) and choose (B).

14. **B**   Choices (A), (C), and (D) all feature repetition of the word *Baltimore*, while (B) does not. Since that suggests that the question is testing concision, check to see whether (B) works. It effectively and correctly links the two ideas, so (B), the most concise answer, is correct.

15. **C**   The writer wants this sentence to reflect the information in the chart as accurately as possible. The order in which the cities are listed in (A) is the order in which they appear in the "City" column. This is a trap answer though, because the *respectively* in the sentence tells us the cities should be listed from largest to smallest. If you scan down the column headed "1880," you can see that Chicago had a bigger population in that year than St. Louis or Boston. Eliminate (A) and (B) as they do not list Chicago first. Check to see that Boston had a larger population than St. Louis. It did, so eliminate (D). The correct answer is (C).

16. **D**   The sentence that begins the second paragraph states that *Baltimore's relatively small population size today seems unremarkable*. Choices (A), (B), and (C) all provide information about Baltimore that may be familiar to people, but none of them address the size of Baltimore's population. Choice (D) does address population size, which connects both to the paragraph as a whole and to the information about the growth in Chicago and St. Louis that is discussed in the rest of the sentence. Choose (D).

17. **D**   The answer choices feature variations of the word *holy*. Look at the rest of the sentence to see what sense of the word you need. This paragraph is explaining how well-suited Baltimore is for shipping, so this sentence requires a word that means something like *very* or *entirely*. Choices (A) and (B) use *holy*, which means *sacred* and does not make sense in this context. Eliminate (A) and (B). Choice (C) uses *holey*, which means *having a lot of holes*; eliminate (C). Choice (D) uses *wholly*, which means *entirely*. The correct answer is (D).

18. **C**   The sentence to be inserted begins with *The answer is*, which suggests that the sentence should be inserted after a question has been posed. Sentence 3 provides the *more interesting question* that the rest of the paragraph works to answer. Eliminate (A) and (B) since it doesn't make sense to answer a question that hasn't been asked yet. Inserting the new sentence between Sentence 3 and the rest of the paragraph provides a concise answer that links the question that is posed and the details that explain the answer. Eliminate (D) and choose (C).

19. **D** The first and last words are changing in these answer choices. Eliminate (A), since it begins with *fore* and the phrase needs to begin with the preposition *for*. The paragraph is talking about what was required for Baltimore to get a big boost in population, so the expression must mean something like *become prominent* or *really stand out*. The word *fore* means *toward the front*, so the expression *come to the fore* means *come to the front*. Neither *four* nor *for* makes sense in the expression. Eliminate (B) and (C) and choose (D).

20. **A** Look at the differences in the answer choices and consider whether you need *to travel* or *traveling* to follow *which enabled cargo*. *To travel* completes the phrase correctly, so eliminate (B) and (D). Compare (A) and (C) and see which preposition completes the idea better. Choice (A) has the sense of traveling by means of water, while (C) has the sense of moving through the water. Choice (A) fits the context of the paragraph better, since the point is that linked bodies of water allowed cargo to be moved easily. Eliminate (C) and choose (A).

21. **C** Verbs are changing in the answer choices. Look to see whether you need a singular or plural verb. The subject of the sentence is *result*, which is singular. Eliminate (A) and (B). The B&O began running in the 1820s, so the past tense makes sense. Eliminate (D) and choose (C).

22. **A** Choices (C) and (D) feature ideas that are touched on in the passage, but neither highlights the main idea of the passage overall or fits well with the focus on railroads in the last two paragraphs. Eliminate them. Choice (B) mentions rail lines explicitly, but look carefully at (A). Its reference to *how connected a city was to other places* encompasses the means of connection (the rail lines and shipping) while emphasizing why those means were important (because they connected the city to other places). Eliminate (B) and choose (A).

Part IV
Math

Chapter 15
Introduction to
SAT Math

INTRODUCTION

If you're aiming for the highest score on the SAT, you probably already have a broad range of math skills. In fact, you probably already know the math required to answer almost every question on the typical SAT Math section. So why aren't you already scoring an 800?

You may be surprised to learn that what's holding you back is *not* content knowledge. Students who score in the high 600s have roughly the same amount of mathematical knowledge as those who score an 800. Knowing more math is not the key—you've likely already learned almost every concept that's on the Math test.

The problem is that on the SAT, the questions are not so much difficult as they are hard to do under timed conditions. They can also contain tricky trap answers. The SAT is not a fair test; in fact, the test writers are out to get you! They restrict your time, then they expect you to do all sorts of time-consuming algebraic manipulation. They make you feel rushed and then give you answers you may get if you calculated something incorrectly or misread the question. They even take away your calculator on one section! To improve your score, you'll need to do four things.

- Learn when to use your calculator and how to get along without it.
- Learn to avoid traps and eliminate careless errors.
- Become familiar with the types of questions that appear on the SAT.
- Learn our strategies for recognizing and defeating these questions.

In this chapter, we'll focus on the first two of these points; in later chapters, we'll cover the other two.

AVOIDING TRAPS AND CARELESS ERRORS

If you want to score a 750 or higher on the Math section, you can't afford to make *any* careless errors. The first thing to do is slow down! This might seem counterintuitive. In order to score an 800, you must answer every single math question correctly. But it doesn't matter if you get all the hardest questions right if you throw it all away on a few silly mistakes on the easier questions. Set a goal *right now* to avoid careless mistakes from here on.

To avoid careless mistakes, burn the following acronym into your brain: RTFQ. This stands for Read The Full Question. Consider the following question:

Example 1:

12 ▬▬▬▬▬▬▬▬▬▬▬▬▬▬

At what point (x, y) does the graph of $2y - x = 6$ intersect the x-axis in the xy-plane?

A) $(0, 3)$

B) $(0, 6)$

C) $(-6, 0)$

D) $(3, 0)$

This is a fairly typical SAT math question. The majority of high scorers will expect to get it right. However, did you catch the trap? Read the full question one more time. Which intercept are you looking for? Your math classes in high school have likely conditioned you to put this equation into the format $y = mx + b$, where b represents the y-intercept. If you did not read the question carefully and simply converted the equation to this format, you could easily fall for (A). However, the question is asking for the coordinates when $y = 0$. RTFQ! Slow down. Take a few extra seconds between reading this question and starting to solve it. Make sure you know exactly what you are looking for.

A closely related skill is Process of Elimination (POE). Focus on the word "process." This implies an action on your part. POE is not something that occurs in your head. You have a pencil; make sure that you use it to cross off wrong answers. Let's consider the above problem one more time. Assume that you read the question carefully and you caught that it was about the x-intercept. Use POE to cross off any answer choices that represent y-intercepts:

Example 2:

12 ▬▬▬▬▬▬▬▬▬▬▬▬▬▬

At what point (x, y) does the graph of $2y - x = 6$ intersect the x-axis in the xy-plane?

A) ~~(0, 3)~~

B) ~~(0, 6)~~

C) $(-6, 0)$

D) $(3, 0)$

Notice how this simple technique allows you to avoid falling for the obvious traps. However, there are some less obvious traps as well. Choice (D) has the right y-coordinate, but this point is not even on this line. Does $2(0) - 3 = 6$? No, it doesn't, but $2(3) - 0 = 6$. Choice (D) is one you might get if you mixed up the x- and y-coordinates. Get rid of this trap as well, and you're left with only one answer.

Example 3:

12

At what point (x, y) does the graph of $2y - x = 6$ intersect the x-axis in the xy-plane?

A) (0, 3)

B) (0, 6)

C) (−6, 0)

D) (3, 0)

The moral of the story is that the SAT is full of traps. Making sure to RTFQ and using your pencil to cross of bad answer choices can improve your score right now, just by helping you avoid careless mistakes.

Try the following questions, chock-full of typical, nasty SAT traps. To get the most out of the drill, don't just do the questions; instead, see if you can spot the traps in the questions and answers. When you're done, check out each explanation of how to crack it. Let's dive in.

13

The population of a certain town increased by 20% in one year. The following year, the town's population decreased by 20%. What was the net effect on the town's population over two years?

A) It increased by 4%.

B) It was unchanged.

C) It decreased by 4%.

D) It decreased by 10%.

Here's How to Crack It

The main trap answer in this question is (B). Many students will be tempted to think that the 20% increase is cancelled out by the 20% decrease. This just goes to show that on the SAT, if you arrive at an answer by simply thinking for a few seconds, that answer is probably wrong. To see why, use some real numbers. Let's say the population was originally 100. A year later, it will be 20% higher, or 120. The population then decreases by 20%, so take 20% of 120 and subtract by the total: $120 - (0.20)(120) = 96$. The population decreased by 4%, so the correct answer is (C).

27

An exponential function is graphed in the xy-plane. If the graph of the function has a y-intercept of 15 and the function is always increasing, which of the following could be the equation of the function?

A) $-15(0.80)^x$

B) $-15(1.20)^x$

C) $15(0.80)^x$

D) $15(1.20)^x$

Here's How to Crack It

Without a good understanding of exponential functions, it is easy to look at the answers and assume that answers with positive 15 are the ones that are increasing. While that is not necessarily true, it's a good bet that the answer in (A) is not increasing, since it has a negative coefficient and a smaller value in the parentheses. After eliminating (A), use your knowledge of intercepts to determine which equation has a y-intercept of 15. This happens when $x = 0$, as an exponent of 0 makes any base equal 1. You can try it on your calculator for this question if you forget that. Choice (B) has a y-intercept of -15, so eliminate that, too. If x was 1 instead of 0, (C) would decrease and (D) would increase, so the correct answer is (D). We'll cover a bit more on exponential growth in the Word Problems chapter.

16

Don's Travel Expenses

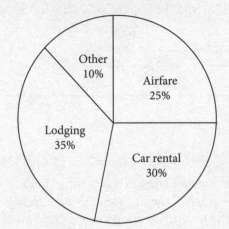

The pie chart above shows how Don spent $360 on a recent business trip. The amount Don spent on car rental was only a portion of the total cost of the car rental, because he shared the cost of the car equally with three other people. What was the total cost of the car rental?

A) $108

B) $270

C) $324

D) $432

Here's How to Crack It

To find what Don spent on car rental, take 30% of $360: (0.30)($360) = $108. Notice that this number is (A). Partial answers often appear on the SAT. To find the correct answer, we need to multiply by four, because Don shared with three other people, so (4)($108) = $432, and the correct answer is (D). The most common mistake on this question is to multiply by three, which would lead you to pick (C). Watch out for traps; they're everywhere!

Notice that the last few problems were accompanied by calculator symbols. That means they are likely to be found in Section 4, where calculator use is permitted. To get you acclimated to test conditions as you work through this book, use the calculator only on those questions that have the appropriate calculator symbol.

Try it on the following questions.

14

$$x^2 + y^2 = 360$$

$$y = -3x$$

If (x, y) is a solution to the system of equations above, what is the value of y^2 ?

A) −18

B) 6

C) 36

D) 324

Here's How to Crack It

First of all, you can eliminate (A) before doing any work—a squared term cannot give you a negative value unless you are dealing with imaginary numbers. One way to solve this is to square both sides of the second equation, so it becomes $y^2 = 9x^2$. Be careful when squaring this term to make sure you get the correct coefficient. You could solve this equation for y^2, but you get a messy fraction. You are less likely to make an error if you plug the value for y^2 into the first equation to get $x^2 + 9x^2 = 360$, or $10x^2 = 360$. Therefore, $x^2 = 36$. Don't pick (C) just yet, though! Remember to RTFQ! You are solving for y^2, and $36 + y^2 = 360$, so $y^2 = 324$. The correct answer is (D).

Designed To Do You Wrong

Notice that (A) gives a value for *y* and (B) gives a possible value for *x*. The wrong answers don't come out of nowhere—they are answers you'd get if you miscalculated or solved for the wrong quantity.

9

If j is any integer such that $4 < \sqrt{j} < 9$, what is the difference between the largest and smallest possible values of j ?

A) 1

B) 3

C) 63

D) 65

Here's How to Crack It

First, square each element of the inequality to get $16 < j < 81$. You may be tempted to simply subtract here: $81 - 16 = 65$. But j is an integer that is *between* these values, so the largest and smallest values for j are 80 and 17, respectively. Therefore, $80 - 17 = 63$, and the correct answer is (C). If you didn't square the inequality, you may have picked (B). If you took the positive square root of the inequality, you may have chosen (A).

TIME MANAGEMENT

You might be wondering at this point how you are supposed to incorporate this advice. Slow down! Use your pencil more! You may think that these techniques will leave you with less precious time for those difficult math questions. However, consider how little time it will actually take to cross off incorrect answer choices with your pencil. If you eliminate incorrect answer choices immediately as they are identified, the time spent is negligible. Reading the Full Question can also seem more time-consuming than skimming the question quickly and beginning work as soon as possible, but, in reality, reading each question carefully and looking for traps often saves time. Students who do this work each problem more efficiently: They understand the question more quickly and are able to apply smart strategies without losing precious seconds rereading each problem. Time management is certainly important. Following are a few techniques you can use to maximize your time.

Order of Difficulty: It's Personal

Why should a high-scoring student care about the difficulty level of a question on the SAT Math sections? If you've got the math skills to do all—or at least, almost all—of the questions on the SAT Math sections, you may think the best approach for you is to dive straight in and do the questions in order. That's not necessarily the best approach, though.

The questions on the Math sections are presented in a loose Order of Difficulty (OOD), so the easier questions tend to be earlier in a section, and the harder questions tend to be later. However, just because the test writers think a question is easy (or hard) doesn't mean it's easy (or hard) *for you*. It's possible you will find the last question on a section to be surprisingly easy; conversely, you may find one in the middle to be excruciatingly difficult. For what it's worth, we have numbered the math problems that you'll encounter throughout this part of the book to correspond with where they'd approximately appear on the test. There are 38 questions on the calculator portion and 20 on the no-calculator portion, so our numbering should give you a good gauge of how POOD can be of benefit to you.

So, remember to use Personal Order of Difficulty (POOD). To maximize your efficiency, don't linger too long on any one question. Do every question that you understand immediately. If you're not sure how to work a question, or if it just seems like it will be too time-consuming, skip it for now.

Once you have reached the end of the section, go back to the ones you skipped. You will now have more time to decipher their meaning and work through to the answer without worrying about other questions that you haven't gotten to yet. Consider the following scenarios for solving for *x*.

Example 4:

(1) $x + 4 > 7$

(2) $2x = 8$

(3) $x^3 + 3x^2 + 3x + 1 = 0$

(4) $\dfrac{x}{4} = \dfrac{3}{5}$

Assume that you have poorly managed your time and you only have two minutes to work these four questions. What would be the advantage of passing over question (3)? Perhaps you could solve it if you had enough time. However, compared to the other three questions, it is much more challenging and time-consuming. If you worked questions (1), (2), and (4), you could then use all of the remaining time you had to puzzle out question (3). If you allowed yourself to get bogged down in solving question (3), you might not have any time left to answer question (4).

Using POOD has two major advantages. First, you will be less likely to either skip or have to rush through easier questions because you wasted too much time on hard ones. Second, since this is a timed test, longer or harder problems can cause your anxiety to build, which might affect your performance on other questions. Saving those tough questions for last will allow you to work more smoothly, efficiently, and confidently through the section.

A NOTE ON CALCULATORS

Most common calculators are allowed on Section 4 of the SAT. Some exceptions include

- Laptops
- Calculators with a QWERTY keyboard
- Cell-phone calculators

If you aren't sure whether your calculator is allowed, check the College Board website (www.sat.collegeboard.org and click on "Test Day Checklist").

Your calculator can definitely come in handy for complicated calculations in Section 4; to be efficient on the test, you'll want to make the best use of it. But be careful! Some questions are designed with "calculator traps" in mind—careless errors the test writers know you might make when you just dive into a problem with your calculator.

Example 5:

Given the function $f(x) = 5x^2 - x - 7$, what is $f(-4)$?

A) −91

B) −83

C) 69

D) 77

This problem can be solved manually or with the calculator—whichever you prefer! But if you use a calculator, be careful with that (−4). What you punch into your calculator should look something like this:

$$5(-4)^2 - (-4) - 7$$

When working with negative numbers or fractions, make doubly sure that you use parentheses. If you don't, a lot of weird stuff can happen, and unfortunately all of the weird, wrong stuff that can happen is reflected in the wrong answer choices. If you ran this equation and found 77, (D), you got the right answer. If not, go back and figure out where you made your calculator mistake.

Types of Calculators

Throughout the rest of the math chapters, we will discuss how to use your calculator when it is allowed and what to do when you can't use it. We recommend you make sure your calculator is acceptable for use on the test and that it can do the following:

- handle positive, negative, and fractional exponents
- use parentheses
- graph functions
- convert fractions to decimals and vice versa
- change a linear equation into $y = mx + b$ format

When calculator use is allowed, use it as needed to avoid careless mistakes, but use it wisely. Set up the problem on paper first, and be careful with negative numbers, fractions, and parentheses.

Working Smarter

The techniques and strategies in this book are not that hard to learn, but they will not be second nature to you. Make sure that you focus on putting them into practice. Your goal is to internalize every strategy in this book. When you have internalized a concept, you no longer consciously think about what to do. You simply do it. Think about some of the equations in Example 4 above. Were you able to look at some of them and immediately know what the answer was without consciously thinking about the math? If so, then you have successfully internalized the concepts necessary to manipulate basic equations when solving for x. Test prep is no different!

Successfully incorporating these techniques requires two things: practice and review. Many of the techniques you will learn from these pages may initially seem awkward. You may even ask yourself why you should try something new if you can already solve the problem another way. This is a valid question; however, at its core it reveals the distinction between a technique and content knowledge. A technique is a transferable skill that you can use on a variety of questions. Content knowledge, while certainly useful, is not necessarily equally applicable to all test questions. Techniques are.

Mastering new skills requires practice. Think about learning a new sport. Your coach explains how to perform an action, such as spiking a volleyball or making a lay-up. You easily comprehend what is being said. "No problem," you think. However, there is a big difference between understanding a concept and having the necessary coordination to complete it. This analogy is comparable to testing techniques. Much of what you read in this manual will seem easy, such as using POE. Only practice, however, will make crossing off wrong answers *every time* second nature to you.

The second reason you should try something different is more pragmatic: If you could hit your goal score already, you wouldn't be reading this book! Do not merely skip to the practice questions and try to work them the old way. Even if you think your way is easier, practice the techniques. Remember that working many practice problems will reinforce all the techniques you currently use. This includes bad habits. Practicing math problems without attempting anything new will never improve your score. It is often said that insanity is doing the same thing over and over again but expecting different results. Do not drive yourself crazy with meaningless practice. Apply what you learn in these pages to every single question you work. You will be pleased with the results.

Finally, review your work. Do not simply tally up your points and pat yourself on the back. Every question missed is a learning opportunity. Ask yourself what happened. Did you have the necessary content knowledge? Did you miss an opportunity to use a new technique? Did you rush and miss a keyword? Did you not correctly apply POE? For every problem, you can identify a reason that you missed it. Over time, you will begin to see patterns emerging. For example, you might notice that you tend to rush through all algebra problems and therefore have more careless errors. The beauty of test prep is once you know what you are doing wrong, that problem will vanish. You will be on guard against making the same mistakes in the future.

Summary

○ Be on the lookout for trap answers on the SAT and eliminate them when you find them.

○ Read each question carefully to understand what it is asking you to do.

○ Slow down and use your pencil to avoid careless errors.

○ Use your Personal Order of Difficulty to ensure efficiency. Save for last questions that you don't understand or that seem time-consuming.

○ When calculator use is allowed, make sure you are still setting the problem up on paper first. Only use the calculator as a last step, when it is necessary to avoid calculation errors.

○ Practice all the new strategies in this book until you can use them well. Review your work to learn from any mistakes that you make.

Chapter 16
Fundamentals, Coordinate Geometry, and Functions

INTRODUCTION

This chapter will focus on the fundamental question types of the SAT Math sections. While there are many legitimate shortcuts that can be made and will be discussed below, ultimately you will simply need to solve many of the questions on the SAT. This chapter will begin with a discussion of math vocabulary words and concepts that appear throughout the SAT. Next, we will discuss functions and the many ways that they can be presented on the SAT. Finally, the chapter will include some drills where you can hone the skills you learned from this chapter.

VOCABULARY

The SAT loves to test vocabulary words. Make sure you're familiar with all of these definitions:

Number	any number, including fractions, integers, decimals
Integer	a number that has no fractional or decimal component
Negative	less than zero
Positive	more than zero
Even	divisible by 2 with no remainder
Odd	divisible by 2 with a remainder of 1
Difference	the result of subtraction
Sum	the result of addition
Product	the result of multiplication
Quotient	the result of division
Ratio	fractional relationship between two amounts
Prime	a number with exactly two distinct factors (1 and itself)
Factor/Divisor	a number by which another number can be divided evenly
Prime factor	a prime number by which another number can be divided evenly
Multiple	a number multiplied by an integer
Remainder	the amount left over after long division
Distinct	different
Consecutive	in order
Absolute value	positive distance from zero
The square of...	x^2
The square root of...	$\sqrt{x}$
Mean	average

Median	middle number of an ordered list (or the average of the two middle numbers)
Mode	most frequently occurring number in a list
Range	the difference between the greatest and least numbers on a list
Percent	divided by 100
Inclusive	including the numbers at the ends of the range
Reciprocal	1 divided by the number
Rational number	a number that can be expressed as a fraction
Radical	a number with a root (a fractional exponent)
Extraneous solution	a solution found using algebra that does not work in the original equation
Linear equation	$y = mx + b$
Exponential equation	$y = c^x$, where c is a constant
Quadratic equation	$ax^2 + bx + c = 0$
Quadratic formula	$x = \dfrac{-b \pm \sqrt{b^2 - 4ac}}{2a}$

MATH FUNDAMENTALS

As we discussed in the introduction, it's very important to Read the Full Question (RTFQ)! Many common errors occur because students miss a key word, rather than not knowing how to work a problem. Consider the following question.

1

If x, y, and z are distinct positive integers and sum to 66, which of the following could be the greatest possible value for x ?

A) 21

B) 22

C) 23

D) 63

Here's How to Crack It

First, underline the key vocabulary words in this problem: *distinct*, *positive*, and *integer*. The problem says that they *sum* to 66. Finally, RTFQ! Notice that you are looking for the "greatest possible value for *x*." Now, use Process of Elimination (POE). In (A), if *x* is 21, then *y* + *z* must sum to 45. Therefore, *y* could be 22 and *z* could be 23. Eliminate (A). Choice (B) is a trap for the student who simply divides 66 by 3 to get an average value of 22. Eliminate (B). Now, consider (C). Be very careful here! If *x* is 23, then *y* + *z* = 43, so *y* could be 21 and *z* could be 22. However, there is nothing in the problem that says the numbers have to *be* consecutive, so eliminate (C) and try (D). If *x* is 63, then *y* + *z* = 3. These have to be distinct, positive integers, but that is OK since one of the variables could be 2 and the other could be 1. Therefore, the credited response is (D).

SOLVING

Some questions on the SAT will require you to use algebraic manipulation to solve equations. Operations done to one side of the equation need to also be performed on the other side of the equation. You have probably done this a lot in math class, so we will focus on some of the strange ways ETS might present solving questions.

Let's look an example of a typical "isolate the variable" question:

6

The electric field inside a spherical shell can be calculated using the equation $E = \dfrac{kqr}{R^3}$, which relates the variables of electric field (*E*), charge (*q*), distance from the center of the sphere to the charge (*r*), and radius of the sphere (*R*) to one another and to a constant (*k*). Which of the following expressions best describes how to find the charge (*q*) that is necessary to create an electric field in a given system?

A) $q = \dfrac{Ekr}{R^3}$

B) $q = \dfrac{ER^3}{kr}$

C) $q = \dfrac{kr}{ER^3}$

D) $q = \dfrac{Ekr}{kR^3}$

Here's How to Crack It

The problem asks you to rewrite the expression in terms of charge (the variable q).

In order to isolate q on one side of the equation, start by multiplying both sides of the equation by the denominator on the right side: $ER^3 = kqr$. Next, divide both sides of the equation by k and r: $q = \dfrac{ER^3}{kr}$, which matches (B).

SYSTEMS OF EQUATIONS AND INEQUALITIES

The SAT presents systems of equations and inequalities in tricky ways. You will need to be able to recognize what the problems are actually asking for, and use that knowledge to find the best approach for solving the equation.

Let's look at a problem that asks you to work with a system of inequalities:

17

Which of the following accurately defines all possible values of $a - b$ if $5 \le a \le 17$ and $9 \le b \le 35$?

A) $-30 \le a - b \le 8$

B) $-18 \le a - b \le -4$

C) $-8 \le a - b \le 30$

D) $13 \le a - b \le 18$

Here's How to Crack It

If a problem asked you to find all the possible values of $a + b$, you could simply stack and add the inequalities. However, when a problem asks you to subtract, multiply, or divide inequalities, you need to test *each end* of the possible ranges against one another. For example, the low end of the a range (5) minus the low end of the b range (9) is −4, while the low end of the a range (5) minus the high end of the b range (35) is −30. Also, the high end of the a range (17) minus the low end of the b range (9) is 8, while the high end of the a range (17) minus the high end of the b range (35) is −18. Use the highest and lowest numbers you calculated as the ends of the range for $a - b$: $-30 \le a - b \le 8$, which matches (A).

Your work for this problem might look like this:

a	b	$a - b$
5	9	−4
5	35	−30
17	9	8
17	35	−18

When a problem presents simultaneous equations, be sure to note what the question is asking for (RTFQ) and find the fastest way to get there. Consider this example:

3

If $4a - 2b = 16$ and $3a - 3b = 15$, then $7a - 5b =$

A) −2

B) 3

C) 11

D) 31

Here's How to Crack It

Solving these simultaneous equations for the values of a and b would be a chore. However, note that the problem isn't asking for the values of a and b; instead, it's asking for the value of $7a - 5b$. What's the easiest way to get to that value? Simply stack and add the equations: $7a - 5b = 25$, which is (D).

You won't always be able to directly stack and add or subtract equations to solve. Let's look at a question that requires a different approach:

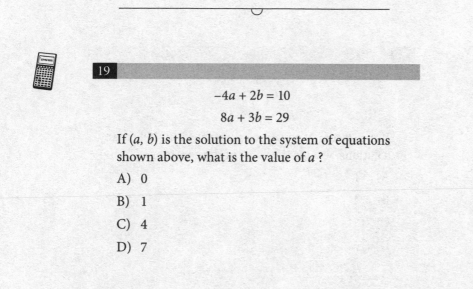

$$-4a + 2b = 10$$
$$8a + 3b = 29$$

If (a, b) is the solution to the system of equations shown above, what is the value of a ?

A) 0

B) 1

C) 4

D) 7

Here's How to Crack It

You can use various methods to solve a question like this: You could solve one equation for a, then substitute the value into the other equation. Alternatively, you can look for a way to change the equations so that they will stack and add to eliminate a variable. In this case, you could multiply the first equation by 2, then stack and add the equations, like this:

$$
\begin{array}{r}
-8a + 4b = 20 \\
+ \quad 8a + 3b = 29 \\
\hline
7b = 49
\end{array}
$$

Now solve to find that $b = 7$, and substitute that value into one of the original equations: $8a + 3(7) = 29$, so $8a + 21 = 29$, $8a = 8$, and $a = 1$, (B).

Another way ETS will test simultaneous equations is to reference the number of solutions a system has. For instance, if a system of linear equations has *infinite solutions*, then the equations are identical (they represent the same line). On the other hand, if a system of linear equations has *no solutions*, then the lines represented are parallel (they have equal slopes).

Let's look at some examples:

7

$$\frac{y-5}{4} = x$$
$$kx - 3y = -15$$

If the system of equations above has infinitely many solutions, what is the value of the constant k ?

A)   1

B)   4

C) 12

D) 16

Here's How to Crack It

Since the problem specifies that the system of equations has *infinitely many solutions*, the equations represent the same line and are essentially identical. Start by putting both equations into the slope-intercept form: $\frac{y-5}{4} = x$ becomes $y = 4x + 5$, while $kx - 3y = -15$ becomes $y = \frac{k}{3}x + 5$. Since these equations must be identical, $\frac{k}{3}$ must equal 4, so $k = 12$, which matches (C).

Now let's try a question in which a system of equations has *no solution*.

10

$$\frac{1}{3}x - \frac{7}{9}y = 2$$

$$36 - tx = -14y$$

Consider the system of linear equations above, in which t is a constant. If the system has no solutions, what is the value of t ?

A) -6

B) $\dfrac{3}{14}$

C) $\dfrac{3}{7}$

D) 6

Here's How to Crack It

Since the problem states that the system has *no solutions*, the equations represent parallel lines (lines with the same slope but different y-intercepts). Start by putting both equations into the slope-intercept form. Clear the fractions in the first equation by multiplying both sides by 9: $\frac{1}{3}x - \frac{7}{9}y = 2$ becomes $3x - 7y = 18$, or $y = \frac{3}{7}x - \frac{18}{7}$. The second equation becomes $y = \frac{t}{14}x - \frac{36}{14}$. Since these equations have the same slope, $\frac{t}{14}$ must equal $\frac{3}{7}$, so $t = 6$, which matches (D).

Another kind of system of equations question may give you a line and an equation that is not linear and ask you for the number of solutions. Here's one to try.

19

$$y = 3x + 2$$
$$y = 4x^2 - 4x + 3$$

How many values of (x, y) satisfy the system of equations above?

A) 0

B) 1

C) 2

D) Infinitely many

Here's How to Crack It

Because the first equation is a line and the second is a quadratic, it is impossible for the two to be equal. This means there cannot be infinitely many solutions to the system of equations; eliminate (A). Next, to determine the number of solutions, begin by combining the equations. Substitute $3x + 2$ for y in the second equation: $3x + 2 = 4x^2 - 4x + 3$. Because this is a quadratic, set it equal to 0 by subtracting $3x + 2$ from both sides: $0 = 4x^2 - 7x + 1$. This doesn't factor nicely, so the easiest way to determine the number of solutions is to consider the discriminant: $b^2 - 4ac$, when the quadratic equation is in the form $0 = ax^2 + bx + c$. If the discriminant is positive, there are two solutions. If it is negative, there are no (real) solutions, and if it is equal to 0, then there is one solution. Plug in $a = 4$, $b = -7$, and $c = 1$ into the discriminant: $(-7)^2 - 4(4)(1) = 49 - 16 = 33$. This is positive, so there are two real solutions; choose (C).

EXTRANEOUS SOLUTIONS

Some equations that involve roots or rational numbers will produce solutions that don't actually work in the original equation. These solutions are referred to as *extraneous solutions*. When the SAT asks for an extraneous solution, solve for the solutions and then plug them back into the original equation to see which one doesn't *actually* work, even though it's a solution.

Let's look at an example:

10

$$b - 4 = 3\sqrt{b}$$

Which of the following is the extraneous solution for b in the equation above?

A) −16

B) −1

C) 1

D) 16

Here's How to Crack It

Square both sides of the equation to get rid of the square root sign: $(b-4)^2 = (3\sqrt{b})^2$, which becomes $b^2 - 8b + 16 = 9b$. Be careful, as there are several traps you can fall into on that step! Move everything to the left side of the equation: $b^2 - 17b + 16 = 0$, which factors into $(b-16)(b-1) = 0$. Therefore, the solutions to the equation appear to be $b = 16$ and $b = 1$. Now, plug both of these values of b into the original equation to see which one of them is extraneous. If you plug $b = 1$ into the original equation, you get $-3 = 3\sqrt{1}$, or $-3 = 3$, which is untrue. Therefore, $b = 1$ is the extraneous solution, and the credited response is (C).

COMPLEX NUMBERS

Occasionally, a mathematical operation will require taking a square root of a negative number. With real numbers, that isn't possible—no real number can be squared to get a negative number. This is where i comes in. The i stands for "imaginary," to distinguish it from "real" numbers, and it equals $\sqrt{-1}$. When i is squared, the result is –1. "Complex numbers" combine real and imaginary numbers in the form $a + bi$, where a is real, and bi is imaginary.

- The imaginary number $i = \sqrt{-1}$.
- Treat i just like a variable, except that $i^2 = -1$.
- $a + bi$ is a complex number, where a is the real component of the number, and bi is the imaginary component of the number.
- Many calculators have an i button and an $a + bi$ mode, which can come in handy if a question on complex numbers comes up in the section of the test that allows calculators.

Let's look at a problem that puts all of these concepts together:

11

Which of the following imaginary or complex numbers is equivalent to $\dfrac{2-3i}{6+4i}$? (Note: $i = \sqrt{-1}$)

A) $-\dfrac{1}{2}i$

B) $\dfrac{1}{3}+i$

C) $-\dfrac{13i}{10}$

D) $\dfrac{6}{5}-\dfrac{13i}{10}$

Here's How to Crack It

Start by getting rid of i in the denominator of the equation. To do so, multiply the expression by $\dfrac{6-4i}{6-4i}$. This works because $6 - 4i$ is the *conjugate* of $6 + 4i$. A *conjugate* is formed by changing the sign of the second term of the binomial. Since $(a + b)(a - b) = a^2 - b^2$, you can do the same thing here to clear i from the denominator: $(6 + 4i)(6 - 4i) = (36 - 16i^2)$. And since $i^2 = -1$, the denominator simplifies to $36 + 16$, which equals 52. You will need to use FOIL to find the new numerator: $(2 - 3i)(6 - 4i) = 12 - 8i - 18i + 12i^2$, which simplifies to $12 - 26i + 12(-1)$, then $12 - 26i - 12$, or simply $-26i$. Therefore, to put it all together, $\left(\dfrac{2-3i}{6+4i}\right)\left(\dfrac{6-4i}{6-4i}\right) = -\dfrac{26i}{52}$, which simplifies to $-\dfrac{i}{2}$, (A).

TRY IT EXERCISE 1

Try these questions on your own. Only use your calculator when it is allowed. See Chapter 20 for complete answers and explanations.

10

For $i = \sqrt{-1}$, what is the product of $(5 + 2i)$ and $(-3 - 4i)$?

A) $-23 - 26i$

B) $-23 - 14i$

C) $-7 - 26i$

D) $-7 - 34i$

19

Which of the following is an extraneous solution to the equation $\dfrac{1}{x-3} + \dfrac{1}{x+3} = \dfrac{12}{2x^2-18}$?

A) -3

B) 0

C) 3

D) 9

$$x^2 < 4$$
$$0 < y^3 < 25$$

If x and y are integers that satisfy the above inequalities, how many distinct possible values are there for $x + y$?

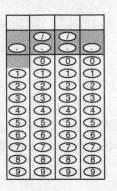

> For further practice, go online to your Student Tools and complete the Chapter 16 Fundamentals Drill and Inequalities Drill.

COORDINATE GEOMETRY

Many questions on the SAT test your knowledge of graphs in the *xy*-plane. You will see questions that ask about the graph of an equation, graphs that ask you to find the equation, and much more. Here is everything you need to know about coordinate geometry on the SAT.

Basic Coordinate Geometry Facts

- The coordinate plane is a system of two perpendicular axes used to describe the position of a point (x, y).
- The *x*-axis is the horizontal axis of the coordinate plane.
- The *y*-axis is the vertical axis of the coordinate plane.
- The origin is the intersection of the *x* and *y* axes and has the coordinates $(0, 0)$.
- Point locations within the coordinate plane are written as (x, y), where *x* denotes the horizontal distance from the origin and *y* denotes the vertical distance from the origin.
- The *y*-intercept is the coordinate at which a line or a function intersects the *y*-axis. Therefore, the value of *x* for the *y*-intercept will always be zero and will take the form $(0, y)$.

- The x-intercept is the coordinate(s) at which a function intersects the x-axis. Therefore, the value of y for the x-intercept will always be zero and will take the form $(x, 0)$. These values are also known as roots, solutions, or zeros of the function.
- Slope is defined as the ratio of vertical change to horizontal change, or $\dfrac{rise}{run}$.

- Slope can always be calculated with two points from the same line, using the formula $m = \dfrac{y_2 - y_1}{x_2 - x_1}$, where m is the slope value, (x_2, y_2) is one point, and (x_1, y_1) is another.
- The slope-intercept form of the equation of the line is $y = mx + b$, where m is the slope, and b is the y-intercept. Both of these values are constants. In this formula, x and y are coordinate values of any point on that line.
- Parallel lines have identical slopes.
- Perpendicular lines have slopes that are negative reciprocals of one another.

Advanced Coordinate Geometry Facts

- A parabola is a graph of a quadratic equation in the xy-coordinate plane. The general form of the equation is $y = ax^2 + bx + c$.
- Parabolas are symmetrical around an axis of symmetry and have a single vertex on the axis of symmetry.
- If a is positive, the graph opens upward. If a is negative, the graph opens downward. When a is positive, increasing its value makes a parabola steeper; If a is negative, decreasing its value also makes a parabola steeper. It may be helpful to think of a as analogous to slope.
- Changing the value of b shifts the parabola's axis of symmetry left or right, in the *opposite* direction. So, a negative value for b means that the axis of symmetry is positive, and vice versa.
- c is the y-intercept of the parabola. For example, if $c = 2$, the coordinates of the y-intercept are $(0, 2)$.
- The y-coordinate of any point can be found by putting the x-value into the standard equation and solving for y.
- Parabolas also can be written using the vertex form of the equation: $y = a(x - h)^2 + k$, where a, h, and k are constants.
- The vertex of the parabola in this form is (h, k).

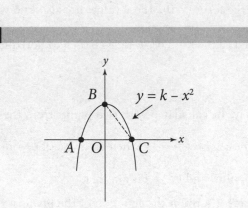

14

The figure above shows the graph of the parabola $y = k - x^2$, where k is a constant. If the coordinates of point A are $(-2, 0)$, what is the length of line segment BC?

A) $\sqrt{5}$

B) $2\sqrt{5}$

C) 6

D) $5\sqrt{2}$

Here's How to Crack It

The parabola $y = k - x^2$ is centered on the y-axis, so if the coordinates of A are $(-2, 0)$, the coordinates of C must be $(2, 0)$. Whenever you have a point on a graph, you can plug it into the equation to find a missing piece. So, plug in $(2, 0)$ to find k: $0 = k - 2^2$, therefore $k = 4$. This tells that the coordinates of B are $(0, 4)$. To find the length of BC, you don't need the distance formula: Just draw a right triangle and use the Pythagorean theorem. The legs of the triangle are 2 and 4, so $2^2 + 4^2 = (BC)^2$, and $BC = \sqrt{20} = 2\sqrt{5}$. The correct answer is (B).

In the *vertex form* of a parabola, which is written as $y = a(x - h)^2 + k$, the value of a also determines the direction and width of the parabola. A question may ask you to convert from the standard form of a parabola to the vertex form, or vice versa. Here's an example.

$$g(x) = (x + 5)(x - 3)$$

Which of the following is an equivalent form of the function g that would be most useful in determining the vertex of the parabola formed when function g is graphed in the xy-plane?

A) $g(x) = (x + 1)^2 - 14$

B) $g(x) = (x + 1)^2 - 16$

C) $g(x) = x^2 + 2x - 15$

D) $g(x) = x(x + 2) - 15$

Here's How to Crack It

The question asks you to convert the equation into the vertex form of the parabola. Before you start, eliminate (C) and (D) because they do not match the vertex form $a(x - h)^2 + k$. To convert the function to vertex form, FOIL the factors together: $g(x) = (x + 5)(x - 3) = x^2 - 3x + 5x - 15 = x^2 + 2x - 15$. Next, you need to "complete the square" in order to convert to the vertex form. Since the vertex form requires the element $(x - h)^2$, add in a constant that will allow you to factor out a squared binomial. In this case, you would need $x^2 + 2x + 1$ to be present so that you can factor it into $(x + 1)^2$. Therefore, rewrite the function by adding a 1 and subtracting a 1: $g(x) = x^2 + 2x + 1 - 1 - 15$. Now you can factor out the squared binomial: $g(x) = (x + 1)^2 - 1 - 15$, which simplifies to $(x + 1)^2 - 16$, (B).

You may also need to complete the square on questions that involve the equation of a circle. Remember that the equation of a circle is $(x - h)^2 + (y - k)^2 = r^2$, where (h, k) is the center of the circle, and r is the radius.

Let's look at an example.

14

$$x^2 - 6x + y^2 - 8y = 0$$

If (h, k) is center of the circle described by the equation above in the xy-plane, what is the value of k ?

A) 2

B) 3

C) 4

D) 5

Here's How to Crack It

Start by working with the x terms. Find the coefficient on the x (−6), divide it in half (−3), and square it (9). Add that value to both sides of the equation to get $x^2 - 6x + 9 + y^2 - 8y = 9$. You can convert the x terms into the square form to get $(x - 3)^2 + y^2 - 8y = 9$. The question only asks for the value of h, which is the x-coordinate of the center when the circle equation is in the form $(x - h)^2 + (y - k)^2 = r^2$. You already have the x terms in that form, so $h = 3$, which is (B).

If you needed to find the center or the radius of the circle, you would complete the square on the y terms in the same way: $-8 \div 2 = -4$, and $(-4)^2 = 16$, so the equation becomes $(x - 3)^2 + y^2 - 8y + 16 = 9 + 16$ or $(x - 3)^2 + (y - 4)^2 = 25$. The center is $(3, 4)$ and the radius is 5.

REFLECTION AND TRANSFORMATION FACTS

- Rotation means turning a line or function around a point called the center of rotation.
- Reflecting a line or a function means creating a mirror image of the graph or function around the line of reflection.
- Lines reflected across the x-axis have slopes that are negatives of each other (*not* negative reciprocals) and y-intercepts that are negatives of each other.
- Lines reflected across the y-axis have slopes that are negatives of each other but the same y-intercept.
- A translation moves a figure without reflecting or rotating it. See the following examples.

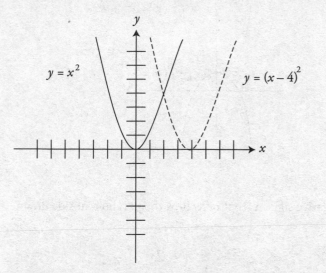

In this example, the graph is translated to the right by adjusting the *x*-coordinate value. If a number is inside the parentheses with the *x*-value, then the graph shifts the number of units opposite the direction of the sign.

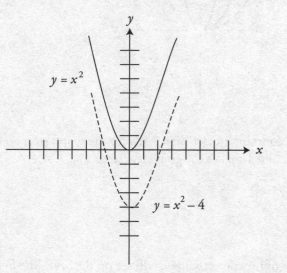

In the example above, the graph is translated down 4 units. Notice that a translation on the *y*-axis is outside the parentheses, and the shift matches the value of the sign.

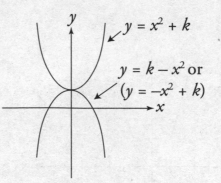

Putting a negative sign in front of x^2 flips the parabola upside down.

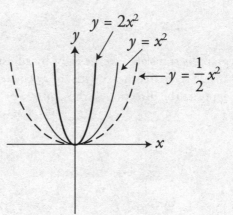

Multiplying x by a constant greater than 1 makes the graph steeper. Conversely, a constant between 0 and 1 makes the graph less steep.

FUNCTIONS

There are two types of functions that you will see on the SAT. The first type is very similar to coordinate geometry and often overlaps significantly with the material discussed earlier. These are often called linear functions. Essentially, a function acts like a machine. A function produces a y-value whenever you put in an x value. A function can have multiple x values for a single y-value, but a function can never have multiple y-values for a single x-value. In other words, a function can move up and down in the xy-plane, but it can never double back on itself. See the following figures.

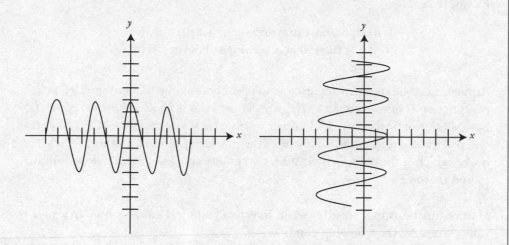

The figure on the left is a function, while the figure on the right is not a function. If you can draw a vertical line that touches more than one point on the graph, it's not a function (this is called the "vertical line test").

Function notation is slightly different from coordinate geometry notation. The y-value is usually written as $f(x)$. In other words, $f(x) = y$. The value (x) represents all the possible x-values for the function. The f alone is not a variable and should not be solved for. It merely denotes the name of the function. If there are multiple functions on a graph, then they are usually denoted using an alphabetical pattern: $f(x)$, $g(x)$, $h(x)$…. As long as you are comfortable following directions, functions should not pose too many issues for you. Consider the following example:

Example 1:

The function $f(x)$ is defined by $f(x) = 3x^2 - 1$. If p is a positive integer, and $4f(p) = 428$, then what is the value of p ?

Begin by simplifying to the basic function by dividing both sides by 4, so $f(p) = 107$. Next, since $f(p) = f(x)$ with a value of p, substitute the given equation for $f(p)$: $3p^2 - 1 = 107$. Now, solve for p: $3p^2 = 108$, $p^2 = 36$, so $p = 6$.

Function questions on the SAT may also require you to process information from charts and graphs. Since $f(x)$ represents the y-coordinate and x represents the x-coordinate, functions can also be understood as a form of point notation. Consider in the following two examples how function notation can be used to represent coordinate graphs.

Example 2:

> If $f(x)$ is a linear function such that $f(1) = 5$ and $f(-1) = 9$, then what is the slope of the graph of $y = f(x)$?

As mentioned in an earlier question, don't get confused by the terminology. A linear function is just a line. Since $f(x) = y$, $f(1) = 5$ can be read as "the function $f(x)$ has a y value of 5 when x is 1." In other words, this is just the point (1, 5). The second pair can be read in the same way: "The function $f(x)$ has a y value of 9 when x is -1," which is the point (-1, 9). With two points on a line, use the slope formula to find that $m = -2$.

Harder functions may require you to interpret graphical data for find an x or a y value. Consider the following example:

Example 3:

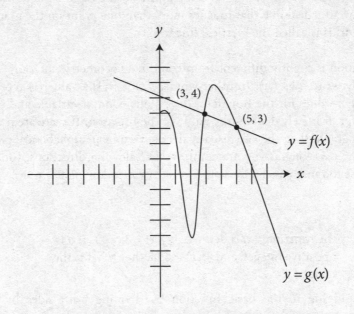

> The figure above shows the graphs of the functions $y = f(x)$ and $y = g(x)$. Which of the following describes all the values of x for which $g(x) \geq f(x)$?

This question is asking you to find all of the values for x for which the line $g(x)$ is above (greater than) the line $f(x)$. The values range from 3 to 5 or $3 < x < 5$. Trap answers on the SAT would include the y-values or would confuse greater than and less than.

Sometimes a question will present you with information about a graph of a function and ask you to make conclusions about the function based on the graph. Here's an example of this type of question:

13

If the function g has four distinct zeros, which of the following could represent the complete graph of g in the xy-plane?

A)

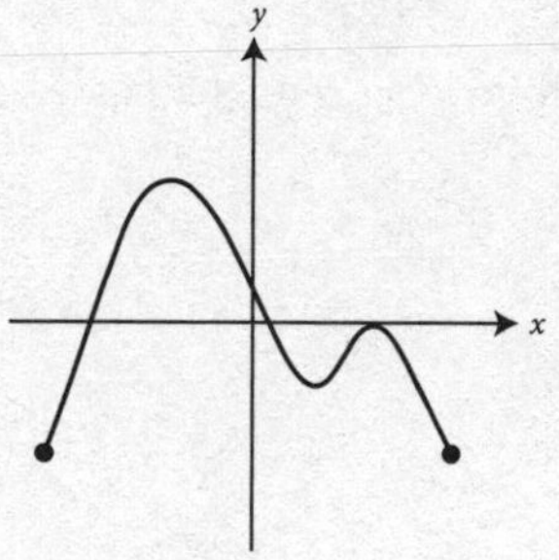

B)

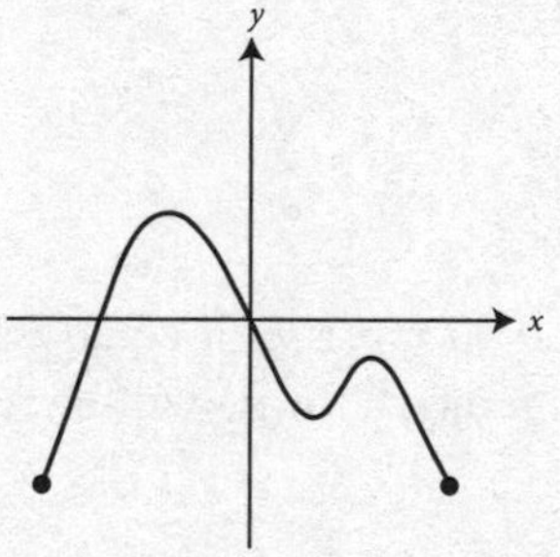

C)

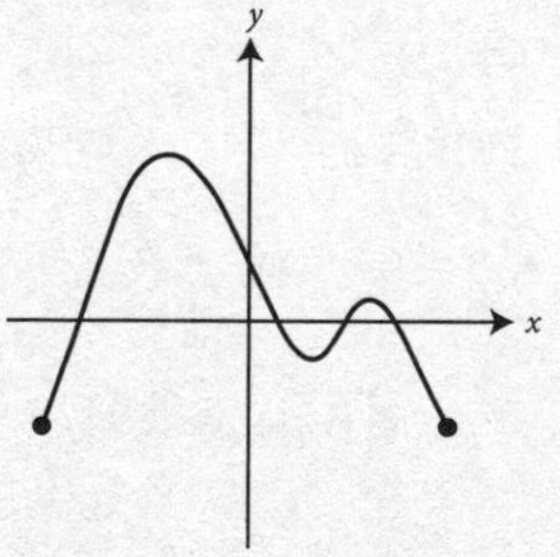

D)

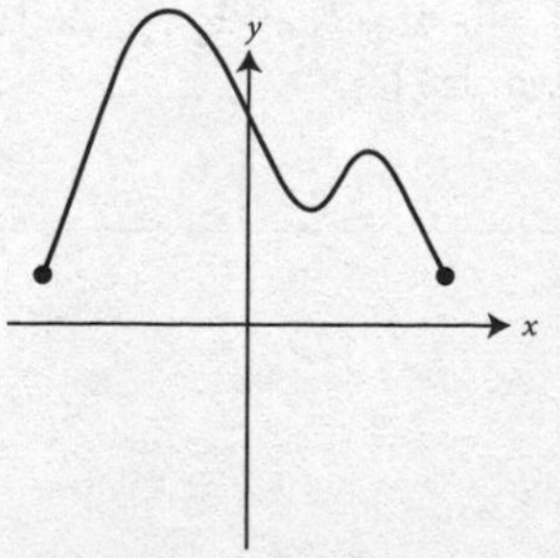

Here's How to Crack It

Zeros are the places where the line and the *x*-axis meet. If the graph has four distinct zeros, it crosses the *x*-axis in four places. Only the function in (C) does this.

The zeros of a function may also be tested in a word problem, such as the following example.

10

Which of the following represents all zeros of the function $f(x) = -\dfrac{1}{4}x^5 + \dfrac{3}{4}x^3 + x$?

A) 2 only

B) –2 only

C) –2, 2

D) –2, 0, –2

Here's How to Crack It

To find the zeros of a function, you must set it equal to zero and solve. Since this function has a power of 5 in it, some factoring will be required.

$$f(x) = -\frac{1}{4}x^5 + \frac{3}{4}x^3 + x$$

$$f(x) = -\frac{1}{4}(x^5 - 3x^3 - 4x)$$

$$f(x) = -\frac{1}{4}x(x^4 - 3x^2 - 4)$$

$$f(x) = -\frac{1}{4}x(x^2 - 4)(x^2 + 1)$$

$$f(x) = -\frac{1}{4}x(x - 2)(x + 2)(x^2 + 1)$$

Therefore, the real zeros are at $x = 0$, $x = 2$, and $x = -2$. The factor $x^2 + 1$ has no real solutions to it. The correct answer is (D).

TRY IT EXERCISE 2

Attempt these questions, either with or without your calculator as shown, then check your answers in Chapter 20.

10

Which of the following represents a polynomial function with roots of $\{-\frac{1}{2}, 3, \text{ and } 3\}$?

A) $f(x) = 2x^3 - 11x^2 + 12x + 9$

B) $f(x) = 2x^3 + 11x^2 + 12x - 9$

C) $f(x) = 3x^2 - 11x + 9$

D) $f(x) = 3x^2 + 11x + 9$

16

Which of the following represents the equation of a quadratic function with vertex (3, 4) that passes through the point (1, 2) ?

A) $y = -2x^2 + 3x - \frac{1}{2}$

B) $y = -\frac{1}{2}x^2 + 3x - \frac{1}{2}$

C) $y = 2x^2 - 3x - \frac{1}{2}$

D) $y = -\frac{1}{2}x^2 - 3x - \frac{1}{2}$

15

$f(x)$ is a curve defined by $f(x) = x^3 - 6x^2 + 11x - 6$. Line $g(x)$ intersects $f(x)$ at the x-coordinate that is the even solution to $f(x)$ and passes through the point (0, 6). If $h(x)$ is a line perpendicular to $g(x)$, then what is the equation of $h(x)$, if $h(x)$ also passes through (0, 6) ?

A) $h(x) = -\frac{1}{3}x + 6$

B) $h(x) = 3x + 6$

C) $h(x) = \frac{1}{3}x + 6$

D) $h(x) = -3x + 6$

If (h, k) is the vertex of the parabola defined by $f(x) = -x^2 + 6x - 8$, what is the value of $h + k$?

For further practice, go online to your Student Tools and complete the Chapter 16 Coordinate Geometry Drill and Functions Drill.

Summary

- Techniques and strategies will definitely help you improve your scores, but you do need to have a solid understanding of basic mathematical concepts. Make sure you have the basics down!

- Problems will often require you to know mathematical terms and their definitions. Familiarize yourself with math vocabulary words prior to the test.

- Solving Equations and Inequalities
  - If a question asks you to solve for an unknown value in an equation or inequality, simply manipulate the equation and isolate the variable.
    - When working with inequalities, you must flip the inequality sign when multiplying or dividing by a negative number.
  - If you are given multiple equations and asked to find the value of an expression, try stacking and either adding or subtracting the equations.
    - Still can't get the expression you need? Try multiplying or dividing the resulting equation to get the desired expression.

- To find an extraneous solution, solve the equation, find the solutions, and plug them back into the original equation. The extraneous solution is the value that doesn't work.

- Imaginary and Complex Numbers
  - You will encounter imaginary numbers on the SAT; when you think about it, this is crazy!
  - Imaginary numbers result from taking the square root of a negative number.
  - $i = \sqrt{-1}$, $i^2 = -1$, and $i^4 = 1$
  - $a + bi$ is a complex number, of which a is real and bi is imaginary.
  - Don't forget to use the i button and the $a + bi$ mode on your calculator!

○ Coordinate Geometry
  • Is there a figure? If not, draw one! Is the provided figure not to scale? Re-draw it!
  • Lines
    • The equation of a line in slope-intercept form is $y = mx + b$, in which m is the slope and b is the y-intercept.
    • Parallel lines have identical slopes; both lines have a slope of m.
    • Perpendicular lines have slopes are negative reciprocals of one another; one line has a slope of m and the other line has a slope of $-\dfrac{1}{m}$.
  • Solving for Distance
    • When asked to solve the distance between two points on a graph, connect the points, construct a right triangle, and find the length of the hypotenuse using the Pythagorean theorem.
  • Parabolas
    • The general form of a parabola is $y = ax^2 + bx + c$.
    • The vertex form of a parabola with a vertex (h, k) is $y = a(x - h)^2 + k$.
  • Plugging in points from the graphs can be helpful on coordinate geometry problems!

○ Functions
  • When working with functions, plug in an x-value to find $f(x)$, or the y-value, or vice-versa.
    • When graphing, the solution of a function would be graphed as $(x, f(x))$.
  • If a question asks about the number of zeroes in a function, simply find the total number of x-intercepts.

- When solving rotation, translation, and reflection questions, sketch the movement on your figure.
  - Rotations should rotate around a point.
  - Reflections provide a mirror image.
  - Translations move the graph up if the number is inside the parentheses, or over if the number is outside the parentheses.

○ As always, make sure you use the global techniques of POE to eliminate obviously incorrect answers!

Chapter 17
Alternative
Approaches

INTRODUCTION

Scoring a 750 or higher on the SAT Math sections requires near perfection. Hardly a single problem can be skipped or answered incorrectly. One of the major challenges is developing the necessary flexibility to deal with every type of problem that the SAT might throw at you. Memorizing the many different equations and formulas needed is one way of beating these problems. While there are formulas you'll want to memorize, there are literally hundreds of formulas and concepts that *might* be helpful on the SAT once in a great while.

Additionally, you must ask yourself what you will do if you can't remember the correct formula for a problem. If you are ever stumped on the SAT, you may not hit the score you want.

As a result, it is vital that you develop alternative strategies for dealing with challenging questions. A successful alternative strategy should do several things: 1) it should guarantee the correct answer; 2) it should be as fast as or faster than applying the "correct" algebraic formula; and 3) it should be applicable to numerous situations.

This chapter will cover two alternative techniques for approaching challenging questions: Plugging In and Ballparking.

PLUGGING IN

Speed and accuracy are a vital combination for acing the Math sections of the SAT. If you had only thirty seconds left on one of the Math sections, which of the following two questions would you rather have?

1

A customer walks into a convenience store to purchase two candy bars valued at 50 cents apiece. If he pays with a ten-dollar bill, how much change will he receive?

A) $6

B) $7

C) $8

D) $9

A customer walks into a convenience store to purchase b bars of candy valued at c cents apiece. If he pays d dollars, which of the following expressions represents his change, in dollars?

A) $d - bc$

B) $bc - d$

C) $\dfrac{bc}{100} - d$

D) $d - \dfrac{bc}{100}$

Without a doubt, you would rather do the first problem, but why? The two problems are nearly identical! They cover the same topic and require the same math. What aspect of these problems makes number two so much more challenging? The answer, of course, is the presence of variables. Even if you're really good at algebra, numbers are easier to work with. As a result, the first problem is very straightforward, despite the need to convert from cents to dollars in order to solve for the change. Algebra, on the other hand, is not as intuitive.

By the way, did you get (D) for both questions? If not, come back and try the second one after you've completed this section!

Fortunately, it is possible to eliminate the need to use algebra on many SAT questions. This strategy is called Plugging In. Consider the following problem:

Which of the following is equivalent to the expression $\dfrac{3x+3}{\sqrt{x+1}}$?

A) $3x + 3$

B) $\sqrt{x+1}$

C) $3\sqrt{x-1}$

D) $3\sqrt{x+1}$

Here's How to Crack It

Instead of considering each choice and determining whether it is equivalent to $\frac{3x+3}{\sqrt{x+1}}$, try Plugging In. Begin by choosing a value for the variable, x. Because you need to take the square root of $x + 1$, choose a value which makes $x + 1$ a perfect square. Try $x = 8$. Make $x = 8$ in the original expression: $\frac{3(8)+3}{\sqrt{8+1}} = \frac{24+3}{\sqrt{9}} = \frac{27}{3} = 9$. Since 9 is the value of the expression in the question, what must be true of the correct answer? The correct answer must also equal 9 when $x = 8$. This is the *target*; circle it on your paper. Now, make $x = 8$ in each answer choice and eliminate what doesn't equal the target value, 9:

A)	$3(8) + 3 = 24 + 3 = 27$	This doesn't match your target; eliminate it.
B)	$\sqrt{8+1} = \sqrt{9} = 3$	This doesn't match your target; eliminate it.
C)	$3\sqrt{8-1} = 3\sqrt{7}$	This doesn't match your target; eliminate it.
D)	$3\sqrt{8+1} = 3\sqrt{9} = 3(3) = 9$	This is the only choice which matches your target; it must be the correct answer.

Consider the speed at which it is possible to move through this problem. Since arithmetic is so much more intuitive than algebra, most of these answers were probably obviously incorrect as soon as you Plugged In. Also, ask yourself which method is more error prone: using knowledge of algebraic principles and number theory in your head, or doing some basic arithmetic on paper?

Plugging In can be used for any and every question that has variables in the answer choices. Just follow these steps:

> 1. Choose a number for the variables in the problem.
> 2. Solve the problem using arithmetic. Circle the solution: This is your *target* number.
> 3. Plug In the numbers you substituted for variables into each answer choice.
> 4. The answer choice that matches your target is the correct answer. Be sure to check all four answers.

Now try another:

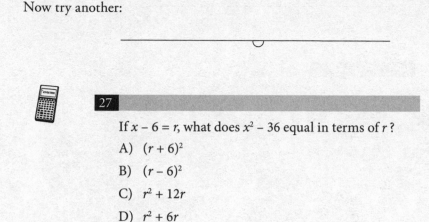

27

If $x - 6 = r$, what does $x^2 - 36$ equal in terms of r?

A) $(r + 6)^2$

B) $(r - 6)^2$

C) $r^2 + 12r$

D) $r^2 + 6r$

Here's How to Crack It

Here there are a couple of variables and a few tricky steps in the algebra, but Plugging In makes the problem much more straightforward. The first step is to choose values for the variables. Since there are two variables that are related, Plug In numbers that make the math as simple as possible. Let's say $x = 8$. Then $8 - 6 = 2$, so $r = 2$. Now solve the problem: $8^2 - 36 = 28$, so 28 is the target. Now, Plug In $r = 2$ into each of the answer choices; the correct answer will equal 28.

A) $(2 + 6)^2 = 8^2 = 64$ This doesn't match your target; eliminate it.

B) $(2 - 6)^2 = (-4)^2 = 16$ This doesn't match your target; eliminate it.

C) $2^2 + 12(2) = 4 + 24 = 28$ This matches your target, but check all four choices!

D) $2^2 + 6(2) = 4 + 12 = 16$ This doesn't match your target; eliminate it.

Therefore, the answer is (C).

When plugging in, be careful which numbers you choose, especially when calculator use is not allowed. Take a look at the next problem, and consider what would happen if you Plug In $b = 1$.

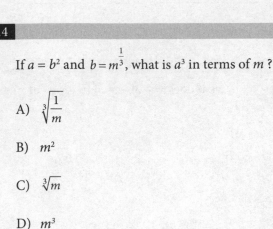

14

If $a = b^2$ and $b = m^{\frac{1}{3}}$, what is a^3 in terms of m ?

A) $\sqrt[3]{\dfrac{1}{m}}$

B) m^2

C) $\sqrt[3]{m}$

D) m^3

Here's How to Crack It

If $b = 1$, then $b^2 = 1$. This means that $a = 1$, and therefore $m^{\frac{1}{3}} = \sqrt[3]{m} = 1$ and $m = 1$. So if you Plug In using 1, then your target is also 1. Now try the answer choices.

A) $\sqrt[3]{\dfrac{1}{1}}$ This matches your target.

B) $1^2 = 1$ This matches your target.

C) $\sqrt[3]{1} = 1$ This matches your target.

D) $1^3 = 1$ This matches your target.

By Plugging In the number 1 for your value, no answer choices were eliminated. In basic terms, avoid numbers that either have unusual properties (such as 0 or 1), or that might make the math more challenging. The acronym **FROZEN** is useful for remembering which numbers to avoid:

    F = fractions
    R = repeating the same value (such as x and y are both 2)
    O = one
    Z = zero
    E = extreme (numbers that are very large or that are very small)
    N = negatives

Let's try this question again. We'll avoid the **FROZEN** numbers and pick values that make the math as simple as possible. In this question, it's easiest to start by working backwards. Since you are taking the third root of m, pick a number that is the cube of an integer, such as 8. If $m = 8$, then $b = 2$ and $a = 2^2 = 4$. The question asks for a^3, so our target is $4^3 = 64$. Now try the answer choices.

A) $\sqrt[3]{\dfrac{1}{8}} = \dfrac{1}{2}$

This doesn't match your target, so eliminate it.

B) $8^2 = 64$

This matches your target, but check all four answers!

C) $\sqrt[3]{8} = 2$

This doesn't match your target, so eliminate it.

D) $8^3 = 512$

This doesn't match your target, so eliminate it.

Therefore, the answer is (B).

As you can see, Plugging In is a powerful technique for improving both speed and accuracy on challenging problems.

Let's look at one more very challenging algebra problem that is made comparatively simple through the use of Plugging In:

30

If $x > 4$, what is the remainder when polynomial $x^4 + x^3 - 14x + 6$ is divided by the binomial $x - 2$?

A) 0

B) 1

C) 2

D) 3

Here's How to Crack It

You may or may not have run across synthetic division or polynomial division in your math classes. However, even if you have, Plugging In works great here. The question is asking for the remainder when one big, ugly thing is divided by a somewhat less ugly thing. Plug In for x to turn this into an arithmetic problem. Because you're dividing by $x - 2$ (and you have your lovely calculator available), make $x = 12$. That way, you end up dividing by 10 and can simply look at the last digit of the answer after you plug in $x = 12$ for the remainder. If $x = 12$, then the polynomial is $12^4 + 12^3 - 14(12) + 6 = 20{,}736 + 1{,}728 - 168 + 6 = 22{,}302$. When you divide 22,302 by $(12 - 2) = 10$, you are simply moving the decimal place over one spot to the left, giving you 2,230.2. The 2 to the right of the decimal place would be your remainder (because you're dividing by 10), so the answer is (C).

PLUGGING IN MORE THAN ONCE

We have discussed checking each answer choice when plugging in. Why do you need to do that? In some cases, you pick a set of "magic numbers" which makes more than one answer choice work (like making $b = 1$ in question 14 above). There are other problems that are set up in such a way that it's likely that you'll need to plug in more than once. Let's look at an example:

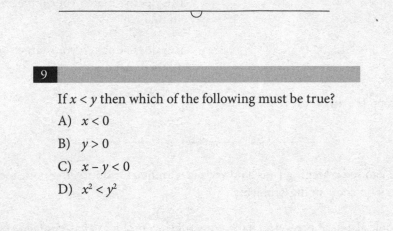

9

If $x < y$ then which of the following must be true?

A) $x < 0$

B) $y > 0$

C) $x - y < 0$

D) $x^2 < y^2$

Here's How to Crack It

As with all Plugging In questions, begin by choosing easy numbers that satisfy the rules of question. For example, $x = 2$ and $y = 3$. Now check each of the answers.

A)	$2 < 0$	Since your x and y satisfy the equation, this is not true, so eliminate it.
B)	$3 > 0$	This is currently true.
C)	$2 - 3 < 0$	This is currently true.
D)	$4 < 9$	This is currently true.

Even though the values you chose for x and y were valid, you were only able to eliminate one answer choice. This is not unusual when plugging in "normal" values for x and y. Remember the FROZEN numbers that we said to avoid? The phrase "must be" includes all possible situations as defined by the equation. Therefore, if $x < y$ the correct answer will be valid even if you plug in a fraction, a repeating number, a one, a zero, an extreme, or a negative. Choose one of the FROZEN numbers and Plug In again. FROZEN numbers can even be mixed and matched: for example, a negative fraction. A quick reminder though: You must choose two values that work in the original problem. For example, in this situation, you cannot make x greater than (or equal to) y.

Try Plugging In again, using a negative value for x and zero for y: so $x = -2$ and $y = 0$. Since (A) has been eliminated already, check only the remaining answers:

A)   Already eliminated

B) $0 > 0$ Not true, so eliminate it.

C) $-2 - 0 < 0$ Still true; keep moving.

D) $(-2)^2 < (0)^2$ Not true, so eliminate it.

Therefore, the answer must be (C).

───────────────○───────────────

Of course, not every problem on the SAT will look like the problems you just did. However, in many cases, Plugging In is still an effective technique. Let's look at some other situations in which Plugging In works wonders, even if using this technique isn't always immediately obvious.

PLUGGING IN ON GRID-INS

As you just saw, checking each answer choice when Plugging In is very important. But what happens when there are no answer choices? Plugging In works well on Grid-In questions when the values are relative to one another. Let's see an example:

───────────────○───────────────

16

If $\dfrac{a}{b-2} = \dfrac{3}{4}$ and $\dfrac{b}{c} = \dfrac{2}{3}$, what is the value of $c - 2a$?

Here's How to Crack It

Let's pick some numbers. If $a = 3$, then $b - 2 = 4$, so $b = 6$. Then, $\dfrac{6}{c} = \dfrac{2}{3}$, so $c = 9$.

Now let's find the answer: The question asks for the value of $c - 2a$, so $9 - 2(3) = 3$.

It's that easy!

———————○———————

Look for relationships between numbers on Grid-In questions; if you spot them, you might have a great opportunity to use Plugging In to make the question a snap!

———————○———————

INTERPRETING VARIABLES, CONSTANTS, AND EXPRESSIONS

Some SAT problems will ask for you to interpret the meaning of part of an equation, inequality, or expression. These problems can seem daunting at first, but approaching the problems systematically and using Plugging In when appropriate will make these questions approachable.

———————○———————

13

Aaron is training for a marathon. He plans to run a total of 5 times each week. Four runs each week (the "short runs") will be the same distance, and each week Aaron will increase the distance of the short runs by a constant amount. The fifth run (the "long run") will increase each week by a constant percentage. Aaron models his total distance, d, in kilometers, w weeks since the beginning of his training plan using the equation $d = 4(5 + 0.5w) + 8(1.1^w)$. What does 0.5 represent in the equation?

A) The increase in total distance each week

B) The number of weeks until Aaron's marathon

C) The increase in distance of each short run each week

D) The increase in distance of each long run each week

Here's How to Crack It

To approach these questions, start by Reading the Full Question and underlining what the question is asking about: the "0.5" in the equation. Next, label what you know in the equation. The variable d represents total distance, and w is the number of weeks since the beginning of training, so the equation is the same as *total distance* = $4(5 + \underline{0.5weeks}) + 8(1.1^{weeks})$. Next, work some Process of Elimination. To begin with, 0.5 is multiplied by *week*, so it doesn't make sense that it represents the number of weeks until the marathon; eliminate (B). The remaining choices discuss distance, which makes sense because the right side of the equation adds up to distance on the left side of the equation. Next, Plug In some numbers to see what happens with different values. You don't have your calculator here, so you want be creative. Normally, when Plugging In you want to avoid 0 and 1, but here your goal is to understand how the equation works, not to find an algebraic answer choice. So see what happens at $w = 0$ and $w = 1$. When $w = 0$, then $d = 4(5 + 0.5(0)) + 8(1.1^0) = 4(5) + 8(1) = 28$ total kilometers, and when $w = 1$, then $d = 4(5 + 0.5(1)) + 8(1.1^1) = 4(5.5) + 8(1.1) = 22 + 8.8 = 30.8$ total kilometers. Between week 0 and week 1, the total distance increased $30.8 - 28 = 2.8$ kilometers, not 0.5, so (A) doesn't fit; eliminate it. Next, compare the remaining answer choices. Both talk about the increase in the distance of runs. The question says that the short runs increase by a constant distance each week, whereas the long run increases by a constant percent. As we'll discuss a bit more in the Word Problems chapter, the formula for linear growth includes multiplication, whereas compounded percent growth involves exponents. The 0.5 is multiplied by w and the other part of the right side of the equation has the exponent. This means that 0.5 must be the increase in short-run distance; choose (C).

These questions can get quite challenging, so if you're serious about getting an elite score on the SAT, be sure to master the approach:

Interpreting Expressions

1. RTFQ: Underline what the question is asking about.
2. Label what you know.
3. POE any choice that doesn't make sense.
4. Plug-and-Play: Plug In for the variables to see what's happening.
5. Compare answer choices and POE until one choice remains.

For these questions, creative use of Plugging In can give you an insight into what's going on in an algebraic expression.

PLUGGING IN WITH GRAPHS AND CHARTS

Process of Elimination and Plugging In can also be useful when the SAT asks you to make inferences from data or graphs. Let's look at an example:

Questions 18 and 19 refer to the following information.

**Population densities of emerald ash borer,
Agrilus planipennis, at various
locations**

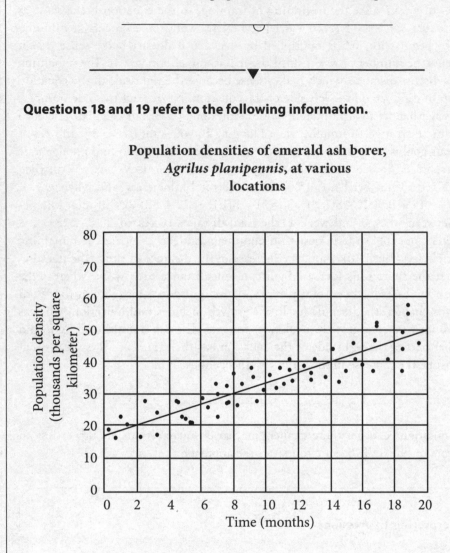

The scatterplot above shows the population densities of emerald ash borer, *Agrilus planipennis*, an invasive insect species which threatens North American ash species. The scatterplot shows the population densities, *p*, of different locations *m* months after the discovery of emerald ash borers in that location.

Which of the following inferences is best supported by the scatterplot above?

A) On average, the population density of a given location increases by 33% each month.

B) At the site with the lowest population density, 17 emerald ash borers per square kilometer were found.

C) A site is expected to have 50,000 ash borers per square kilometer 20 months after discovery of ash borers.

D) At a given location, the population of ash borers is expected to stop increasing and stabilize eventually.

Here's How to Crack It

Whenever you are confronted with a chart or graph, always read the axes. Here, the vertical axis is "Population density (thousands per square kilometer)" and the horizontal axis is "Time (months)." Next, because the question wants the best-supported inference, go right to Process of Elimination. For (A), you can Plug In using the graph. The line of best fit goes through the points (2, 20) and (8, 30). You can determine the average percent increase per month over that interval by finding the average increase and seeing what percent that is of the first point. The population density increased by 80 − 20 = 60,000 per square kilometer over 8 − 2 = 6 months, making an average increase of $\frac{60,000}{6}$ = 10,000 per month. This is an increase of $\frac{20,000-10,000}{20,000} \times 100$ = 50%, not 33%. Eliminate (A). Choice (B) ignores that the vertical axis is in *thousands* per square kilometer; the lowest point would be 17,000, not 17, insects per square kilometer; eliminate (B). For (C), at 20 months, the line of best fit is at 50, which represents 50,000 insects per square kilometer (remember the units!), so keep (C). While (D) may be true, the scatterplot only shows an increase, so the data doesn't support a leveling off of the population; eliminate (D) and choose (C).

As you just saw, many SAT problems that feature charts, graphs, or other visual representations of data are great opportunities to Plug In. In fact, in many cases the key to Plugging In on these problems is to use the numbers given in the graphic, rather than do all the hard work that the test-writers want you to do. Let's look at another question based on the same scatterplot:

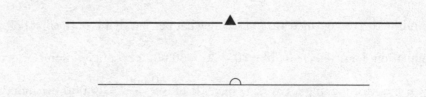

Which of the following equations represents the line of best fit of the scatterplot above?

A) $p = 0.33m + 17$

B) $p = 1.67m + 17$

C) $p = 0.33^m$

D) $p = 17m + 0.33$

Here's How to Crack It

You can spend a lot of time analyzing the entire line, but your job isn't to come up with the equation for the line of best fit on your own; instead, you only need to pick from one of the four provided choices. Pick a point on the graph: at 2 months, the population density is 20,000 insects per square kilometer. Make $m = 2$ in each answer choice and eliminate any in which p isn't close to 20. Only (B) is anywhere close (rounding makes (B) 20.33, which is much closer than the other choices).

Ultimately, Plugging In is a great tool in your toolbox. It can increase both speed and accuracy, especially on challenging questions. In order to achieve your goal score, you must have a method for approaching every question on the SAT, and Plugging In is often the fastest and safest way to go. Plugging In can also give you a way into a question that seems confusing or daunting. Look for opportunities to plug in any time you see variables in the answer choices or relationships between numbers or when you feel an urge to solve algebra equations.

Here are a few Plugging In questions for you to try. Be sure to only use your calculator on those questions with a calculator symbol next to them! Read the explanations when you are finished to ensure that you are using the Plugging In technique correctly. Then review the questions from the previous chapter to see if Plugging In could be used on any of them to make your work easier or faster.

TRY IT EXERCISE 1

See Chapter 20 for answers and explanations. Only use your calculator when permitted.

12

The weight of a certain shipment of apples may not deviate from 50 pounds by more than 5 pounds. If W is the weight, in pounds, of the shipment, which of the following represents all possible values of W?

A) $|W - 5| \leq 50$

B) $|W - 50| \leq 5$

C) $|W + 50| \leq 5$

D) $|W - 5| \geq 50$

18

The wholesale price of a boat is x dollars. At an auction, the boat sells for y percent more than the wholesale price. Don later purchases the boat at z percent below the auction price. Which of the following expressions represents the price, in dollars, that Don paid for the boat?

A) $x\left(1 + \dfrac{y}{100}\right)\left(1 - \dfrac{z}{100}\right)$

B) $x\left(1 + \dfrac{y}{100}\right)\left(1 + \dfrac{z}{100}\right)$

C) $x\left(\dfrac{xy}{100}\right)$

D) $x\left(\dfrac{xy}{100} + \dfrac{xz}{100}\right)$

20

Which of the following expressions is equivalent to $3^{2x} \times 27^{\frac{1}{2}x}$?

A) 3^x

B) $3^{\frac{7}{2}x}$

C) $3^{\frac{9}{2}x}$

D) $3^{\frac{13}{2}x}$

27

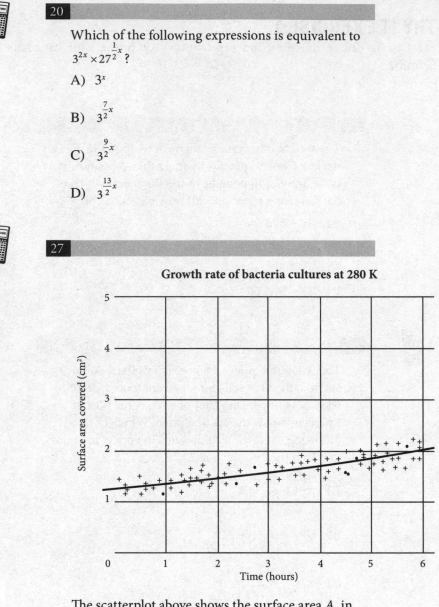

Growth rate of bacteria cultures at 280 K

The scatterplot above shows the surface area A, in cm², of standard petri dishes covered by bacteria grown at 280 Kelvin h hours after being placed in the temperature-controlled refrigerator. Which of the following best describes the curve of best fit?

A) $A = 1.1^h + 1.25$

B) $A = 0.9^h + 1.25$

C) $A = 1.122^h$

D) $A = 1.1^h + 0.25$

15

If $x \neq -3$, $\dfrac{x^5 - 2x^4 - 13x^3 + 14x^2 + 24x}{x+3} =$

A) $x^4 + x^3 - 10x^2 - 16x - 24 - \dfrac{72}{x+3}$

B) $x^4 + 5x^3 + 2x^2 - 8x$

C) $x^4 + x^3 + 16x^2 + 62x + 164 - \dfrac{492}{x+3}$

D) $x^4 - 5x^3 + 2x^2 + 8x$

> For further practice, go online to your Student Tools
> and complete the Chapter 17 Plugging In Drill.

BALLPARKING

The other technique that can increase your accuracy and speed on the SAT is Ballparking. Rather than working a multiple-choice question all the way to the exact answer, you can sometimes get right to the only answer in the ballpark by using Process of Elimination on answers that aren't anywhere close to what the right answer has to be.

One place where Ballparking is especially helpful is on the No Calculator section of the Math. Let's look at some examples of situations where Ballparking is much faster than doing long calculations.

8

If $\dfrac{x}{11} - \dfrac{3}{11} = 79$, what is the value of $x - 3$?

A) 82

B) 237

C) 869

D) 2,607

Here's How to Crack It

Start by Reading the Full Question. You need to find $x - 3$, which is straightforward once you realize that multiplying both sides by 11 will clear the fractions on the left side of the equation and give you $x - 3 = 79 \times 11$. So you reach for your favorite calculator…but then remember this is the No Calculator section! Fret not! Look at the answer choices: They are very far apart indeed. Round 79 up to 80 and 11 down to 10. The answer has to be somewhere near 80 × 10 = 800. Only (C) is anywhere near 800, so it must be the answer.

———————◯———————

When you don't have access to your calculator, Ballparking can save tons of time and let you avoid tedious, arduous, wearisome calculations. However, even when you *can* use your calculator, sometimes it's still faster to use Ballparking rather than grabbing your calculator and punching some numbers:

———————◯———————

19

Number of participants in Grand Prix Tournaments by location, 2014 and 2015

	2014	2015
Montreal	2,978	3,213
Quebec City	1,782	1,702
Toronto	3,098	3,982
Vancouver	2,321	2,355

The two-way table above shows the number of participants in Grand Prix Tournaments in four Canadian cities in 2014 and 2015. Which city had the greatest ratio of participants in 2014 to participants in 2015?

A) Montreal

B) Quebec City

C) Toronto

D) Vancouver

Here's How to Crack It

If you want to compare ratios, convert to fractions. Here, you want to express each city as $\dfrac{\text{participants in 2014}}{\text{participants in 2015}}$. Write the fraction for each city next to its answer choice:

A) Montreal $\dfrac{2,978}{3,213}$

B) Quebec City $\dfrac{1,782}{1,702}$

C) Toronto $\dfrac{3,098}{3,982}$

D) Vancouver $\dfrac{2,321}{2,355}$

You might now be tempted to grab your calculator and turn each fraction into a decimal, but only Quebec City has a numerator greater than the denominator, so Quebec City's ratio must be greater than 1, whereas the other three choices will have ratios less than 1. Now you know that Quebec City, (B), is the answer *without* having to punch all these numbers into your calculator!

Sometimes questions want you to explicitly use Ballparking. Here's an instance:

28

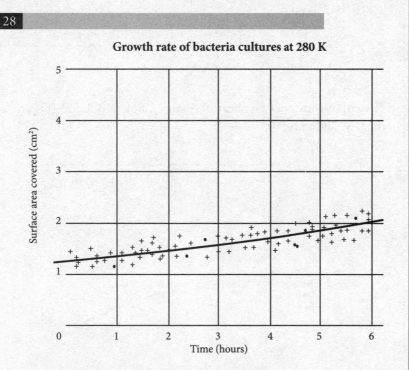

Growth rate of bacteria cultures at 280 K

The scatterplot above shows the surface area A, in cm², of standard petri dishes covered by bacteria grown at 280 Kelvin h hours after being placed in the temperature-controlled refrigerator. Which of the following is closest to the projected surface area covered at 8 hours?

A) 2 cm²

B) 3 cm²

C) 4 cm²

D) 5 cm²

Here's How to Crack It

First, the curve is already at 2 cm² at 6 hours, so 2 cm² doesn't make sense for 8 hours; eliminate (A). Next, 8 hours isn't on the chart. So take your pencil and extend the curve and the vertical axis:

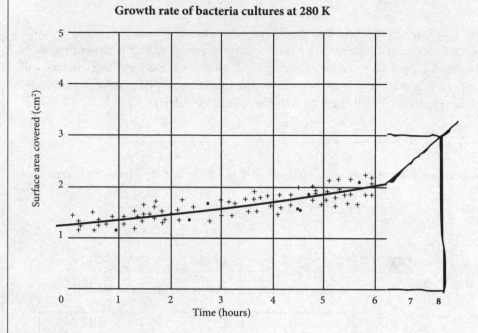

Growth rate of bacteria cultures at 280 K

The curve ends up a bit short of 3 cm². Choices (C) and (D) are far too high, so the best option is (B).

TRY IT EXERCISE 2

Here are a few questions to try Ballparking on. Use the technique, even if you know how to do the question "for real." Changing the way you approach the SAT is the key to changing your score! Oh, and don't forget to leave your calculator to the side for any question without a calculator symbol! Answers can be found in Chapter 20.

9

On a backpacking trip, Jane started by walking north at a rate of 6 kilometers per hour for $\frac{3}{8}$ of her total walking time. She then walked east at a rate of 3 kilometers per hour for the rest of the time. The distance that Jane covered while walking north was what fraction of the total distance she walked?

A) $\frac{1}{3}$

B) $\frac{3}{8}$

C) $\frac{5}{11}$

D) $\frac{6}{11}$

13

If $7(x^2 - 3) = 679$, then $x^2 + 3 =$

A)   10

B)   103

C)   685

D)   4,759

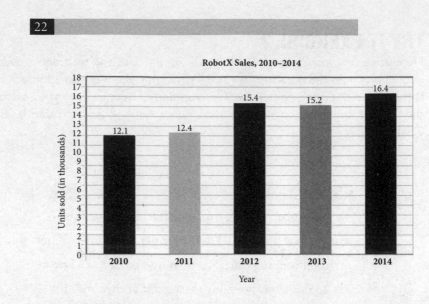

The figure above shows the total sales per year at RobotiX from 2010 through 2014. Which year had the greatest percent increase in units sold over the previous year?

A) 2011

B) 2012

C) 2013

D) 2014

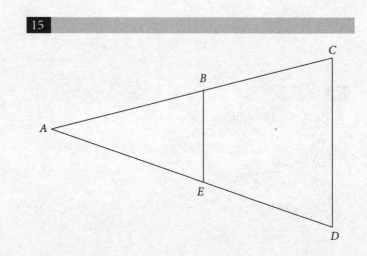

In the figure above, $BE \parallel CD$, E is the midpoint of AD, and $BE = 3$. What is the value of CD?

A) 1.5

B) 3

C) 4

D) 6

Summary

- Using alternative techniques is the key to nailing the SAT Math.
  - Alternative techniques must be accurate and faster than doing the question "the right way."
  - Alternative techniques are tools for your toolbox. They do NOT completely replace knowing the math for every question!

- Plugging In turns many crazy algebra problems into straightforward arithmetic questions.

- Steps to Plugging In:
  - Assign values for the variables.
  - Solve the problem using numbers. Find the answer to the question. This is the Target Value. Circle it!
  - Using your assigned values, Plug In the numbers into each answer choice.
  - The answer choice that matches your target is the correct answer. Be sure to check all four choices!

- Questions that ask you to interpret expressions are also great opportunities to Plug In:
  - RTFQ: Underline what the question is asking about.
  - Label what you know.
  - POE any choice that doesn't make sense.
  - Plug-and-Play: Plug In for the variables to see what's happening.
  - Compare answer choices and POE until one choice remains.

- For charts, graphs, and other sorts of data, look to Plug In data points into answer choices, rather than coming up with algebraic expressions of the information. Your job is to pick the right answer choice, NOT to do all the hard statistical analysis yourself!

- ○ Ballparking is another great alternative technique.
  - • Avoid long calculations on the no calculator section by using POE on any answer choice not in the ballpark.
  - • Try Ballparking rather than using your calculator on data analysis questions.
  - • Look to Ballpark when ETS gives you a figure in a Geometry question.

Chapter 18
Word Problems and Other Hot Topics

INTRODUCTION

On the SAT, word problems can present some special difficulties. The test writers love these problems because there are many ways that they can lead you into traps. This chapter presents the most effective strategies for avoiding these traps, and it covers the topics that are most likely to trip you up on hard problems.

USE BITE-SIZED PIECES

The first step in conquering word problems is to break the question into bite-sized pieces. After you Read the Full Question (RTFQ), go back to the beginning. As soon as you find something simple to do, do it! Let's use the question below as an example.

6

In a particular bowl of candy-coated chocolates, there are twice as many red pieces as brown ones, three times as many green pieces as brown ones, and half as many yellow pieces as green ones. If there are a total of 75 candy-coated chocolates in the bowl, how many of them are not yellow?

A) 10

B) 15

C) 55

D) 60

Here's How to Crack It

Remember to Read the Full Question (RTFQ) first, and underline what the question is asking for. Now go back to the beginning and take it one bite-sized piece at a time.

> In a particular bowl of candy-coated chocolates, there are twice as many red pieces as brown ones...

You could tackle this piece of information by saying that red = $2x$ and brown = x. Now tackle the next bite-sized piece.

> ...three times as many green pieces as brown ones...

Since brown was x, green must be $3x$. Move on to another bite-sized piece.

> …and half as many yellow pieces as green ones.

Since green was $3x$, yellow must be $\frac{1}{2}(3x) = 1.5x$. Move on to another bite-sized piece.

> If there are a total of 75 candy-coated chocolates in the bowl…

Since 75 is the number of red, brown, green, and yellow pieces, you can say that $2x + x + 3x + x = 75$. So $7\frac{1}{2}x = 75$, and thus $x = 10$. Do not go to the answer choices yet! Very likely, 10 is there and is a wrong answer. Instead, you should finish Reading the Full Question so that you know what the question is actually asking for.

> … how many of them are not yellow?

Notice that the question is <u>not</u> asking for x, but rather for $2x + x + 3x$, which equals $6x$, or 60. The correct answer is (D).

———————◯———————

Using bite-sized pieces will help you break problems into a series of simple, manageable steps, improving both your accuracy and efficiency.

START WITH THE MOST STRAIGHTFORWARD PIECE

The example above was relatively simple because it presented the pieces in a logical order. But this won't always happen on harder SAT questions. Two of the test writers' favorite tricks are to make you do unnecessary work and to mix up the logical order, hiding the most useful information in the middle or near the end of the problem. Take a look at the next example.

———————◯———————

7

Which of the following expressions is equivalent to $(2a^2b^3c^4d^5)^3$?

A) $8a^6b^6c^{12}d^{15}$

B) $8a^6b^6c^7d^{15}$

C) $8a^6b^9c^{12}d^{15}$

D) $8a^6b^9c^7d^{15}$

Here's How to Crack It

Is it helpful to calculate $(2a^2)^3$? What about $(d^5)^3$? In this case, a quick scan of the answer choices tells you that this would be a waste of time. But what happens if you calculate just $(b^3)^3$? That lets you quickly get rid of two wrong answer choices, (A) and (B). When you compare the remaining ones, you only have to calculate $(c^4)^3$ to get rid of another wrong answer choice, (D), and select the correct answer, (C). What if, instead, you started by calculating $(c^4)^3$? Again, you can quickly get rid of two wrong answer choices, (B) and (D), and then you would only have to calculate $(b^3)^3$ to get rid of another wrong answer choice, (A), and select the correct answer, (C). Always use process of elimination as you work the problem, or POE-as-you-go. Don't waste time working all the way through it.

Let's practice using bite-sized pieces with a word problem, eliminating after each piece.

4

Anthony is joining a *tae kwon do* class that charges a monthly membership fee of $19.99. A tax of 7% is applied to the monthly membership fee, and an additional graduation fee of $15 is charged each time he moves up a belt level. If Anthony moves up 2 belt levels in n months, which of the following represents his total charge, in dollars, for that period of membership?

A) $1.07(19.99n + 30)$

B) $1.07(19.99n) + 30$

C) $1.07n(19.99 + 2n)$

D) $1.07n(19.99) + 2n$

Here's How to Crack It

The first two lines of the word problem tell you that the base fee is $19.99 plus 7% tax for each month. All four answer choices start off with exactly that information $(1.07$ times 19.99 times $n)$, so starting with this initial information will waste your time. The middle part of the word problem tells you that he moves up two belt levels, which means an extra $30. You can eliminate (C) and (D) at this point, since $2n$ would be 4, which isn't in the question. Since there is no mention of a tax being applied to that $30, you can also eliminate (A), and now you can select the only remaining option, (B).

To summarize: Break the problem into bite-sized pieces, and start with the most straightforward piece, which is not necessarily the first piece of the problem.

PLUG IN THE ANSWERS (PITA)

In the previous chapter, we saw how useful it can be to Plug In whenever there are variables in the answer choices. A closely related technique is Plugging In the Answers (PITA for short). When the answers contain numbers rather than variables, see if you can Plug In the Answers! Let's look at an example.

10

A cargo ship currently holds two-thirds of its maximum capacity by weight. If seven tons of cargo were added to the ship, it would hold 75% of its maximum capacity. What is the maximum capacity, in tons, of the ship?

A) 48

B) 60

C) 84

D) 96

To Plug In the Answers, follow these simple steps:

1. Label the answer choices to avoid careless mistakes and trap answers.
2. If the question asks for the greatest or smallest value, start there. Otherwise, start with one of the answers in the middle.
3. Work the steps, using Bite-Sized Pieces.
4. Eliminate answers that are too big or small.
5. When one of the answers works—STOP.

Here's How to Crack It

First, label the answer choices. In this case, the answers represent the maximum capacity of the ship, so write something like "max" over the answer choices. Since the question is asking for the greatest value ("maximum"!), start with (D) and work through the problem in bite-sized pieces. We need to find two-thirds of 96, which is 63. Then we need to add 7 more tons, so we have 70. Finally, we ask whether 70 is 75% of 96. That is false, so (D) is incorrect. Here's what your work should look like so far:

A cargo ship currently holds two-thirds of its maximum capacity by weight. If seven tons of cargo were added to the ship, it would hold three-fourths of its maximum capacity. What is the maximum capacity, in tons, of the ship?

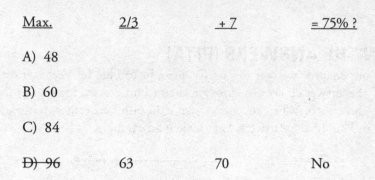

Max.	2/3	+ 7	= 75% ?
A) 48			
B) 60			
C) 84			
~~D) 96~~	63	70	No

Does it matter which answer we try next? Remember that we're looking for a maximum! So let's try (C). Two-thirds of 84 is 56. Add 7 more tons and we have 63. Is 63 equal to 75% of 84? Yes, it is, so (C) is the correct answer. Here's what your work should look like now:

A cargo ship currently holds two-thirds of its maximum capacity by weight. If seven tons of cargo were added to the ship, it would hold three-fourths of its maximum capacity. What is the maximum capacity, in tons, of the ship?

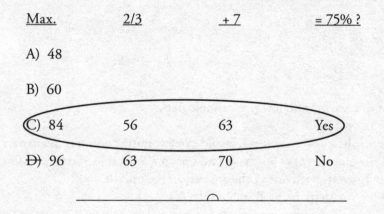

Max.	2/3	+ 7	= 75% ?
A) 48			
B) 60			
C) 84	56	63	Yes
~~D) 96~~	63	70	No

Remember how you have to check all the answers when you Plug In your own number? Well, when you Plug In the Answers, you don't need to check all four answers! There is only one correct answer, so stop as soon as you find it.

Let's try a more difficult problem.

15

During the 93 days of summer, the number of tourists at a certain resort can be modeled by the function $n(d) = \frac{1}{5}d^2 - 14d + c$, where c is a constant and $n(d)$ represents the number of visitors on day number d for $1 \le d \le 93$. The number of visitors on day number 20 was equal to the number of visitors on what number day?

A) 40

B) 50

C) 60

D) 70

Here's How to Crack It

This problem is tougher than the last, but it can be beaten by the same approach. Start by labeling the answers; they represent the number of a day (for example, the 40th day, the 50th day, etc.). Now work the problem in bite-sized pieces. First, we need to know the number of visitors on the 20th day, so plug 20 into the function: $n(20) = \frac{1}{5}(20)^2 - 14(20) + c$. This simplifies to $-200 + c$. What's c? We don't know, so we can either just leave it or else plug in our own number for c. Either way will work. Say we leave it; the total we are looking for is $-200 + c$.

Now tackle the answer choices, starting with one of the answers in the middle. Say we start with (B). Plug 50 into the function: $n(50) = \frac{1}{5}(50)^2 - 14(50) + c$. This simplifies to $-200 + c$. Success! Choice (B) is the correct answer, and you are done working this problem! How does that feel?

As you can see, if the question is not asking for a greatest or least value, it pays to start with either (B) or (C). If your first choice is not the correct answer, you can usually tell which direction you should go: to the lower or to the higher number.

However, you should always remember there is an exception to this rule. As we've seen, when a question asks for the *least* value (or for the *greatest* value), you should start with the smallest (or the largest) answer choice. Sometimes, the fact that the test-writers are doing this can be difficult to see. Let's try an example.

8

Linda has four children: Adam, Baron, Karin, and Darren. Each child was born exactly three years apart. In 2015, their combined ages were 34 years. What was the age in years of the youngest child in 2012?

A) 1

B) 2

C) 3

D) 4

Here's How to Crack It

Again, start by labeling the answer choices. They represent the age of the youngest child in 2012. Since the problem asks for the age of the youngest child, you start working in bite-sized pieces with (A), the smallest number. The next column could contain the sum of the ages of the four children in 2012, which in this case is: $1 + 4 + 7 + 10 = 22$. The final column should contain the sum of the ages of the four children in 2015. This is 3 years later, so you want to add 3 years for each child, or 12 years all together. In this case, that would be $22 + 12 = 34$. Finally, you ask whether your calculation equals 34. Since it does, you select (A), and you are done!

As you can see, PITA is a very useful strategy: It can save you time and bail you out when you don't know how to solve a question. Remember, when you PITA, do the following:

1. Label the answer choices.
2. If the question asks for the greatest or smallest value, start there. Otherwise, start with one of the answers in the middle.
3. Work the steps, using Bite-Sized Pieces.
4. Eliminate answers that are too big or small.
5. When one of the answer works—STOP.

To practice Plugging In the Answers, try the drill below. Then go back though the previous chapters and see if Plugging In the Answers would increase your speed on any of the questions you've already solved.

TRY IT EXERCISE 1

See Chapter 20 for complete answers and explanations. Only use your calculator when you are allowed to do so.

11

A physics student was conducting experiments to determine the correct equation to describe the trajectory of a ball that was thrown straight up into the air from a height of five feet above the ground with an initial velocity of 3 feet per second. If the height of the ball is given by the equation $h = 5 + 3t - 2t^2$, where h = height in feet and t = time in seconds, at which of the following values for t will the ball have the greatest height?

A) 0.75

B) 1

C) 1.5

D) 2.5

18

Mrs. Johnson earns $60 more per week than Mr. Johnson. If three-fifths of Mrs. Johnson's weekly salary is equal to two-thirds of Mr. Johnson's weekly salary, how much do the Johnsons earn together in one week?

A) $540

B) $780

C) $960

D) $1,140

13

If a and c are positive integers such that $\dfrac{2}{5}a = b$ and $b = \dfrac{3c^2}{4}$, what is the least possible value of a?

A) 30

B) 36

C) 42

D) 48

> For further practice, go online to your Student Tools
> and complete the Chapter 18 PITA Drill.

HOT TOPICS

You may not yet realize it, but the SAT is pretty predicable. The test writers like to recycle the same old topics, year after year. Below are some of the SAT's greatest hits, with some helpful strategies to get you through these questions.

Percents

With percent questions, it's often helpful to translate English to math. The following terms come up frequently, so make sure you know how to translate them.

English	Math
percent (%)	divide by 100
of	multiply
is, are	equals, costs
what, what number, some number	x (or any variable)

Let's try an example.

8

A study found that 10% of Americans have a diagnosable personality disorder. If only 5% of people with personality disorders seek psychological treatment, and there are 320 million Americans, how many Americans with personality disorders (in millions) seek psychological treatment?

A) 1.6

B) 3.2

C) 6.4

D) 7.2

Here's How to Crack It

Remember to use bite-sized pieces and translate. The phrase "10% of Americans" can be translated as $\frac{10}{100}$ (320 million) = 32 million. The phrase "5% of people with personality disorders" can now be translated as 5% of 32 million, or $\frac{5}{100}$ (32 million) = 1.6 million. The correct answer is (A).

Arithmetic concepts are often tested with charts and tables. The test writers hide the data you need in the graphic, so you have to pull the right numbers out. Let's try an example.

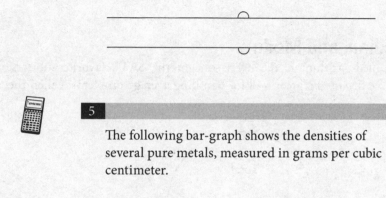

5

The following bar-graph shows the densities of several pure metals, measured in grams per cubic centimeter.

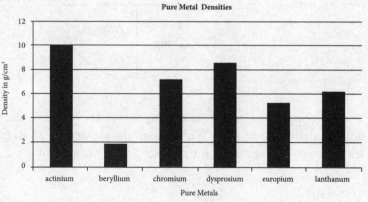

The density of beryllium is approximately what percentage of the density of actinium?

A)   5

B)   10

C)   20

D) 500

Here's How to Crack It

Plug in the numbers from the chart: The density of beryllium is approximately 2 g/cm³, and the density of actinium is approximately 10 g/cm³. So you can read the question in this way:

2 is approximately what percentage of 10?

Now translate the English into math. $2 = \dfrac{x}{100} \cdot 10$, which reduces to $2 = \dfrac{x}{10}$, so $x = 20$, which is (C).

Mean, Median, and Mode

Average (also called "arithmetic mean") is one of the SAT's favorite subjects. Fortunately, we've invented a great tool for handling average problems, called the average pie.

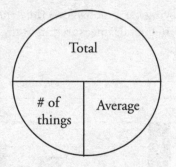

In any average calculation, three components are involved: the total, the number of things, and the average. What makes the average pie so useful is that it represents, in easy-to-read form, the following three versions of the calculation.

$$\frac{\text{Total}}{\text{\# of things}} = \text{Average} \qquad \frac{\text{Total}}{\text{Average}} = \text{\# of things} \qquad \text{\# of things} \times \text{Average} = \text{Total}$$

Any time you have two of the components, you can easily find the third by using the pie. Just think of the horizontal bar as a division symbol, and the vertical bar as a multiplication symbol. Let's look at a sample question.

3

The average (arithmetic mean) weight of five gold
bars is 9 pounds. After two more bars are added, the
average weight increases to 11 pounds. What is the
average weight, in pounds, of the two bars that were
added?

A) 13

B) 14

C) 15

D) 16

Here's How to Crack It

Start with the first (bite-sized) sentence. The number of things is 5 and the average
is 9, so multiply to find the total and fill in the pie.

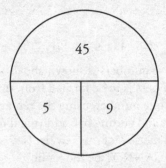

Now do the same for the next sentence. There are 7 things, and the average is 11,
so the total is 77.

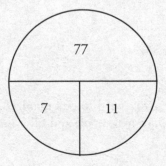

Finally, to tackle the last sentence, make a new pie. There are two things, and the
total is 77 − 45 = 32, so divide to get the average, which is 16, and the correct answer is (D).

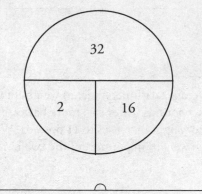

Along with average, the SAT likes to throw in the related concepts of median and mode. Just remember that median is the middle number of an ordered list, and mode is the number (or numbers) that occurs most often in an ordered list. Try a question.

24 ▬▬▬▬▬▬▬▬▬▬▬▬▬▬▬▬▬▬

[1, 3, 9, 10, 17]

A list of five numbers is shown above. A new list of seven numbers is to be formed from the list above by repeating one number, using the remaining numbers once each, and adding one additional number. If the mean and median of the new list is 9, which of the following CANNOT be the mode?

A) 3

B) 9

C) 10

D) 17

Here's How to Crack It

This is a tough question, so you need to be organized. You know that the mean (average) of the new list is 9, so make a pie and fill it in.

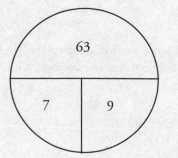

Since the original total is $1 + 3 + 9 + 10 + 17 = 40$, and the new total has to be 63 in order for the mean to be 9, the repeated number plus the new number must equal 23.

You also know that the median is 9, so draw 7 spots and put 9 in the middle.

__   __   __   <u>9</u>   __   __   __

Now, PITA! Start with (B). If the mode is 9, that means the repeated number must be 9. We need to add 23, so the new number is $23 - 9 = 14$. Fill in your list:

<u>1</u>   <u>3</u>   <u>9</u>   <u>9</u>   <u>10</u>   <u>14</u>   <u>17</u>

The median is still 9, so (B) checks out, which means it's <u>NOT</u> the answer.

Which answer should we try next? It's hard to tell, so if you're not sure, pick a direction and go! Let's try (C). If the mode is 10, that's the number we repeat, so the new number is $23 - 10 = 13$. Now fill in the list again.

<u>1</u>   <u>3</u>   <u>9</u>   <u>10</u>   <u>10</u>   <u>13</u>   <u>17</u>

This time, the median is 10, but since the question states that the median is 9, 10 cannot be the mode, and the correct answer is (C).

One of the keys to mean, median, and mode questions is to stay organized. Using the average pie and writing everything down will help you to avoid overlooking important pieces of the puzzle.

Mean, Median, and Mode are the three big statistical concepts you can expect to see on the SAT. Since mean, median, and mode measure the middle (MMM MM!), they are called measures of central tendency. In addition to knowing about the middle of your data, sometimes you want to know about how far the data are spread, or how evenly they are spread. The next two concepts help you do just that.

Range and Standard Deviation

Range is a simple concept: the distance from the lowest to the highest number. Standard Deviation is a less simple concept, but in a nutshell, it measures the evenness of your data. Let's illustrate both concepts with a concrete example.

Say you poll twenty people in a fast food restaurant on a given day and time. You find that the wealthiest person there makes $400,000 per year, the poorest person there makes $10,000 per year, and everybody else is somewhere in between. Based on this information alone, you can calculate the range of incomes: $400,000 − $10,000 = $390,000. This number does give you some information about the people in the restaurant that day, but not much.

To know more, you would want to know the mean, median, and/or mode. Let's say you figure out that the mean income of your twenty people is $70,000 per year. This information answers some questions, but leaves others open. Maybe eighteen people make around $55,000 per year, and just two make much less or much more. In that case, most of the people make about the same income: That means that your data have low variability, and so you would have a small standard deviation. But maybe five people make between $10,000 and $30,000; another five make between $30,000 and $60,000; another five make between $60,000 and $70,000; another four make between $75,000 and $100,000, and just one makes $400,000. In that case, people have very different incomes: That means that your data have high variability, so you would have a higher standard deviation.

Luckily, you will never have to calculate a standard deviation for the SAT! Let's see how the SAT might test your knowledge of range and standard deviation.

15

A billionaire visiting a fast food restaurant decides to give $20,000 to everyone in the restaurant. What effect does this gift have on the mean and standard deviation of the patrons' incomes for that year?

A) It would increase the mean and the standard deviation.

B) It would increase the mean but have no effect on the standard deviation.

C) It would decrease the mean and the standard deviation.

D) It would decrease the mean but have no effect on the standard deviation.

Here's How to Crack It
Since standard deviation is a measure of how spread-out or even the data is, the only things that change it are changes to individual data points. If data points are removed or added, or if some increase or decrease while others stay the same, the standard deviation will be affected. In this case, the income of all patrons in the restaurant changed, and the income changed by the same amount for everyone. The standard deviation would therefore be the same, so eliminate (A) and (C). Everyone would have more money this year, so the average or mean income would increase, making (B) the right answer.

Sampling Error and Margin of Error

Some SAT Math questions will feel more like the questions you'd find on a science test. They may give you the data from an experiment and ask questions about it. If you encounter questions that ask about the sampling error of a study, identify the variables and determine whether the conclusion is supported by the experiment or study. When considering the validity of study, check to ensure that the study was conducted on an unbiased sample that is representative of the target population, the conclusion is supported by the data, and the conclusion is based solely on the acquired data.

1

VRT is a company interested in testing out a new virtual reality device to determine whether or not the device will be popular among suburban moms. VRT decides to do product testing at four soccer tournaments around the country, requesting that all interested individuals take part in a live demonstration in each stadium's lobby. After conducting the testing, VRT collected the data, finding that 65% of the suburban moms who participated were interested in purchasing the virtual reality device. Based on this finding, would VRT be justified in claiming that the majority of suburban moms would likely purchase the new virtual reality device?

A) Yes; the majority of suburban moms who participated in the live demonstration indicated that they would likely purchase the new virtual reality device.

B) Yes; VRT's study used a representative sample of the target population, indicating that the conclusion is accurate.

C) No; while 65% of the suburban moms who participated in the study indicated that they would likely purchase the virtual reality device, the sample failed to accurately represent the target population.

D) No; the majority of suburban moms indicated that they would not purchase the new virtual reality device.

Here's How to Crack It

When you encounter questions that ask about the validity of a conclusion, you want to examine the information provided, eliminating answer choices that fail to support the data. In this scenario, VRT wished to determine whether or not suburban moms would be interested in purchasing the new virtual reality device. However, the sample that VRT used was not representative of the target population. Indeed, VRT only went to four locations nationwide that were holding soccer tournaments. Not only did VRT limit the sample by only gathering data from four locations, but VRT also failed to account for the fact that not all suburban moms have children who play soccer. To make matters worse, VRT requested that individuals test the product in the lobby, meaning that only those who were interested in the product would attend the demonstration. Accordingly, VRT would not be justified in claiming that the majority of suburban moms would likely purchase the new virtual reality device as the sample was not representative of the target population; choose (C).

You may also encounter questions that ask discuss confidence intervals and margins of error, measures used to determine that a sample population is representative of the real-world population. Consider a survey with a confidence level of 95% and a margin of error of $\pm$ 5. In this scenario, the results should be repeated within 5 percentage points of the sample results 95 out of 100 times.

2

KittenFoodz Incorporated conducted a random survey of 2,500 cat owners from around the United States. 1,750 of the respondents stated that they buy grain-free cat food, while the remainder stated that they do not purchase grain-free cat food. After analyzing the results, KittenFoodz Incorporated determines that the survey results have a margin of error of 4%. Which of the following best represents the range for the percentage of the nation's cat owners who do not purchase grain-free cat food?

A) 26–34%

B) 30–38%

C) 66–74%

D) 70–78%

Here's How to Crack It

In order to determine the range for the percentage of the nation's cat owners who do not purchase grain-free cat food, you must first find the percent of surveyed cat owners who do not purchase grain-free cat food. The question states that of the 2,500 cat owners surveyed, 1,750 of them purchase grain-free cat food. In turn, the number of surveyed cat owners who do not purchase grain-free cat food is 2,500 − 1,750 = 750. Next, determine the percentage of cat owners who do not purchase grain-free cat food by dividing the number of people who do not purchase grain-free cat food by the total number of individuals surveyed: $\frac{750}{2,500} = 0.3 = 30\%$. Since the margin of error is 4%, the range for the percentage of the nation's cat owners who do not purchase grain-free cat food is 30% ± 4%, or 26%–34%. Choice (A) is the correct answer.

UNIT CONVERSION

The SAT can also test proportions with questions about unit conversions and scale drawings. Try this one:

In tabletop gaming, 28 mm scale figurines are at a 1:64 scale to their real-world equivalents. The above minotaur figurine is 43 millimeters (mm) tall. If this figurine uses 28 mm scale, then how tall would the equivalent real-world minotaur be, rounded to the nearest foot? (Note: 1 foot = 304.8 millimeters)

Here's How to Crack It

Use proportions to convert the units to feet. First, figure out how many millimeters tall the real-world minotaur would be by setting up a proportion:

$$\frac{1}{64} = \frac{43\,mm}{x\,mm}$$

Solve for x by cross-multiplying: $x = (43)(64) = 2{,}752$ mm. Next, set up another proportion using the conversion factors. Remember to label your units and have the same units in the numerators and denominators of each fraction:

$$\frac{1\text{ foot}}{304.8\text{ mm}} = \frac{x\text{ feet}}{2{,}752\text{ mm}}$$

Cross-multiply to get $304.8x = 2{,}752$. Divide both sides by 304.8 and you get $x = 9.03$, which rounds to 9 feet.

PROBABILITY

Here's the basic definition of probability:

$$\text{Probability} = \frac{\text{number of desired options}}{\text{number of possible options}}$$

Let's try a question.

1

Blood Type	Number of Americans
A+	108,800,000
A–	19,200,000
B+	32,000,000
B–	6,400,000
AB+	12,800,000
AB–	3,200,000
O+	118,400,000
O–	19,200,000

The chart above shows the number of Americans living in the United States that have a particular blood type. Based on the information provided, what is the probability that a randomly selected American in the United States will have neither an A or O blood type?

A)   5%

B)   17%

C)   57%

D)   83%

Here's How to Crack It

In order to determine the probability that a randomly selected American in the United States will have neither an A nor O blood type you must first find the total population. Add the individual populations to find that the total population is 108,800,000 + 19,200,000 + 32,000,000 + 6,400,000 + 12,800,000 + 3,200,000 + 118,400,000 + 19,200,000 = 320,000,000. Next, you to find that the total population of Americans living in the United States that have neither A nor O blood types. Add the B+, B–, AB+, and AB– populations together to find this total to be 32,000,000 + 6,400,000 + 12,800,000 + 3,200,000 = 54,400,000. Finally, you can determine the probability that a randomly selected American in the United States will have neither an A or O blood type by dividing the population that has neither A nor O blood types by the total population of Americans living in the United States; $\frac{54,400,000}{320,000,000} = 17\%$. Select (B).

SEQUENCES

Like several of the topics in this chapter, the most important thing to do with SAT sequences is to organize them. If a question asks you about the first six terms of a sequence, make slots for each term and label them, like this:

1st   2nd   3rd   4th   5th   6th

___   ___   ___   ___   ___   ___

It also helps to look for patterns that will make the question easier to manage. Let's try an example.

9

$$\frac{1}{j}, \frac{1}{2}, \frac{j}{4}, \ldots$$

In the sequence shown above, the first term is $\frac{1}{j}$ for all values of j greater than 2. Each term after the first is equal to the preceding term multiplied by a constant. Which of the following, in terms of j, is equal to the sixth term of the sequence?

A) $\dfrac{j^2}{16}$

B) $\dfrac{j^3}{16}$

C) $\dfrac{j^3}{32}$

D) $\dfrac{j^4}{32}$

Here's How to Crack It

Did the phrase "in terms of" ring a bell? If you thought to Plug In, that was a smart choice! Since $j > 2$, let's see what happens if we plug in $j = 3$. Then, the first three terms are $\frac{1}{3}, \frac{1}{2}$, and $\frac{3}{4}$. It's not easy to spot the relationship between these numbers. Is each term really the preceding term multiplied by a constant? It's hard to tell, so let's plug in another number that makes the math easier. If $j = 4$, then the first three terms are $\frac{1}{4}, \frac{1}{2}$, and 1. Now we can see the relationship. Each term is double the previous term! Armed with this knowledge, you should make a diagram for the first six terms:

1st	2nd	3rd	4th	5th	6th
$\frac{1}{4}$	$\frac{1}{2}$	1	2	4	8

The sixth term is 8, so that's our target. Now plug $j = 4$ into the answers, and pick the one that equals 8; it's (D).

GROWTH AND DECAY

Sequences reflect numbers changing in a pattern over time. If a population increases by a set factor or percent over time, it is said to be growing exponentially. Things like compound interest, the spread of viruses, or population growth of bacterium might show this sort of growth. Similarly, if it shrinks by a set factor or percent, it is showing exponential decay. The amount of radiation in an isotope or the drug concentration in a person's body decrease in this way over time. Unlike growth at a constant rate, which involves multiplication and a linear graph, exponential growth involves exponents, hence the name.

When the growth is a **percent** of the total population, the formula for exponential growth or decay is

$$\textit{final amount} = \textit{original amount} \, (1 \pm \textit{rate})^{\textit{number of changes}}$$

When the growth is a **multiple** of the total population, the formula for exponential growth or decay is

$$\textit{final amount} = \textit{original amount} \, (\textit{multiplier})^{\textit{number of changes}}$$

Use this knowledge to make the next question easier.

────────────○────────────

1

Researchers at Cat-In-A-Tube are working on technology that infuses kittens with glow cells that allow cats to glow in the dark. After much work, the researchers have created glow cells that reproduce at a rate of 32% each day. If the researchers start with two glow cells, what is the minimum number of days before the researchers have 550 glow cells?

A) 20

B) 21

C) 22

D) 23

Here's How to Crack It

In order to determine the minimum number of days before the researchers have 550 glow cells, it is helpful to know the formula for growth: *final amount = original amount* $\times$ $(1 + rate)^n$, where n = the number of changes. Here, you are told that the researchers start with two glow cells and that the population grows at a rate of 32% each day. Accordingly, the growth equation will be $550 = 2(1.32)^n$. Since the question provides numerical answer choices in ascending order, and asks you to find the minimum number of days to have 550 glow cells, you can use PITA to tackle this question! If you start with (B), the number of glow cells after 21 days will be $550 = 2(1.32)^{21}$; $550 = 2(340.45)$; $550 = 680.90$. Since the question asks you to find the minimum number of days it takes to create 550 glow cells, you can now eliminate (C) and (D). Next, check (A). Here, the number of glow cells after 20 days will be $550 = 2(1.32)^{20}$; $550 = 2(257.92)$; $550 = 515.83$. Since you have not reached the minimum number of glow cells, eliminate (A) and select (B).

────────────○────────────

EQUATIONS

Although Plugging In and PITA are extremely valuable strategies, once in a while you just have to write equations and solve. This often happens near the end of the grid-in section. When you're faced with this situation, translate the word problem carefully, and pay close attention to what the problem is asking for. Let's try an example.

33

Two rival cell-phone companies have different rate structures. Company X charges a flat rate of $0.15 per minute. Company Y charges $0.25 per minute for the first five minutes, and $0.10 for each minute after the first five. If a call costs the same amount with either plan, how long, in minutes, does that call last?

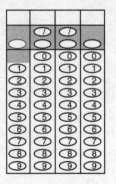

Here's How to Crack It

Let's break this down into bite-sized pieces. We'll say that x = the number of minutes. A call with the company X costs $0.15x$. A call with company Y costs—be careful here—$5(0.25) + 0.1(x - 5)$. The two calls cost the same amount, so set them equal to each other and solve; you should get $x = 15$, so the correct answer is 15.

Sometimes a question will require two variables, so you'll need to write two equations. Try the next question.

17

On Saturday, Abeke participated in a long-distance race. After the race, he learned that 11 more runners finished before him than finished after him. He also learned that the total number of runners who finished the race was four times the number of runners who finished after him. How many runners finished the race before Abeke did?

Here's How to Crack It

When we first discussed bite-sized pieces, we said that the test writers will often hide the most useful information near the end of a problem. That's definitely the case here. The second sentence is much easier to handle than the first, so let's deal with it first. But even before that, draw a map or picture of the problem! The total is four times the number who finished after Abeke. Let's say the total = t, and the number who finished after Abeke = x. Therefore, $t = 4x$. Now let's translate the first sentence. If x runners finished after Abeke, then $x + 11$ finished before him, and the total number is $x + (x + 11) + 1$ (we have to count Abeke), which simplifies to $2x + 12$. Now we can write a second equation: $t = 2x + 12$. From the first equation, substitute $4x$ for t in the second equation, so now you have $4x = 2x + 12$. Solve this to get $x = 6$.

Wait! Stop! Don't forget to RTFQ! The question asks how many runners finished *before* Abeke, which is $x + 11$, so the correct answer is $6 + 11 = 17$. No matter how pleased you are when you've solved a question, don't forget to READ THE FULL QUESTION.

The acceleration rate, a, of a panther is based on the change in velocity, ΔV, in meters per second, and the duration of the time interval at which each of the velocity measurements was taken, ΔT. If $a = \dfrac{V_2 - V_1}{T_2 - T_1}$, which of the following expresses the duration of the time interval in terms of a and V?

A) $T = \dfrac{V_2 - V_1}{a_2 - a_1}$

B) $T_2 - T_1 = \dfrac{V_2 - V_1}{a}$

C) $T = \dfrac{V_2 - V_1}{a}$

D) $T_2 - T_1 = \dfrac{V_2 - V_1}{a_2 - a_1}$

Here's How to Crack It

While you could Plug In on this question, you are unable to use your calculator and the equation is relatively straightforward to manipulate. By crossing out the phrase "in terms of a and V," you know that you need to find the duration of the time interval, ΔT, which is expressed as $T_2 - T_1$ in the provided equation, $a = \dfrac{V_2 - V_1}{T_2 - T_1}$. Accordingly, you can eliminate (A) and (C) because they are simply looking at T, not ΔT expressed as $T_2 - T_1$. Next, manipulate the equation, $a = \dfrac{V_2 - V_1}{T_2 - T_1}$ by multiplying both sides of the equation by $T_2 - T_1$ to find that $a(T_2 - T_1) = V_2 - V_1$. Finally, isolate $T_2 - T_1$ by dividing both sides of the equation by a to find that $T_2 - T_1 = \dfrac{V_2 - V_1}{a}$. Accordingly, eliminate (D) and select (B).

TRY IT EXERCISE 2

Questions 27 and 28 refer to the following information.

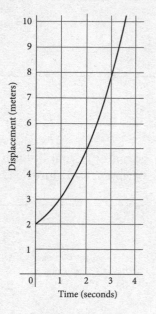

When acceleration is constant, change in displacement is directly proportional to time and proportional to the square of time. This is expressed by the Merton rule: $x = x_0 + v_0 t + \frac{1}{2}at^2$, where x is the final displacement, x_0 is the initial displacement, v_0 is the initial velocity, a is acceleration, and t is time in seconds. The graph above shows the displacement of an object under constant acceleration.

27

Which of the following expresses t in terms of x, x_0, v_0, and a?

A) $t = \dfrac{-v_0 \pm \sqrt{(v_0)^2 - 2a(x_0 - x)}}{a}$

B) $t = \dfrac{-v_0 \pm \sqrt{(v_0)^2 - 4a(x_0 - x)}}{2a}$

C) $t = \dfrac{-v_0 \pm \sqrt{(v_0)^2 - 2a(x_0 - x)}}{(x_0 - x)}$

D) $t = \dfrac{-v_0 \pm \sqrt{(v_0)^2 - 4a(x_0 - x)}}{2(x_0 - x)}$

According to the graph and equation above, what is the value of *a* if the initial velocity is 0.5 m/s ?

A) 0.25

B) 0.5

C) 1.0

D) 2.0

▲

For further practice, go online to your Student Tools and complete the Chapter 18 Arithmetic Drill.

Summary

- Don't choke when you see long word problems. Instead, break down the question into manageable, bite-sized pieces and RTFQ.

- When you see word problems with numbers in the answer choices that are in either ascending or descending order, PITA. When you find the right answer, pick it and move on!

- When dealing with percent questions, translate the English words into math terms.

- Remember that Mean, Median, and Mode measure the middle (MMM MM).
  - Mean is the average; draw an average pie to keep yourself organized.
  - Median is the number in the middle of a set; make sure you put your numbers in order.
  - Mode is the most frequently occurring number in a set.

- You won't have to calculate a standard deviation on the SAT, but you should know that standard deviation indicates how data is distributed across a given range.

- When asked about sampling error, ensure that the data collection was done properly, the sample is representative of the target population, and the conclusion is based on the data.

- Margin of error tells you how representative a study is compared to the target population.

- When converting between different units, create a proportion.

o Probability can be thought of as $\dfrac{\textit{what you want}}{\textit{total number of possibilities}}$.

   • If a question asks you to find the probability that one event *and* another event will occur, multiply the individual probabilities together.

   • If a question asks you to find the probability that one event *or* another event occurs, add the individual probabilities together.

o When working with sequences, organize and label the terms in the sequence. It'll make your life much easier.

o Growth and Decay

   • For questions about exponential growth or decay when growth is a percent of the total population, use the formula *final amount = original amount* $(1 \pm \textit{rate})^{\textit{number of changes}}$.

   • For questions about exponential growth or decay when growth is a multiple of the total population, use the formula *final amount = original amount* $(\text{multiplier})^{\textit{number of changes}}$.

o When working with equations, isolate the variable in question.

o Make sure that you only use your calculator when you are allowed to do so!

Chapter 19
Plane Geometry

INTRODUCTION

Plane geometry makes up a small part of the SAT—at most, you will see 6 plane geometry questions over the entire test. Beating tough geometry problems is all about putting together puzzle pieces. Many students struggle with geometry because, unlike algebra, they cannot see the end result as easily. If this is you, try to think of geometry as a puzzle. First, you find the corner pieces. Next, you build the edges. Finally, you finish the interior. Geometry is the same way. There are three steps to beating any geometry problem.

- If there's no figure, draw your own, if a figure is noted as not drawn to scale, re-draw it.
- Write any information from the problem directly on the figure.
- Write down any formulas you need, and add in any information from the problem.

Always start by drawing the figure if one is not provided. Next, label the figure with all the information that you know. Last, always write down any formulas you need. These steps are comparable to finding the corner and edge pieces of a puzzle. Once these are in place, you will often be able to see what the next step is. Consider the following.

17

A square is inscribed in a circle with a circumference of 8π. What is the area of the square?

Here's How to Crack It

At first glance this may seem to be a very challenging problem. Don't panic. Instead, begin by drawing the figure:

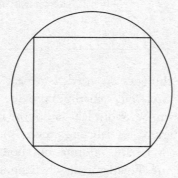

Now, label the figure. The only information that the problem provides is the circumference of the circle, which is 8π. Now, write down formulas. The problem asks for the area of the square. The formula for the area of a square is $A = s^2$, where A is the area of the square and s is the length of each side. To solve this problem, you need to somehow find the length of one of the sides of the square. Next, since the problem provided the circumference, write that down as well: $C = \pi d$ (or $C = 2\pi r$). Put the information from the problem into this equation to find that $8\pi = \pi d$, so the diameter is 8. Now, add this information to the figure. A diameter is any line segment that extends from one edge of a circle to another while passing through the center of a circle. Be sure to add the information to the figure in a way that helps with the square:

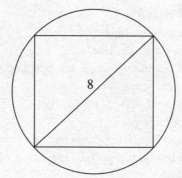

As you can see from this figure, the diameter of the circle is the same distance as the diagonal of the square. Whenever a square is bisected, two special right triangles are formed with angle measures of 45°-45°-90°. The side lengths of this triangle are fixed as well into the following ratio: $s:s:s\sqrt{2}$, where s are the legs of the triangle and $s\sqrt{2}$ is the hypotenuse. Use this ratio to solve for s: $s\sqrt{2} = 8$, so $s = \dfrac{8}{\sqrt{2}}$. Congratulations, you have finally found the last piece of the puzzle you needed. At the beginning of this example, you determined that in order to find the area of the square, you needed the length of the sides. Finish the problem by solving for the area of the square: $s^2 = \left(\dfrac{8}{\sqrt{2}}\right)^2 = \dfrac{64}{2} = 32$. The answer is 32.

———————

To review, three basic techniques are needed to beat every geometry question. A figure is necessary; the SAT will sometimes provide the figure and sometimes force you to create your own. Secondly, label all of the information that the problem gives you about the figure. The labeling process should continue throughout the problem. As you discover more information about the problem, be sure to continue labeling your figure. Finally, many challenging geometry questions appear unsolvable at first glance. To avoid the panic that this feeling may cause, write down formulas for every measurement mentioned in the problem. Writing down the formulas will ensure that you do not make math errors, will give you a goal, will give you some starting math to do, and will often lead you directly to the solution.

Since formulas are so important, the following pages will list and review the different formulas that will appear on the SAT. Each section is followed by a "Try It Drill" that will challenge you to apply the basic approach to geometry while using the facts you just reviewed.

Angle and Line Facts

- There are 90° in a right angle.
- There are 180° in a straight line.
- Two lines that meet at a 90° angle are <u>perpendicular</u>.
- The sign for perpendicular is ⊥ .
- Two lines that never intersect are <u>parallel</u>.
- The sign for parallel is ‖.
- A point where two lines intersect is called a vertex (plural: vertices).
- When two lines intersect, opposite angles are equal and adjacent angles sum to 180°.
- Bisect means to divide an angle exactly in half.
- A line has no width and extends infinitely in both directions.
- On the SAT, if something looks like a straight line, it is actually straight.
- On the SAT, if a line appears to pass through a point, then it does actually pass through that point.
- A line segment is part of a line that has two endpoints.

TRY IT EXERCISE 1

After you try these questions, go to Chapter 20 to check your answers. Remember to leave that calculator alone on questions with no calculator symbol.

3

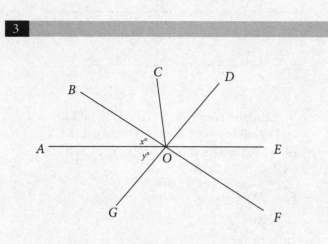

Note: Figure not drawn to scale.

In the figure above, lines *AE*, *BF*, and *DG* all intersect at vertex *O*. If $x + y = 70°$ and if line *CO* bisects angle *BOD*, then what is the measure of angle *BOC*?

A) 20°

B) 40°

C) 55°

D) 75°

4

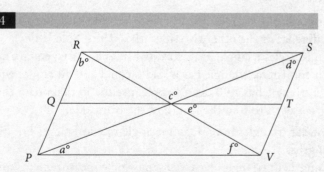

In the figure above, *RS* ∥ *QT* ∥ *PV*. Which of the following must equal 180°?

A) $a + b + c$

B) $a + c + e$

C) $b + c + d$

D) $c + e + f$

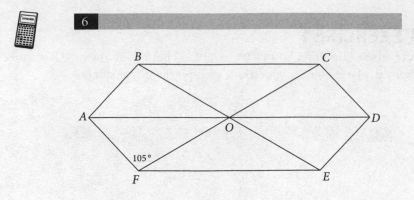

In the figure above, $BC \parallel AD \parallel FE$, and lines AD, BE, and CF all intersect at point O. If $BA \perp AF$, and $BE = CF$, then what is the measure of BOC?

A) 75

B) 90

C) 105

D) 120

TRIANGLE FACTS

- There are 180 degrees in a triangle.
- The longest side is opposite the largest angle.
- The shortest side is opposite the smallest angle.
- Equal angles have equal opposite sides (and vice versa).
- The height of a triangle is *always* perpendicular to its base.
- Area = $\frac{1}{2}bh$.
- Any side of a triangle must be less than the sum and greater than the difference of the other two sides (the "Third Side Rule").
- An isosceles triangle has two equal sides and two equal angles.
- An equilateral triangle has all sides equal and all angles equal.
- If a triangle has a 90 degree angle, use the Pythagorean theorem, or $a^2 + b^2 = c^2$, to find the length of the third side.
- Similar triangles have the same angle measurements but different side lengths.
- Congruent triangles have the same angle measurements and side lengths.
- In a special right triangle with angles 30-60-90 degrees, the sides are in the fixed proportion of $x : x\sqrt{3} : 2x$. This special triangle is half of an equilateral triangle.

- In a right isosceles triangle, the angles measure 45-45-90 degrees and the sides are in a fixed proportion of $x: x: x\sqrt{2}$. This special right triangle is half of a square.

- On the SAT, the following special right triangles commonly appear: 3-4-5; 6-8-10; 5-12-13.

TRY IT EXERCISE 2

Work these questions, with or without your calculator as indicated, then check the answers in Chapter 20.

1

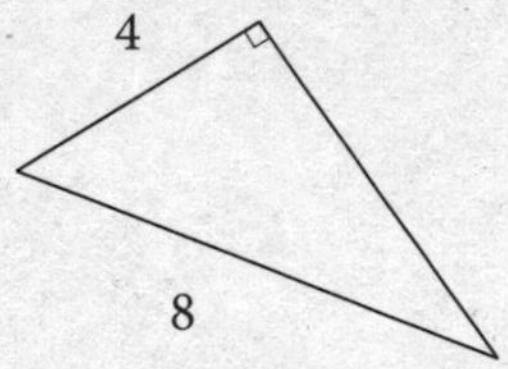

What is the area of the triangle above?

A) $8\sqrt{3}$

B) 16

C) $16\sqrt{3}$

D) 32

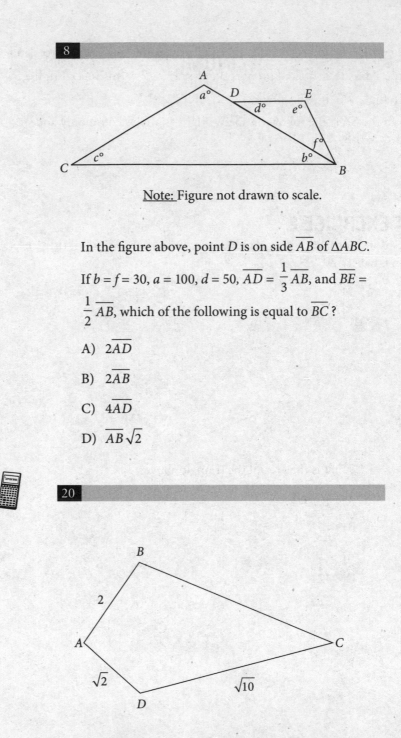

8

Note: Figure not drawn to scale.

In the figure above, point D is on side $\overline{AB}$ of $\triangle ABC$. If $b = f = 30$, $a = 100$, $d = 50$, $\overline{AD} = \dfrac{1}{3}\overline{AB}$, and $\overline{BE} = \dfrac{1}{2}\overline{AB}$, which of the following is equal to $\overline{BC}$?

A) $2\overline{AD}$

B) $2\overline{AB}$

C) $4\overline{AD}$

D) $\overline{AB}\sqrt{2}$

20

In the figure above, line segments AC and BD are perpendicular and intersect at point O (not shown). If $AO = DO$, then what is the ratio of the area of triangle ACD to the area of triangle ABC?

A) 1 to $\sqrt{3}$

B) 1 to 2

C) 1 to 3

D) $\sqrt{3}$ to 1

RIGHT TRIANGLES TRIGONOMETRY FACTS

- The three trigonometric ratios used to solve right triangle problems on the SAT are sine (sin), cosine (cos), and tangent (tan).
- Use SOH-CAH-TOA to remember these ratios:

  - SOH : Sin = $\dfrac{Opposite}{Hypotenuse}$

  - CAH: Cos = $\dfrac{Adjacent}{Hypotenuse}$

  - TOA: Tan = $\dfrac{Opposite}{Adjacent}$

- "Opposite" refers to the side directly across from an angle, "Adjacent" refers to the side next to an angle, and "Hypotenuse" is the side across from the right angle.
- Since the hypotenuse is always the longest side, both the sin and cos values must be less than 1.
- Complementary angles are a pair of angles whose measures add to $90°$. In a right triangle, the two angles that aren't right angles are complimentary.
- The sine of an angle is equal to the cosine of its complementary angle.

TRY IT EXERCISE 3

After you try these questions, go to Chapter 20 to check your answers. Remember to leave that calculator alone on questions with no calculator symbol.

11

In right triangle ABC (not shown), if sin $CAB = \dfrac{7}{25}$,

and the perimeter of triangle ABC is 14, which of the

following is closest to the length of BC?

A) 1.75

B) 6

C) 6.25

D) 7

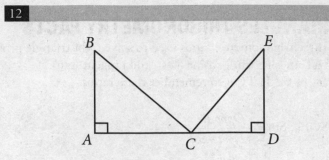

In the triangles shown above, if $BC \perp CE$, which of the following statements must be true?

A) $AC = ED$

B) $\dfrac{AB}{AC} = \dfrac{DE}{CD}$

C) $\dfrac{AB}{BC} = \dfrac{CD}{CE}$

D) $\dfrac{BC}{AC} = \dfrac{CE}{CD}$

Sam is standing at the edge of the roof of a building looking straight ahead. He then directs his gaze downward 63° and sees a pothole 10 meters from the base of the building. If Sam's eye level is 1.2 meters above the rooftop, which of the following is closest to the height of the building?

A) 5.13 meters

B) 18.43 meters

C) 19.63 meters

D) 20.83 meters

CIRCLE FACTS

- There are 360 degrees in a circle.
- A radius r is the distance of *any* line that extends from the center of the circle to a point on its edge.
- All radii in a circle are equal.
- The straight line distance from one point on the circle to another, passing through the center, is the diameter (d).
- The diameter is the longest possible line in the circle.
- The diameter is twice the radius.
- A chord is any line segment from one point on the edge of a circle to another.
- The diameter is the longest possible chord.
- Circumference is the distance around the circle.
- Circumference = πd or $2\pi r$.
- An arc is any portion of the circumference.
- Arc measure is proportional to the size of its central angle.
- To calculate arc length, use the following formula:

$$\frac{part}{whole} = \frac{central\ angle}{360°} = \frac{arc}{2\pi r}$$

- The formula for the area of circle is $A = \pi r^2$.
- A sector is any portion of the area of a circle that is bounded by two radii and an arc.
- The sector area is proportional to the central angle measure.
- In order to find a sector area, use the following formula:

$$\frac{part}{whole} = \frac{central\ angle}{360°} = \frac{sector\ area}{\pi r^2}$$

- Any line that is tangent to a circle is perpendicular to the radius of the circle at the point where the radius and the tangent line intersect.

TRY IT EXERCISE 4

Work these questions, either with or without your calculator as you see fit, then check the answers in Chapter 20.

7

A homeowner is buying a circular rug for a square room that has an area of 144 square feet. If the homeowner wants the rug to be centered in the room with 1 foot of space between the edge of the rug and any wall, which of the following is closest to the largest possible area of the circular rug, in square feet?

A) 25

B) 80

C) 100

D) 115

15

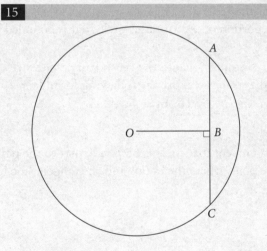

In the figure above, *A* and *C* are points on the circumference of circle *O*. If the area of the circle is 64π and the measure of minor arc *AC* is 4π, then what is the length of line segment *BO* ?

A) 4

B) $4\sqrt{2}$

C) 8

D) $8\sqrt{2}$

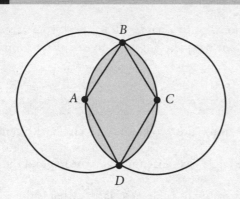

In the figure above, *A* and *C* are the centers of the circles and *B* and *D* are the points of intersection. If the perimeter of the shaded region is 40°, what is the perimeter of quadrilateral *ABCD* ?

A)   40

B)   60

C)   80

D)   120

CIRCLES: TRIGONOMETRY FACTS

- Radians are another way to measure angles.
- A full circle has 2 radians.
- To convert an angle measure between degrees and radians use either of the following formulas:

$$\text{degrees} = \frac{radians \times 180}{\pi} \qquad \text{radians} = \frac{\pi \times \text{degrees}}{180}$$

- Arc lengths can be easily calculated given radian angle measures with the following formula:
  - $s = \theta r$, where S is the arc length, r is the radius, and θ is the central angle of the arc in radians
- The unit circle is a circle with a radius of 1 centered at (0, 0).
- Angle measures on the unit circle are calculated from the positive *x*-axis and move counter-clockwise.
- Negative angle measures move clockwise from the positive *x*-axis.
- The sine of any angle is the *y*-value of the corresponding point on the unit circle.
- The cosine of any angle is the *x*-value of the corresponding point on the unit circle.

TRY IT EXERCISE 5

After you try these questions, go to Chapter 20 to check your answers. Remember to leave that calculator alone on questions with no calculator symbol.

6

Points A and C are two points on a circle with center O. If the circle has a circumference of 16π and the radian measure of angle AOC is $\dfrac{5\pi}{4}$, what is the length of minor arc AC?

A) 4π

B) 5π

C) 10π

D) 12π

21

Given that $\dfrac{7\pi}{6} < x < \dfrac{5\pi}{3}$, where x is in radians, which of the following could be the value of $\sin x$?

A) $-\dfrac{\sqrt{3}}{2}$

B) $\dfrac{-1}{2}$

C) $\dfrac{1}{2}$

D) $\dfrac{\sqrt{3}}{2}$

If $\tan \theta$ is $\dfrac{1}{\sqrt{3}}$ and θ is in radians, which of the following could be the value of $\theta + \dfrac{\pi}{2}$?

A) $\dfrac{-\pi}{6}$

B) $\dfrac{5\pi}{4}$

C) $\dfrac{7\pi}{6}$

D) $\dfrac{5\pi}{3}$

THREE-DIMENSIONAL FIGURE FACTS

- Three dimensional space is called volume.
- The volume of a figure is found by calculating the area of one side and multiplying that by the measurement of the 3rd dimension.
- A rectangular solid is a 3D figure made from rectangles in which opposite faces have the same areas.
- A cube is a rectangular solid in which all sides are equal.
- The volume of a cube is s^3, where s is the side length.
- A line that connects adjacent vertices in a rectangular solid is called an "edge."
- The volume of a rectangular solid is $V = lwh$, where l is the length, w is the width, and h is the height.
- The longest diagonal in a rectangular solid is given by the formula $a^2 + b^2 + c^2 = d^2$, where a, b, and c are the length, width, and height.
- A right circular cylinder is a figure in which the base and top are circles and the sides are perpendicular to the base.
- The volume of a right circular cylinder is $V = \pi r^2 h$, where r is the radius of the circular base, and h is the height of the cylindrical side.
- A right circular cone is a figure that tapers smoothly from the base, which is a circle to a point directly above the center of the circle. The height, drawn from this point to the center of the base, is perpendicular to the base.
- The volume of a right circular cone is $V = \dfrac{1}{3}\pi r^2 h$, where r is the radius of the circular base and h is the height of the cone.
- A pyramid is a figure with a rectangular base and four congruent triangular sides that meet at a point directly above the center of the rectangular base.
- The volume of a pyramid is $V = \dfrac{1}{3}lwh$, where l and w and the length and width of the base, and h is the height of the pyramid.

- A sphere is a figure that is perfectly round, with every point on its surface equidistant from its center.

- The volume of a sphere is $V = \dfrac{4}{3}\pi r^3$, where r is the radius of the sphere.

- The reference box at the beginning of the Math sections provides the formulas for the volume of the shapes already mentioned. Make sure you know which ones are there.

- If a questions asks for the volume of a shape not listed in the reference box, the test will provide the formula to you in the question.

TRY IT EXERCISE 6

Work these questions, either with or without your calculator as indicated, then check the answers in Chapter 20. Don't forget to look at the reference box to find the formula you need, even if you think you know it already.

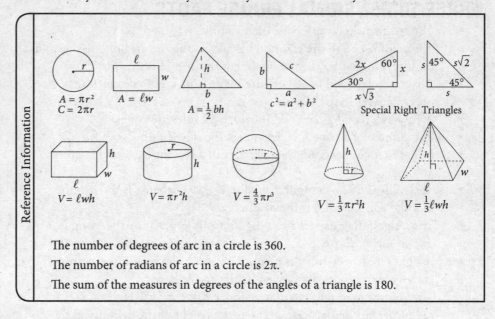

The number of degrees of arc in a circle is 360.

The number of radians of arc in a circle is 2π.

The sum of the measures in degrees of the angles of a triangle is 180.

13

A right circular cone and a right circular cylinder have equal heights and the volume of the cylinder is twice that of the cone. What is the radius of the cylinder if the base radius of the cone is 3 cm and the volume of the cone is 18π cm³ ?

A) $\sqrt{2}$

B) 2

C) $2\sqrt{3}$

D) $\sqrt{6}$

26

A cube with a volume of 64 cubic inches is inscribed in a sphere so that all vertices of the cube touch the sphere. What is the volume, in cubic inches, of the sphere?

A) $16\pi\sqrt{3}$

B) $32\pi\sqrt{3}$

C) $64\pi\sqrt{3}$

D) $128\pi\sqrt{3}$

17

The radius of right circular cylinder A is half of that of right circular cylinder B. Cylinder A has a volume of 100π cubic centimeters and a height of 4 centimeters. If the volume of cylinder B is 200π cubic centimeters, what is the height of cylinder B ?

BALLPARKING AND GEOMETRY

Ballparking is also a great technique on Geometry questions. Most of the time, the figures ETS provides are drawn to scale. (The exceptions are when ETS puts "Note: Figure not drawn to scale" under the figure.) When the figure is drawn to scale, you can Ballpark to eliminate answers that don't fit with the figure, and sometimes narrow the answers down to just one without a ton of extra work.

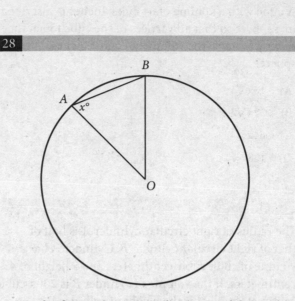

28

In the figure above, O is the center of the circle and $x = 67.5°$. If the area of the circle is 64π, then what is the area of triangle ABO?

A) 12

B) $16\sqrt{2}$

C) 12π

D) $32\sqrt{2}$

Here's How to Crack It

This is a tricky question. If you're not sure how to solve it, or you think you might not have time, consider Ballparking instead. Also, you can use Ballparking to eliminate trap answers before beginning to actually solve a problem.

The first step of Ballparking is to generate a rough estimate of what value you are looking for. The figure is drawn to scale, so carve up the circle into multiple triangles of the same size as the one in the problem. Use your pencil to extend the lines of triangle ABO into diameters. Then keep adding lines until you have filled up the circle.

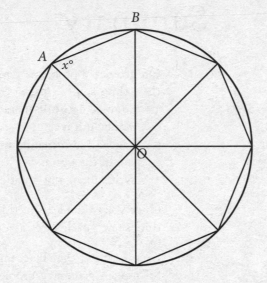

Eight triangles of similar shape fit inside the circle; therefore, the area of the triangle is going to be a little less than $\frac{1}{8}$ of the area of the circle. Since the area of the circle is 64π, then the area of the triangle is going to be just less than 8π. Continue ballparking by rounding the value of π to 3. Therefore, you need an answer choice whose value is just below $8 \times 3 = 24$. Now look at the answers and use POE aggressively:

A)	12	This is too small, eliminate it.
B)	$16\sqrt{2}$	$\sqrt{2}$ is about 1.4, so this is about 22.4. It's close, so keep it!
C)	12π	This is too large, so eliminate it.
D)	$32\sqrt{2}$	This is too large, so eliminate it.

Therefore, the answer is (B).

Now that you know how to Ballpark on geometry questions, be on the lookout for opportunities to do it going forward.

Summary

○ On geometry problems remember to do these three steps.
- Draw a figure if there isn't one, or redraw it if it's not to scale.
- Label all information from the problem in the figure.
- Write down any equations you need.

○ Once you've done these things just take things one puzzle piece at a time!

○ Keep in mind that Plugging In is a useful tool in geometry problems too. Just make sure you follow the rules of geometry with any numbers you pick.

○ Remember your special triangles.
- 45-45-90 with sides of x: x: $x\sqrt{2}$
- 30-60-90 with sides of x: $x\sqrt{3}$ $2x$
- 3-4-5, 6-8-10, and 5-12-13 right triangles

○ Use SOH-CAH-TOA, be careful to mark the reference angle, and keep in mind that for complementary angles the sine of one angle is the cosine of the other.

○ To calculate arc lengths or sector areas use a part to whole proportion:

$$\frac{part}{whole} = \frac{central\ angle}{360°} =$$

$$\frac{arc}{circumference} = \frac{sector\ area}{circle\ area}$$

○ Remember that π radians is 180°: You can use this fact to convert between the two.

○ Since you know the sign of sine, cosine, and tangent in every quadrant, use these as a Process of Elimination tool on trigonometry questions with the unit circle.

○ Ballparking can be a useful tool on geometry questions to save time and help you avoid careless errors.

○ Review this chapter as needed for all the specific geometry facts we've covered.

Chapter 20
Math Exercises:
Answers and
Explanations

CHAPTER 16: FUNDAMENTALS, COORDINATE GEOMETRY, AND FUNCTIONS

Try It Exercise 1

10.   C   Treat the imaginary number i just like any other variable, except that whenever i^2 appears, replace it with -1. Start by using FOIL to multiply the complex numbers: $(5 + 2i) \times (-3 - 4i) = -15 - 20i - 6i - 8i^2$, which simplifies to $-15 - 26i - 8i^2$. Now, replace i^2 with -1: $-15 - 26i - 8(-1) = -15 - 26i + 8$, which simplifies to $-7 - 26i$, (C).

19.   C   An extraneous solution is one that won't work when put back into the original equation. At a glance, it looks like -3 and 3 will make the equation undefined, but which one? When a problem asks for an extraneous solution, go ahead and solve the problem like you normally would, but at the end, plug each solution back into the original equation to see if it actually works. In this case, add the two fractions together by finding a common denominator: $\dfrac{x+3}{(x+3)(x-3)} + \dfrac{x-3}{(x+3)(x-3)} = \dfrac{12}{2x^2 - 18}$, which simplifies to $\dfrac{x+3+x-3}{(x+3)(x-3)} = \dfrac{12}{2x^2 - 18}$. Simplify the right side of the equation by dividing the top and the bottom of the fraction by 2: $\dfrac{x+3+x-3}{(x+3)(x-3)} = \dfrac{6}{x^2 - 9}$. Simplify the numerator and FOIL together the denominator on the left side: $\dfrac{2x}{x^2 - 9} = \dfrac{6}{x^2 - 9}$. Therefore, $2x = 6$ and $x = 3$. However, the solution $x = 3$ is extraneous, since using 3 for x would cause the denominator of the fraction $\dfrac{1}{x=3}$ to equal zero, so $x = 3$ cannot be used in the equation, and therefore 3 is an extraneous solution to the problem. Choice (C) matches.

31.   4   This question deals with the basic properties of integers as they are squared or cubed. Any squared value will be positive, so x can be either negative or positive. On the other hand, y can only be positive, since its cube is positive (a cubed negative number will always result in a negative). Remember to RTFQ! The question asks for distinct values of $x + y$. Start by writing down all possible values for x and y. Since x^2 is less than 4, the only possible values for x are -1, -1, 0, and 1. Since y^3 is less than 25 but greater than zero, the possible values for y are 1 and 2. Since there are three values for x and two for y, you might assume the answer is $3 \cdot 2 = 6$. But like most easy short cuts on the SAT, this is a trap. Write it out! Sum the values systematically:

$$-1 + 1 = 0$$
$$-1 + 2 = 1$$
$$0 + 1 = 1$$
$$0 + 2 = 2$$
$$1 + 1 = 2$$
$$1 + 2 = 3$$

Since the distinct values of $x + y$ are 0, 1, 2, and 3, the answer is 4.

Try It Exercise 2

10. **A** When given the zeros of a function, you are given x-values which are the solutions to the factors of the function. Rewrite the zeros and multiply out the terms to determine the function.

$$x = -\frac{1}{2} \qquad\qquad x = 3 \qquad\qquad x = 3$$

$$x + \frac{1}{2} = 0 \qquad\qquad x - 3 = 0 \qquad\qquad x - 3 = 0$$

To remove the fraction in the first factor, multiply that factor by 2 to get $2x + 1 = 0$.

$$
\begin{aligned}
f(x) &= (2x + 1)(x - 3)^2 \\
&= (2x + 1)(x^2 - 6x + 9) \\
&= 2x^3 - 12x^2 + 18x + x^2 - 6x + 9 \\
&= 2x^3 - 11x^2 + 12x + 9
\end{aligned}
$$

The correct answer is (A).

16. **B** Recall that the vertex form of a parabola is $y = a(x - h)^2 + k$. Plug in the vertex and the given point to find the value of a.

$$
\begin{aligned}
2 &= a(1 - 3)^2 + 4 \\
2 &= a(-2)^2 + 4 \\
2 &= 4a + 4 \\
-2 &= 4a \\
-\frac{1}{2} &= a
\end{aligned}
$$

Now, plug your value of a into the vertex form and expand it out. Watch the signs!

$$y = -\frac{1}{2}(x-3)^2 + 4$$

$$y = -\frac{1}{2}(x^2 - 6x + 9) + 4$$

$$y = -\frac{1}{2}x^2 + 3x - \frac{9}{2} + 4$$

$$y = -\frac{1}{2}x^2 + 3x - \frac{1}{2}$$

The correct answer is (B).

15. **C**   If only calculator use was allowed on this one! You could graph $f(x)$ and find the even solution immediately. To begin solving this one, you must first factor $f(x)$. The first factor is not obvious, so this requires a little guess and check on your part. You must first look to the coefficient of the x^3 term, 1, and the y-intercept term, −6. Determine the factors of both:

Factors of −6:   ±1, ±2, ±3, ±6

Factors of 1:   ±1

Determine a value to try as a factor by dividing factors of 6 by the factors of 1. Let's check the first one, 1/1, or just 1. If 1 were a solution, then that would mean that $(x - 1)$ would be a factor of the polynomial. Test it out by dividing $f(x)$ by $(x - 1)$:

$$
\begin{array}{r}
x^2 - 5x + 6 \\
x-1 \overline{) \ x^3 - 6x^2 + 11x - 6} \\
-(x^3 - \ x^2) \\
\hline
-5x^2 + 11x \\
-(-5x^2 + \ 5x) \\
\hline
6x - 6 \\
-(6x - 6) \\
\hline
0
\end{array}
$$

Success! A good rule of thumb when you must guess a factor is to start small. It works out that way more often than not. What this tells us is that $f(x)$ factors to $(x - 1)(x^2 - 5x + 6)$. Now factor the rest of the expression so you can figure out the even x-value of the solutions.

$(x - 1)(x^2 - 5x + 6) = (x - 1)(x - 2)(x - 3)$

This means that your solutions are at x = 1, 2, and 3. The only even solution is x = 2, which equates to the coordinate (2, 0). Now take the coordinate in conjunction with what you know regarding $g(x)$. You also know it passes through (0, 6), and with two points, you can determine the slope of the line.

$$m_g = \frac{rise}{run} = \frac{6-0}{0-2} = \frac{6}{-2} = -3$$

To start working on $h(x)$, recall that the question said it is perpendicular to $g(x)$, so you must find the slope by calculating the negative reciprocal.

$$m_h = \frac{1}{3}$$

To find the equation of $h(x)$, you just need the y-intercept, or the point where $x = 0$. The question gave you the point $(0, 6)$, so you already have that information. Therefore, the equation is $h(x) = \frac{1}{3}x + 6$. The correct answer is (C).

33. 4 Begin by completing the square to write the function in the vertex form of a parabola. Watch the signs!

$$
\begin{aligned}
f(x) &= -x^2 + 6x - 8 \\
&= -(x^2 - 6x) - 8 \\
&= -(x^2 - 6x + 9 - 9) - 8 \\
&= -(x^2 - 6x + 9) - (-9) - 8 \\
&= -(x^2 - 6x + 9) + 9 - 8 \\
&= -(x - 3)^2 + 1
\end{aligned}
$$

Therefore, the vertex is at $(3, 1)$, and $h = 3$ and $k = 1$. Therefore, $h + k = 4$.

CHAPTER 17: ALTERNATIVE APPROACHES

Try It Exercise 1

12. B Plug In! The weight of the shipment must be within 5 pounds of 50 pounds, so start with $W = 50$. Because you're looking for the choice that describes all possible values of W, the correct answer must be true when $W = 50$. Choices (C) and (D) are false for $W = 50$, so eliminate them. Next, you want to Plug In again. If you try $W = 55$, both choices (A) and (B) are true; the same is the case for $W = 45$. What you want to try is a number *outside* the range; make $W = 44$ and eliminate answer choices that are *true* with that value. If $W = 44$, choice (A) is still true; eliminate (A) and choose (B).

18. A Don't panic with labor-intensive problems such as this. Instead, get rid of the algebra by Plugging In. Also, don't worry about making the numbers realistic. Set the price of the boat as $x = 100$ since this number works well with percentages. Make the markup at auction $y = 20$ and the

discount $z = 10$. Now use these numbers to find the price of the boat. Since the markup is 20%, the auction price of the boat is $120. Don later purchased the boat for 10% off. 10% of $120 is $12, so the final purchase price is $108. This is the target number. Now plug those numbers into a calculator: (A) is the only one that matches your target. The answer is (A).

20. **B** Challenging exponent questions are among some of the fastest questions on the SAT when you use Plugging In. Set $x = 2$ and run the numbers through the calculator: $3^4 \times 27^1 = 2{,}187$. This is the target. Now, Plug In $x = 2$ to the answers. Only (B) matches this target.

27. **D** Plug In, using points from the curve. Look for places where it is easy to determine where the curve is. At $h = 6$, $A = 2$. Plug in $h = 6$ and eliminate any choice that does not make $A = 2$. This eliminates (A) and (B). Try another point. At $h = 0$, $A = 1.25$. Choice (C) does not work for this value; eliminate (C) and choose (D).

15. **D** Plug In! Pick an easy number, since calculator use is not allowed. Make $x = 2$. The question then becomes $\dfrac{(2)^5 - 2(2)^4 - 13(2)^3 + 14(2)^2 + 24(2)}{2+3} = \dfrac{32 - 2(16) - 13(8) + 14(4) + 48}{5}$ $= \dfrac{32 - 32 - 104 + 56 + 48}{5} = \dfrac{0}{5} = 0$. This is your target; circle it. Make $x = 2$ in each choice and eliminate any choice that does not equal 0. (Note: you can eliminate (A) and (C) without solving entirely because the fractions at the end will leave a decimal, making it impossible for those two answers to equal 0 when $x = 2$.) The only choice that works is (D).

Try It Exercise 2

9. **D** Jane spends a little less than half her time walking a *lot* faster, so it stands to reason that she would cover more than half the total distance at the faster speed. Another way to look at this is that if she spent half as much time walking at 6 k.p.h. as she did walking 3 k.p.h., the two speeds would balance out, and she would cover the same distance at both speeds. But if that were the case, she would spend $\dfrac{1}{3}$ of her time walking at the faster speed. Since she spends more than $\dfrac{1}{3}$ of her time walking fast, she will cover more than half the distance at the faster speed. Notice that only (D) is a fraction greater than $\dfrac{1}{2}$, so (D) is the only possible answer.

If you want to solve this question exactly, you can use the formula rate $\times$ time = distance. Let's say her total time is x. At the beginning, her distance is $6 \times \dfrac{3}{8}x = \dfrac{18}{8}x$. For the second part, her distance is $3 \times \dfrac{5}{8}x = \dfrac{15}{8}x$. Therefore, her total distance is $\dfrac{18}{8}x = \dfrac{15}{8}x = \dfrac{33}{8}x$. To find the answer,

divide $\dfrac{18}{8}x$ by $\dfrac{33}{8}x$ to get $\dfrac{6}{11}$.

Alternatively, you could Plug In on this problem. Suppose Jane's total walking time is 6 hours.

First, she walks 3 hours at 6 k.p.h. for a distance of $3 \times 6 = 18$ kilometers. Next, she walks 5 hours

at 3 k.p.h. for a distance of $5 \times 3 = 15$ kilometers. Her total distance was $18 + 15 = 33$; the north-

bound part of the trip was $\dfrac{18}{33} = \dfrac{6}{11}$. Either Plugging In or Ballparking works great here; the worst

strategy is the one you learned in math class. Remember, the goal is to get the question right by the

easiest method.

13. **B** The answer choices are really far apart, and you're not allowed a calculator, so this is a great opportunity to Ballpark. Round 679 up to 700: $7(x^2 - 3) = 700$. Divide both sides by 7: $x^2 - 3 = 100$. To
get to $x^2 + 3$, add 6 to both sides and you get $x^2 + 3 = 106$. This is really close to 103, and really far
from every other answer choice, so choose (B).

22. **B** Ballpark! First, eliminate (C) because 2013 was a decrease, not an increase, over 2012's sales. 2011
is only a tiny increase over 2010, whereas 2012 is a huge jump from 2011; (A) is definitely not
as big of an increase as (B), so eliminate (A). 2012 is $15.4 - 12.4 = 3{,}000$ units more than 2011,
whereas 2014 is only $16.4 - 15.2 = 1{,}200$ units more than 2013. Furthermore, the percent change
formula means you will be dividing 2012 by a smaller number (12,400) than what you'll be dividing 2014 by (15,200), so 2012 will clearly be the greater percent increase; choose (B).

15. **D** Can you ballpark on geometry questions? The figure is drawn to scale, so definitely try Ballparking. CD is definitely longer than BE, so eliminate choices (A) and (B). CD is more likely to be
twice BE than only be a little more than BE, so choice (D) makes more sense given the diagram
provided.

Alternatively, this question is testing similar triangles. Both triangle ABE and triangle ACD share

angle A. Because BE and CD are parallel, the other corresponding angles are also congruent, so the

triangles are similar. If E is the midpoint of AD, then $AE = \dfrac{1}{2}AD$, so $BE = \dfrac{1}{2}CD$. If $BE = 3$, then

$3 = \dfrac{1}{2}CD$, making $CD = 6$. We'll cover more about geometry in a later chapter.

CHAPTER 18: WORD PROBLEMS AND OTHER HOT TOPICS

Try It Exercise 1

11. **A** This is a great question to use Plugging In the Answers. Each answer represents a possible value of t, so plug them in for t in the equation and see which gives you the greatest height. Calculator use is allowed, so it should be fairly painless. Usually, you would start in the middle when using PITA, but this quadratic function, or an upside-down parabola. Therefore, the values for h will go up, then back down, so try all the given values of t in the answer choices. For (A), if $t = 0.75$, $h = 5 + 3(0.75) - 2(0.75)^2 = 6.125$. Follow the same steps to find that at $t = 1$, $h = 6$; at $t = 1.5$, $h = 5$; and at $t = 2.5$, $h = 0$. The greatest height, 6.125, occurred when $t = 0.75$, so the correct answer is (A).

18. **D** In this question, you may need to mix a bit of basic algebra with Plugging In the Answers. Start with (B). If the Johnsons earn \$780, we need to find what each of them earns. Let's say Mr. Johnson's earnings are x. Then, Mrs. Johnson's are $x + 60$, so $2x + 60 = 780$ and $x = 360$. Therefore, Mr. Johnson earns \$360, and Mrs. Johnson earns \$420. Now, does $\frac{3}{5}(420) = \frac{2}{3}(360)$? No, so (B) is incorrect. Keep trying until you get to (D). If the Johnson's earn \$1,140, then $2x + 60 = 1,140$ and $x = 540$, so Mr. Johnson earns \$540 and Mrs. Johnson earns \$600. Now check again: Does $\frac{3}{5}(600) = \frac{2}{3}(540)$? Yes, so the correct answer is (D).

13. **A** Since this question is asking for the *least* possible value, we should start with (A). If $a = 30$, then $\frac{2}{5}(30) = 12 = b$, and $12 = \frac{3c^2}{4}$, so $c^2 = 16$, and c (which must be positive) is 4. The question specifies that a and c must be positive integers, and they are, so (A) works, and there is no need to check any other answers.

Try It Exercise 2

27. **A** The answer choices are a clue for this question: The form of the answers is similar to the quadratic formula. There's also both a t and a t^2 in the original equation, which means the equation is quadratic with regards to t. Start by rearranging the equation into standard form

with t as x. This means you want the form to be $0 = at^2 + bt + c$. Subtract x from both sides:

$0 = x_0 + v_o t + \dfrac{1}{2} at^2 - x$. Rearrange to have the t terms in descending order by degree: $0 = \dfrac{1}{2} at^2$

$+ v_o t + x_0 - x$. This means the a term is $\dfrac{1}{2}a$, the b term is v_o, and the c term is $x_0 - x$ (neither of

these terms are multiplied by t, so they must be c). Insert these values into the quadratic formula:

$t = \dfrac{-v_0 \pm \sqrt{\left(v_0\right)^2 - 4\left(\dfrac{1}{2}a\right)\left(x_0 - x\right)}}{2\left(\dfrac{1}{2}a\right)}$. This isn't quite any answer choice, but you can eliminate (C)

and (D) because the wrong terms are in the denominator. Simplify by multiplying the $\left(\dfrac{1}{2}a\right)$

terms by the coefficients and you get $t = \dfrac{-v_0 \pm \sqrt{\left(v_0\right)^2 - 2a\left(x_0 - x\right)}}{a}$, which is (A).

28. **C** There are a ton of unknowns in the equation. You need to use points from the graph to solve for

the different unknowns. Start with $t = 0$. At $t = 0$, displacement, x, is 2. This makes the equation

$2 = x_0 + 0.5(0) + \dfrac{1}{2}a(0)$, which simplifies to $2 = x_0$. Now, pick another point where t is not 0 and

make $x_0 = 2$. At $t = 2$, $x = 5$. Input into the equation: $5 = 2 + 0.5(2) + \dfrac{1}{2}a(2)^2$. Simplify: $5 = 2 + 1 +$

$2a$, then $5 = 3 + 2a$, so $2 = 2a$, and $a = 1$, (C).

CHAPTER 19: PLANE GEOMETRY

Try It Exercise 1

3. **C** There are several ways to solve this one. Here is an efficient way. Line BF has 180 degrees. Since
$x + y = 70$ degrees, then angle GOF must be 110 degrees. Since opposite angles are congruent, angle
BOD is also 110 degrees. Finally, since line CO bisects this angle, angle BOC is half this size, or 55
degrees. The answer is (C).

4. **B** To tackle this problem efficiently, try penciling in every angle that's equal. Like this:

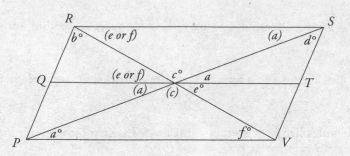

Note that angles *e* and *f* are also equal, as indicated above. Now we can clearly see that *a*, *c*, and either *e* or *f* make up straight line *QT*. Therefore, the correct answer is (B).

6. **D** This one is tricky. Draw in lines *BF* and *CE*. Since lines *BE* and *CF* are equal lengths, *BCEF* must be a rectangle. The diagonals of a rectangle intersect at their midpoints, so point *O* is actually the midpoint of *BE* and *CF*. Therefore, $BO = FO = CO = EO$. Since *AD* intersects point *O* and is parallel to *BC* and *EF*, it must bisect $\angle BOF$, so angles *BOA* and *FOA* must be congruent, which also means that angles *BAO* and *FAO* are also congruent. Since $\angle BAF$ is 90°, angles *BAO* and *FAO* must be 45° each. There are 180° in a triangle, so angles *BOA* and *FOA* are each 30°. Finally, there are 180 degrees in a line, so $\angle BOA + \angle FOA + \angle BOC = 180°$, so $\angle BOC = 180° - 30° - 30° = 120°$, (D).

Try It Exercise 2

1. **A** Don't let the diagram throw you. The base of a triangle is always perpendicular to its height.

    The long way to solve this is to use the Pythagorean Theorem to find the length of the third side: $4^2 + b^2 = 8^2$, so $b^2 = 48$ and $b = 4\sqrt{3}$. Now, put this into the area formula for a triangle: $\frac{1}{2}(4)(4\sqrt{3}) = 8\sqrt{3}$.

    The faster way to solve is to recognize that this is a 30-60-90 right triangle. Since two sides of a right triangle determine the third side, any right triangle in which the hypotenuse is twice one of the legs *must* be a 30-60-90 right triangle. If you recognize this, it can save you some time on calculations. Either way, the answer is (A).

8. **C** Remember the three steps for Geometry:

    1 – Draw the figure

    2 – Label the info

    3 – Write the formula(s)

Step 1 – They've given you a figure, so you don't need to draw anything.

Step 2 – Write in the information they've given you: $b = f = 30$, $a = 100$, $d = 50$. If you continue to determine all of the angle measurements, you'll find that these are two similar triangles.

Step 3 – Write the formula(s). There aren't actually any formulas that you need to solve this question (apart from the basic formulas for the sum of angles in a triangle and for similar triangles).

Once you recognize the similar triangles, the next step is to Plug In for the unknown lengths of the sides they've given in the question: $\overline{AD} = \frac{1}{3}\overline{AB}$. Plug in 2 for $\overline{AD}$, which means that $\overline{AB}$ is 6, $\overline{BD}$ is 4, and $\overline{BE}$ is 3. Next, use a proportion to determine $\overline{BC}$: $\frac{\overline{AB}}{\overline{BE}} = \frac{\overline{BC}}{\overline{BD}}$ or $\frac{6}{3} = \frac{\overline{BC}}{4}$. So $\overline{BC} = 8$. That's the target. Now go back to the answers and plug in the appropriate side lengths to determine which answer choices match 8, and only (C) does.

20. **A**   Start by drawing line segments AC and BD, and label their intersection as O. Since AO and DO are the same lengths, $\angle AOD$ is a 45-45-90 right triangle (*any* right triangle with two legs that are the same is automatically a 45-45-90). Since the hypotenuse is $\sqrt{2}$, $AO = DO = 1$. See the figure below:

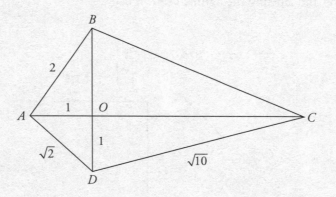

As mentioned two questions ago, any right triangle in which the hypotenuse is twice on of the legs must be a 30-60-90 right triangle, so BO is $\sqrt{3}$. Now, use the Pythagorean theorem to find the length of OC, which is 3. Next, use the area formula of a triangle to find the area of triangles ABC and ACD. Area of $ABC = \frac{1}{2}(\sqrt{3})(4) = 2\sqrt{3}$ and area of $ACD = \frac{1}{2}(1)(4) = 2$. Finally, set this into a ratio, being careful to match the order asked in the question: Area of ACD to area of ABC, so 2 to $2\sqrt{3}$, which reduces to 1 to $\sqrt{3}$. The correct answer is (A).

Try It Exercise 3

11. **A** Begin by sketching a right triangle and labeling the points *A*, *B*, and *C*. It does not matter which vertices you label as which as long as you *CAB* is not your right angle. No matter how you draw the figure, the side opposite from *CAB* is *BC*, so side *BC* corresponds to 7, whereas the hypotenuse corresponds to 25. If you are not familiar with the 7-24-25, you can use the Pythagorean theorem to figure out that the third side must correspond to 24. Now, add up these three values to get a total of 56. Since you know that the perimeter of *ABC* is actually 14, you can set up a proportion: $\frac{14}{56} = \frac{BC}{7}$. Therefore, the value of *BC* is 1.75.

12. **C** The question tells you that $BC \perp CE$, so mark angle *BCE* as a right angle in your figure. Now you should be able to see that angles *BCA* and *DCE* are complementary angles and therefore the sine of one is equal to the cosine of the other. Choice (C) reflects this relationship. Both (B) and (D) mismatch corresponding sides, and note that (A) is wrong because the triangles are similar, but not necessarily congruent.

15. **B** Start by sketching and labeling the figure as shown below:

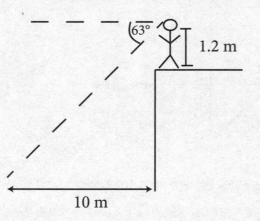

(Note: Make sure you read carefully to determine where the 63° angle is!)

Now, you can figure out that angle opposite to the 10 meters is complementary to 63°, so it must be 27°. Since you want to determine the adjacent side, you should use tangent. Set up your equation: $\tan 27° = \frac{10}{adjacent}$. Using a calculator, you can determine that the adjacent side, the vertical height of the triangle we sketched, is 19.63 meters. Be careful though, this is the height from Sam's eye-level to the ground, but the problem tells us that his eye-level is 1.2 meters high, so the building must be 19.63 − 1.2 = 18.43 meters tall.

Try It Exercise 4

7. **B**   Begin by drawing the figure described. The room is square and has an area of 144 ft². Since the area of a square is s^2, then each side of the room measures 12 ft. Next, draw the circular rug in the center of the room. Be sure to leave 1 foot of space between the rug and each wall. The figure should now appear similar to the one below:

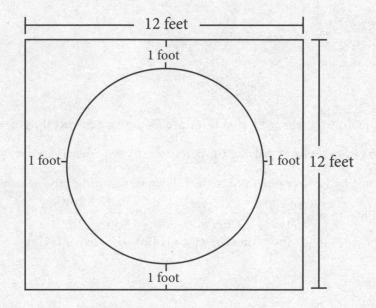

Since there is 1 foot of space on each side, the diameter of the rug must be 10ft and the radius 5 ft. The area of a circle is $A = \pi r^2$, so $A = 5^2\pi$ or 25π. This translates to an actual value of about 78.5 square feet, but we're looking for the closest answer, which is (B).

15. **B**   Begin by drawing lines AO and CO in order to highlight the minor arc distance better. Since the problem mentions the area of the circle, write down the formula $A = \pi r^2 = 64\pi$. Therefore, $r = 8$, which is the distance of AO and CO. The problem mentions an arc length, so calculate the circumference: $C = 2\pi r = 16\pi$. Now, use a proportion to find the measure of central angle AOC:

$\dfrac{x}{360°} = \dfrac{4\pi}{16\pi}$, where x is the central angle measure. Central angle AOC is 90°, which is bisected by line segment *BO*. Therefore, there are two 45-45-90 triangles. The hypotenuse *AO* is 8, so use the properties of a 45-45-90 triangle to find that *BO* is $\frac{8}{\sqrt{2}} = 4\sqrt{2}$. The answer is (B).

19.   **D**   This is a tricky problem. However, always begin by labeling what is known. Any line from the center of a circle to a point on the circle is a radius. Therefore, in order to find the perimeter of *ABCD*, you need to find the radii of circles *A* and *C*. First, draw line segment *AC*. Since *A* and *C* are the centers of the circle, but also lie on the circumference of the other circle, these two circles must be identical.

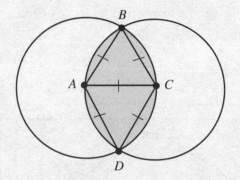

All radii are equal, so the shaded region is formed from two equilateral triangles. Work with only one of the two circles. Start by halving the perimeter to 20π. Since there are two equilateral triangles, $\angle BAD$ must be 120°, or one-third of the full circle. Knowing this, we can set up a proportion to find the radius: $\frac{\text{inscribed angle}}{360} = \frac{\text{arc}}{\text{Circumference}}$, so $\frac{120}{360} = \frac{20\pi}{2\pi r}$. When we solve for *r*, we get $r = 30$. Multiply by 4 to get the perimeter, which is 120. The answer is (D).

Try It Exercise 5

6.   **C**   Solving arc length with radian measures is pretty straightforward: Just use the formula $S = r\theta$. Since the circumference is 16π, the diameter must be 16, and the radius is 8. All you have to do is multiply $\frac{5\pi}{4}$ by 8 to get an arc length of 10π.

21.   **A**   Start by considering the sign of the answer. If $\frac{7\pi}{6} < x < \frac{5\pi}{3}$, then *x* is in either the third or fourth quadrant, and since sine values are *y*-value on the unit circle, all of these values will be negative. Eliminate (C) and (D). Now, it gets a little trickier. You may notice that $\sin\frac{7\pi}{6}$ is (B) and $\sin\frac{5\pi}{3}$ is (A). However, since the inequality excludes both of these values, we need to figure out whether (A) or (B) occurs somewhere else within this range of *x* values. A sin value of $\frac{-1}{2}$ occurs twice on

the unit circle: $\frac{7\pi}{6}$ and $\frac{11\pi}{6}$, and a sin value of $\frac{-\sqrt{3}}{2}$ occurs at $\frac{4\pi}{3}$ and $\frac{5\pi}{3}$. Only $\frac{4\pi}{3}$ is included within the given range, so (A) is correct.

28. **D** Take this one step at a time. Since the tan θ is positive, it must be in the first or third quadrant. Therefore, $\theta + \frac{\pi}{2}$ must be in the second or fourth quadrant. We can therefore eliminate (B) and (C). Now, you can plug in either of the remaining answers. Let's start with (A). If $\theta + \frac{\pi}{2} = \frac{-\pi}{6}$, then $\theta = \frac{-2\pi}{3}$. Use your calculator to check tan $\frac{-2\pi}{3}$. It's not $\frac{1}{\sqrt{3}}$, so eliminate (A) and the answer must be (D).

Try It Exercise 6

13. **D** The first thing you should solve for is the height of the cone using the formula from the reference box: $V = \frac{1}{3}\pi r^2 h$. You get $18\pi = \frac{1}{3}\pi(3)^2 h$, so $18\pi = 3\pi h$. Therefore, $h = 6$. Now draw and label the cylinder using this information. The volume of the cylinder is twice that of the cone, or 36π, and the formula for the volume of a cylinder is $V = \pi r^2 h$. Thus, $36\pi = \pi r^2(6)$, $r^2 = 6$, and $r = \sqrt{6}$. The answer is (D).

26. **B** You are given the volume of the cube, so start there. $V = s^3$, so $64 = s^3$ and $s = 4$. The longest diagonal of the cube will be the diameter of the sphere, so find the diagonal using the "super-Pythagorean" formula: $a^2 + b^2 + c^2 = d^2$. Since this is a cube, all the sides are the same, so $4^2 + 4^2 + 4^2 = d^2$, and $d = \sqrt{48} = 4\sqrt{3}$ (if you don't want to simplify roots, you can just convert to decimals on your calculator). Divide by two to find the radius, which is $2\sqrt{3}$. Now plug that into the formula given in the reference box for the volume of a sphere: $V = \frac{4}{3}\pi r^3 = \frac{4}{3}\pi(2\sqrt{3})^3 = 32\pi\sqrt{3}$.

17. **2** Begin by drawing the figure, labeling it, and writing down the volume formula for a right circular cylinder: $V = \pi r^2 h$. Now, put the information from the problem into the formula: $100\pi = \pi r^2(4)$ and solve for r; you should get $r = 5$. Now draw and label cylinder B. The radius of B is twice that of A, so $r = 10$. Now, put this information into the volume formula and solve for the height: $200\pi = \pi 10^2 h$, so $h = 2$.

Chapter 21
Math Drill 1—No Calculator Section

The following is a brief sampling of math problems on a variety of topics as they would appear on the No Calculator section of the test. The instructions for that section are included, so that you can get used to them now and not need to waste any time figuring them out on test day. There is no answer sheet for the multiple-choice questions—just work out your answers and circle the right answer choices. For grid-ins, read the instructions carefully and mark your answers in the provided grids. Make sure to leave your calculator alone as you work these problems!

Math Drill 1

DIRECTIONS

For questions **1-15**, solve each problem, choose the best answer from the choices provided, and fill in the corresponding circle on your answer sheet. For questions **16-20**, solve the problem and enter your answer in the grid on the answer sheet. Please refer to the directions before question 16 on how to enter your answers in the grid. You may use any available space in your test booklet for scratch work.

NOTES

1. The use of a calculator **is not permitted**.
2. All variables and expressions used represent real numbers unless otherwise indicated.
3. Figures provided in this test are drawn to scale unless otherwise indicated.
4. All figures lie in a plane unless otherwise indicated.
5. Unless otherwise indicated, the domain of a given function f is the set of all real numbers x for which $f(x)$ is a real number.

REFERENCE

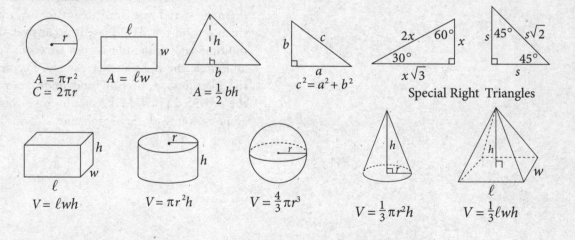

The number of degrees of arc in a circle is 360.
The number of radians of arc in a circle is 2π.
The sum of the measures in degrees of the angles of a triangle is 180.

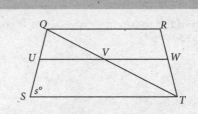

2

If $n \geq m$, which of the following must be true?

A) $m - n > 1$

B) $n - m \leq 1$

C) $m + n \geq 0$

D) $m - n \leq 0$

4

If $\dfrac{5}{\sqrt{10}}h = \dfrac{3}{\sqrt{2}}$, then what is the value of h?

A) $\dfrac{3}{\sqrt{2}}$

B) $\dfrac{5}{\sqrt{2}}$

C) $\dfrac{3}{\sqrt{5}}$

D) $\dfrac{3}{5}$

5

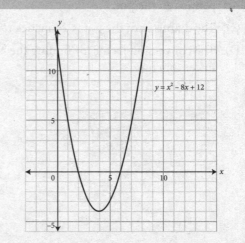

Note: Figure not drawn to scale.

In the figure above, $\overline{QR} \parallel \overline{UW} \parallel \overline{ST}$ and $\overline{QV} = \overline{UV}$. If the measure of $\angle QVW$ is 122°, what is the value of s ?

A) 29

B) 58

C) 61

D) 116

7

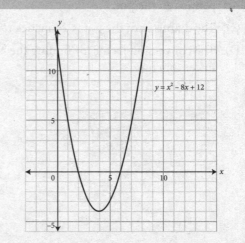

Which of the following equations, when graphed in the xy-plane above would create a system of equations with solutions at points (3, –3) and (8, 12) ?

A) $3x - y = 12$

B) $-3x + y = 12$

C) $x - 3y = 12$

D) $-x + 3y = 12$

8

Which of the following expressions is equivalent to $4^{2y}\,8^y$?

A) 2^{3y}

B) 2^{5y}

C) 2^{7y}

D) 4^{3y}

11

A palm tree is planted in a pot. The monthly growth rate of the tree can be modeled as $y = 0.15x + 14$, where x represents the number of months since the tree was planted, and y is the total height of the tree, in inches. Which of the following statements is true?

A) The tree grows 14 inches per month.

B) The tree was 14 inches tall when it was planted in the pot.

C) The diameter of the pot is 14 inches.

D) The conversion factor for finding the height in centimeters is 14.

12

$$BMI = \frac{w}{h^2} \times 703$$

A physician wants to determine if her patient is at a healthy weight for his height. She calculates his Body Mass Index (BMI) using the equation above, where w is the patient's weight in pounds and h is his height in inches. If the patient is 70 inches tall, which inequality best represents the approximate weights that would suggest that the patient has a BMI greater than 25 ?

A) $w > 175$

B) $w < 175$

C) $w > 150$

D) $w < 150$

14

$$3x - 19y = 17y + 6$$
$$x = 6y + 3$$

Based on the system of equations above, what is the value of the quotient $\dfrac{x}{y}$?

A) $\dfrac{1}{6}$

B) $\dfrac{2}{3}$

C) 4

D) 24

DIRECTIONS

For questions 16-20, solve the problem and enter your answer in the grid, as described below, on the answer sheet.

1. Although not required, it is suggested that you write your answer in the boxes at the top of the columns to help you fill in the circles accurately. You will receive credit only if the circles are filled in correctly.

2. Mark no more than one circle in any column.

3. No question has a negative answer.

4. Some problems may have more than one correct answer. In such cases, grid only one answer.

5. **Mixed numbers** such as $3\frac{1}{2}$ must be gridded as 3.5 or 7/2. (If [3 1 / 2] is entered into the grid, it will be interpreted as $\frac{31}{2}$, not as $3\frac{1}{2}$.)

6. **Decimal Answers:** If you obtain a decimal answer with more digits than the grid can accommodate, it may be either rounded or truncated, but it must fill the entire grid.

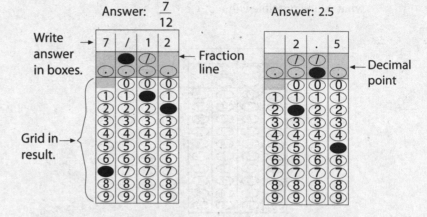

Acceptable ways to grid $\frac{2}{3}$ are:

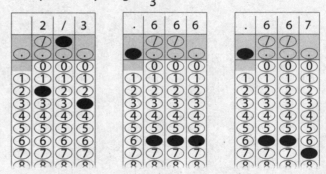

Answer: 201 – either position is correct

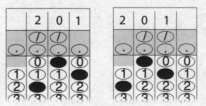

NOTE: You may start your answers in any column, space permitting. Columns you don't need to use should be left blank.

Let the function f be defined by $f(x) = \dfrac{\left(x^2 - x\right)}{x}$, where x is an integer and $x \neq 0$. If $10 < f(y) < 14$, what is one possible value of y ?

If $\dfrac{1}{z} + \dfrac{4z + 2}{z^2 + 11z} = \dfrac{12z - 24}{z^2 + 11z}$, what is the value of z ?

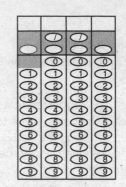

Chapter 22
Math Drill 2—
Calculator
Permitted Section

The following is a small selection of math problems on a range of concepts as they would appear on the Calculator Permitted section of the test. The instructions for that section are included, so that you can become familiar with them now and save time on test day. There is no answer sheet for the multiple-choice questions—just work out your answers and circle the right answer choices. For grid-ins, read the instructions carefully and mark your answers in the provided grids. Calculator use is permitted on all of these questions, so use it to avoid making careless mistakes when necessary, but always set up the problem on paper first.

Math Drill 2

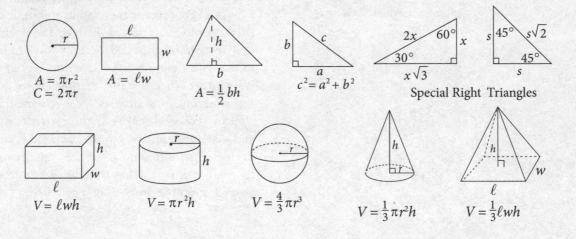

5

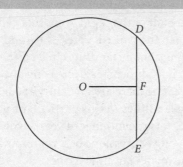

Note: Figure not drawn to scale.

In the figure above, the circle has center O and area 169π. The midpoint of $\overline{DE}$ is F, and $\overline{OF} = 12$. What is the length of $\overline{DE}$?

A) 5

B) 10

C) 13

D) 26

8

A store reduces the price of a pair of shoes by 15 percent. If the sale price is r dollars, which of the following is the closest approximation of the original price, in dollars, of the shoes, in terms of r ?

A) $1.18r$

B) $1.15r$

C) $1.10r$

D) $0.87r$

12

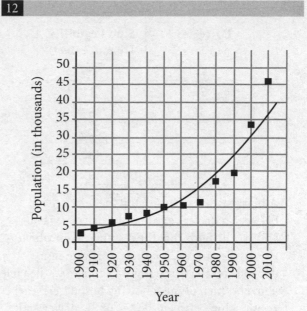

Year

The scatterplot diagram above shows the population of Warren County, Iowa, in thousands of people, since 1900. The curve of best fit shown has a y-intercept of 3,400. Which of the following statements is true about the population of Warren Country, Iowa, given this y-intercept?

A) The median population for Warren County, Iowa, from 1900 to 2000 was 3,400.

B) On average, the population of Warren County, Iowa, increased by 3,400 every 10 years.

C) The population of Warren County, Iowa, in 1900 was exactly 3,400.

D) The population of Warren County, Iowa, in 1990 was approximately 3,400.

15

Driver Age (Years)	Sign Legibility Distance (feet)
15	550
25	512
31	487
35	472
42	443
50	409

A biostatistician is studying the relationship between a driver's age and the driver's visual ability. She finds that the distance from which the driver can read a certain highway sign depends on the driver's age, as shown in the table above. Which of the following best describes the relationship between the age of the driver and the sign legibility?

A) The relationship is approximately exponential, since for every year, the sign legibility distance decreases by approximately 15%.

B) The relationship is approximately exponential, since for every year, the sign legibility decreases by approximately 25%.

C) The relationship is approximately linear, since for every year, the sign legibility distance decreases by approximately 4 feet.

D) The relationship is approximately linear, since for every year, the sign legibility distance decreases by approximately 8 feet.

17

As a result of the rapid growth of cell phone usage in the United States, the number of people using telephone landlines in a certain small town in California is decreasing at a rate of 25% per year. If there are currently 150,000 people using landlines in this particular town, and x represents the number of years, which of the following expressions best represents the trend in the town's landline usage?

A) $150,000(0.25)^x$

B) $150,000(0.25)x$

C) $150,000(0.75)^x$

D) $150,000(0.75)x$

20

$$f(x) = (x^2 - 2x - 35)(x + 5)(x + c)$$

The function f above is a polynomial function where c is a constant. If $(-5, 0)$ and $(3, 0)$ are points on the graph of $f(x)$, what is the product of the zeros of f?

A) -525

B) -105

C) 105

D) 525

23

An athletic trainer coaches only athletes who play football, baseball, and soccer. In a certain month, 3 football players were coached for every 7 baseball players, and 6 soccer players were coached for every football player. If the total number of athletes coached that month was between 375 and 400, how many soccer players were coached?

A) 42

B) 72

C) 98

D) 252

26

Scott takes three times as long to pack 12 boxes as Jean takes to pack 7 boxes. What is the ratio of Scott's average packing rate to Jean's average packing rate?

A) 2:3

B) 4:7

C) 7:4

D) 7:12

DIRECTIONS

For questions 31-38, solve the problem and enter your answer in the grid, as described below, on the answer sheet.

1. Although not required, it is suggested that you write your answer in the boxes at the top of the columns to help you fill in the circles accurately. You will receive credit only if the circles are filled in correctly.

2. Mark no more than one circle in any column.

3. No question has a negative answer.

4. Some problems may have more than one correct answer. In such cases, grid only one answer.

5. **Mixed numbers** such as $3\frac{1}{2}$ must be gridded as 3.5 or 7/2. (If is entered into the grid, it will be interpreted as $\frac{31}{2}$, not as $3\frac{1}{2}$.)

6. **Decimal Answers:** If you obtain a decimal answer with more digits than the grid can accommodate, it may be either rounded or truncated, but it must fill the entire grid.

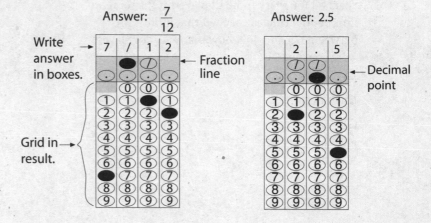

Answer: $\frac{7}{12}$ Answer: 2.5

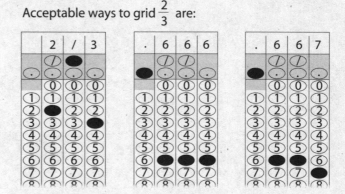

Acceptable ways to grid $\frac{2}{3}$ are:

Answer: 201 – either position is correct

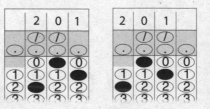

NOTE: You may start your answers in any column, space permitting. Columns you don't need to use should be left blank.

32

The function f is defined by $f(x) = 4x + 3$. If $3 \cdot f(r) = 93$, what is the value of r ?

33

A jar contains glass beads of equivalent weights. If 47 glass beads have a total weight of 3.2 ounces, and the maximum capacity of the jar is 4 pounds, how many glass beads can the jar hold? (Note: 16 ounces = 1 pound)

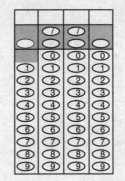

Chapter 23
Math Drills:
Answers and
Explanations

MATH DRILL 1

2. **D** With variables in the question and variables in the answers, you should Plug In on this question. Also, because it asks what MUST BE true, you should be prepared to Plug In more than once. So if $m = 2$ and $n = 3$, (A) is $2 - 3 > 1$, which is false, so eliminate it. Choice (B) is $3 - 2 \leq 1$, which is true, so leave it in. Choice (C) equals $2 + 3 \geq 0$, which is true, so leave it in. Choice (D) is $2 - 3 \leq 0$, which is also true. Now choose two different numbers. Pay particular attention to the ways they're trying to trick you: Try plugging in the same value for both integers, or try a negative number or zero since there are no restrictions on what kind of values you can plug in. Let's say both m and n equal 0. Choice (B) becomes $0 - 0 \leq 1$, which is true, so leave it. Choice (C) becomes $0 + 0 \geq 0$, which is true again, so leave it. Choice (D) becomes $0 - 0 \leq 0$, which is true as well. Now try negative values, like $m = -6$ and $n = 0$. Choice (B) is false, with $0 - (-6) \leq 1$ or $6 \leq 1$. Eliminate it. Choice (C) says $-6 + 0 \geq 0$, which is not true, so get rid of it. The answer is (D): $-6 - 0 \leq 0$.

4. **C** Plugging In the Answers could get ugly here, and it might be hard to tell which direction to go if your first try doesn't work. Solve this one instead. Multiply both sides of the equation by $\sqrt{10}$ to get $5h = \dfrac{3\sqrt{10}}{\sqrt{2}}$. The $\sqrt{10}$ on the right side can be rewritten as $\sqrt{2 \times 5}$ or $\sqrt{2} \times \sqrt{5}$. The $\sqrt{2}$ in the numerator and the denominator cancel out, leaving $5h = 3\sqrt{5}$. Divide both sides by 5 to get $h = \dfrac{3\sqrt{5}}{5}$. This doesn't match any of the answers exactly, but (D) can definitely be eliminated. Choice (C) is the closest, so work with that answer to get the root out of the denominator. Multiply the fraction in the answer by $\dfrac{\sqrt{5}}{\sqrt{5}}$, which will not change the value of the answer. The answer becomes $\dfrac{3}{\sqrt{5}} \times \dfrac{\sqrt{5}}{\sqrt{5}} = \dfrac{3\sqrt{5}}{5}$, which is the value you found for h.

5. **C** Any time you see parallel lines, you need to be thinking about the angles they create. Extend the parallel lines so the angles are easier to see. If $\angle QVW$ is 122°, then $\angle QVU$ is 58°. The question also says that $\overline{QV} = \overline{UV}$, so you know that the angles across from those sides are equal; with 180° in a triangle, and 58° already accounted for, that means $\angle VQU$ and $\angle VUQ$ are both 61°. Then, using parallel lines, you can determine that angle s will also be equal to 61°, or (C).

7. **A** When given points that represent the solutions of the system of equations, test those points out in the given equations. If they work in both equations, they are the solutions to the system. Start with point (8, 12) since it doesn't have any negative values to complicate things. The point is clearly on the graph of the parabola, so try it in the answer choices. Plugging it into (A) results in $3(8) - 12 = 12$, or $24 - 12 = 12$. This is true, so (A) might be the answer. You could check (8, 12) in all the other answer choices to see if any work or just check (3, −3) in (A). The second option is quicker: (A) becomes $3(3) - (-3) = 12$, or $9 + 3 = 12$, which is also true, so the answer is (A).

8. **C** Anytime a question asks you to manipulate exponents, remember that exponent rules apply only to the expressions with the same base, so start by converting each expression into the same base. Both 4 and 8 are powers of 2, so you should get $4^{2y} \cdot 8^y = (2^2)^{2y} \cdot (2^3)^y = 2^{4y} \cdot 2^{3y} = 2^{7y}$, which is (C).

11. **B** Start by labelling the parts of the equation. The question says that y is the height of the tree in inches and x is the number of months since the tree was planted. So the equation is really *height in inches* = 0.15(*months*) + 14. Does this tell you anything about the diameter of the pot, or the height in centimeters? No, so eliminate (C) and (D). Now plug in some numbers to see if (A) or (B) is true. For (A), plug in 1 for x to find that the height after 1 month is 14.15 inches. If $x = 2$ months, the tree is 14.3 inches. The tree did not grow 14 inches, so (A) is false and (B) must be true. When the tree is planted, $x = 0$, so the height is 14 inches.

12. **A** Plugging In could work here, but it might be tricky without a calculator. Instead, set up the inequality and solve it. You want BMI > 25, so plug in what is given into the BMI formula. The inequality becomes $\frac{w}{70^2} \times 703 > 25$. This looks a bit ugly to deal with, so round 703 to 700, which will still give you the "approximate" weights. Also, rewrite 70^2 as 70×70 to make it easier to reduce before solving. Now the inequality is $\frac{w}{70 \times 70} \times 700 > 25$. Cancel one of the 70s in the denominator with the 700, leaving 10 in the denominator, or $\frac{w}{70} \times 10 > 25$. Now reduce the 10 and the 70 to get $\frac{w}{7} > 25$. Finally, multiply both sides by 7 to get $w > 175$.

14. **D** Start by simplifying the first equation by adding $19y$ to both sides to get $3x = 36y + 6$. Looking at the two equations, it doesn't seem possible to get anything into the form $\frac{x}{y}$ that the question asks for. It will be necessary to solve for x and y. You could substitute the value of x in the second equation into the first equation or divide the first equation by 3 so they are both written as $x =$ something, then set those two parts equal. Use whichever method is least likely to cause you to make a careless error, especially since you can't use a calculator.

Substitution: Put $6y + 3$ in for x in the equation $3x = 36y + 6$ to get $3(6y + 3) = 36y + 6$. This becomes $18y + 9 = 36y + 6$ or $18y = 3$. Therefore, $y = \frac{1}{6}$.

Setting the equations equal: Dividing the first equation, $3x = 36y + 6$, by 3 results in $x = 12y + 2$. Set this equal to the second equation to get $12y + 2 = 6y + 3$, so $6y = 1$ and $y = \frac{1}{6}$.

Regardless of how you arrive at the value for y, plug this value into the simpler second equation to find that $x = 6\left(\frac{1}{6}\right) + 3 = 1 + 3 = 4$. Now take the quotient $\frac{x}{y} = \frac{4}{\frac{1}{6}} = 4 \times 6 = 24$, which is (D).

16.   **12, 13, or 14**

You have variables, so Plug In! Since you can't use your calculator, start out small with $y = 5$ to see what you get. $25 - 5$ is 20, divided by 5 is 4: That doesn't meet the requirement that the function needs to be larger than 10. Try plugging in 10, which yields 9—closer! Try again with 11, which gives you EXACTLY 10. Be careful, though; the question said the function must be LARGER than 10, so y cannot be equal to 11. That's enough information, though, to know that some integers larger than 11 will satisfy the condition, so you can answer 12. Actually solving this would show that 13 and 14 also work for y.

18. $\dfrac{37}{7}$ or **5.28** or **5.29**

To add the fractions on the left side of the equation, you need a common denominator. One way to do that is to use the Bowtie Method—multiply the denominator of the first fraction by the numerator of the second fraction to get a new numerator for the second fraction, and multiply the denominator of the second fraction by the numerator of the first fraction to get the new numerator of the first fraction. The denominator of both fractions will be the product of the existing denominators. You can then add the fractions together easily.

In this case, however, that would change the denominator of the second fraction, which already matches that of the fraction on the right side of the equation. Instead, find a way to make the denominator of the first fraction match the other two. The binomial $z^2 + 11$ can be rewritten as $z(z + 11)$, so to get z looking like $z^2 + 11$, multiply the numerator and denominator of the first fraction by $\dfrac{z + 11}{z + 11}$. The left side becomes $\dfrac{1(z + 11)}{z(z + 11)} + \dfrac{4z + 2}{z^2 + 11z} = \dfrac{z + 11}{z^2 + 11z} + \dfrac{4z + 2}{z^2 + 11z} = \dfrac{5z + 13}{z^2 + 11z}$.
Now, since the denominators match on both sides, you know that $5z + 13 = 12z - 24$. Subtract $5z$ from both sides to get $13 = 7z - 24$, then add 24 to both sides to get $37 = 7z$. Finally, divide both sides by 7 to get $z = \dfrac{37}{7}$. On a calculator, this would equal 5.28 or 5.29, so technically, those answers are acceptable as well. Since this is in the No Calculator section, though, stick with the fraction as long as it fits in the grid.

MATH DRILL 2

5. **B** Remember the three steps for Geometry:

      1 – Draw the figure

      2 – Label the info

      3 – Write the formula(s)

      Step 1 – A figure is already provided.

      Step 2 – Label $\overline{OF}$ = 12, and identify that $\overline{DF}$ and $\overline{EF}$ are congruent.

      Step 3 – Write the formula for area of a circle, since that's what they've provided. $A = \pi r^2$. Solve to find $r = 13$. The radius isn't drawn in, so draw in either $\overline{OD}$ or $\overline{OE}$. You will now see that you have a right triangle with one leg of 12 and a hypotenuse of 13, which should trigger your memory of Special Right Triangles: 5-12-13. That means that both $\overline{DF}$ and $\overline{EF}$ are 5. Be careful as you read the question: It's asking for $\overline{DE}$, which has a length of 10, *not* $\overline{DF}$ or $\overline{EF}$, both of which are 5. The credited response is (B).

8. **A** Start by Ballparking: If r is the sale price of the shoes, the original price must be greater than r. Therefore, (D) is too small. Variables in the question and answers are good indicators to use Plugging In! Since the question deals with percentages, start with $100 for the original price of the shoes. The price is reduced 15%, which means it is now $85, or r. The question is asking for the original price, which makes $100 the target. Plug $85 into the answer choices to find the one that comes closest to $100. Choice (A) is $100.30 and (B) is $97.75. Choice (A) is closer and is therefore the closest approximation.

12. **D** A scatterplot shows distinct data points, one dot for each paired x- and y-coordinate. Process of elimination can be used to get rid of (A) and (B). The median will be somewhere near the middle of the graph, or specifically the average of the population values of 1950 and 1960, which is around 10,000. The average is harder to calculate, as you'd have to add all the population values and divide by 12, the number of data points, but it has nothing to do with the y-intercept of the curve. A line or curve of best fit is often drawn to show the best approximation of the majority of data. It can be used to get an idea of where new data points might fall on the graph, but it is only an educated guess. The y-intercept on the curve of best fit for this graph can estimate the population in 1900, which is $x = 0$ on the graph, but it won't be exact. In fact, you can see that the point for 1900 falls just slightly below the curve of best fit. This makes (D) the correct answer.

15. **C** To determine how much the sign legibility distance is changing as a function of the driver's age, take two sets of data from the chart. Start with an age of 15 years and go to an age of 25 years. This is an increase in age of 10 years. Over that increase in age, sign legibility distance goes from 550 feet to 512 feet. This is a decrease of 550 – 512 = 38 feet. To find the decrease per year, divide 38

by 10 to get 3.8 or approximately 4 feet per year. This makes (C) look like it might be correct, but try it one more time to make sure the relationship holds. The increase from 35 to 42 years reflects a difference of 7 years, over which sign legibility distance decreases from 472 or 443 feet, which is a difference of 29 feet. Per year, that's 29 ÷ 7 = 4.12 feet. Again, this is approximately 4 feet per year, so (C) is correct. If the relationship were exponential, the values for the sign legibility distance would be decreasing at a more rapid rate.

17. **C**   There are a couple of different ways to approach this question. You can do some busywork on your calculator and then plug values into the answer choices in order to determine which one matches your data. It would probably be easier to do some quick process of elimination with the answer choices. Since the number of people using landlines is decreasing at a rate of 25% per year, we know that this is an exponential relationship, and thus we can eliminate (B) and (D), which are linear equations (no exponent). Choice (A) is a tricky one, since the number 25 is in the question stem, but the correct answer is actually (C). Since the rate is decreasing 25% each year, that means that each year the number of landline users is 75% of what it was the previous year—hence answer (C).

20. **B**   The zeros of a function when graphed in the xy-plane are the places where the function crosses the x-axis. They may also be referred to as roots, solutions, or x-intercepts. No matter what they are called, they are the places where $y = 0$. The question actually gives two such places: $(-5, 0)$ and $(3, 0)$. This tells you that -5 and 3 are two of the zeros of f. When finding the solutions or roots of a polynomial, you factor it and set each binomial equal to zero. The $(x + 5)$ binomial gives you the root -5. Factor the $(x^2 - 2x - 35)$ part of f to see if the other given root, 3, comes from that or from $(x + c)$. Factoring $(x^2 - 2x - 35)$ gives you $(x - 7)(x + 5)$, so the roots of that part are 7 and -5. This means that the root of 3 comes from $(x + c)$, and you now have all the roots. The graph of f crosses the x-axis at -5, 3, and 7. Remember not to count the -5 twice: The graph of a function can only cross the x-axis once at a given value of x. So the product of the zeros is $(-5)(3)(7) = -105$, which is (B).

23. **D**   Use the Ratio Box to keep your information organized. The first relationship given is 3 football players for every 7 baseball players, so enter those values into the Ratio line. The next piece says 6 soccer players for every football player; since you've already put 3 in for football players, you can't just put in 6 for soccer. Set up a proportion: $\dfrac{6 \text{ soccer}}{1 \text{ football}} = \dfrac{x \text{ soccer}}{3 \text{ football}}$, and you'll find that you should actually enter 18 on the ratio line under soccer.

Next, add all the numbers on the Ratio line (3 + 7 + 18 = 28) and enter that under the Total on the Ratio line. The next piece of information given is that the total actual number of players coached in the month was between 375 and 400, so you'll have to do a bit of Ballparking to determine your multiplier. The Total on the Ratio line (28) is pretty close to 30, and to get from 30 to at least 375 you'll have to multiply by at least 11 or 12. Try 12, and see what your actual number becomes: $28 \times 12 = 336$; that's not big enough, so try 13 or 14: $28 \times 13 = 364$, which still isn't quite big enough. $28 \times 14 = 392$, which is exactly in the range you're looking for. Write 14 in every space on the Multiplier line.

Now, don't go crazy doing all the math to figure out how many athletes in each sport were trained! The question asks only about how many soccer players were coached, so only do what you need to answer the question! The correct answer is (D).

FOOTBALL	BASEBALL	SOCCER	TOTAL
3	7	18	28
14	14	14	14
		252	392

26. **B** One of the ways the SAT makes questions challenging is by combining multiple concepts into one problem. This question is a ratio question, but there's also information missing, and it asks for the ratio of their averages, not their time or actual number of boxes packed. Start by Plugging In for the missing information so you can actually work with values. The missing information is the amount of time it takes each of them to pack different numbers of boxes. So, say Jean takes 2 hours to pack 4 boxes; if it takes Scott three times as long to pack his 12 boxes, it takes him 6 hours.

Next use a Rate Pie (the same thing as an Average Pie, but with Distance/Work on the top, Time on the bottom left and Rate on the bottom right) to determine their individual rates:

Scott:

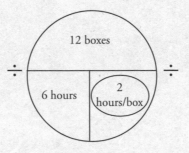

Jean:

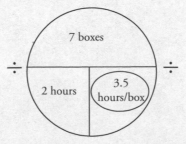

The last step is to find the ratio of Scott's average to Jean's average. Currently, it looks like 2:3.5, but it's unusual for the SAT to have decimals in average questions, so you'll need to convert that into whole numbers: 4:7, which is (B). Notice that (C) is a trap answer: It reverses the ratio, so read the question carefully!

32. **7** Start by dividing $3 \cdot f(r) = 93$ by 3 to get to the value of $f(r)$, 31. Then set the original function equal to 31 and solve:

$$f(x) = 4x + 3$$
$$f(r) = 4r + 3$$
$$31 = 4r + 3$$
$$\underline{-3 \qquad -3}$$
$$\frac{28}{4} = \frac{4r}{4}$$
$$7 = r$$

33. **940** Solve this using proportions: $\dfrac{16 \text{ ounces}}{1 \text{ pound}} = \dfrac{x \text{ ounces}}{4 \text{ pounds}}$ will tell you that the capacity of the jar is 64 ounces. Next, set up a proportion of beads to ounces: Solve $\dfrac{47 \text{ beads}}{3.2 \text{ ounces}} = \dfrac{x \text{ beads}}{64 \text{ ounces}}$ by cross-multiplying to get $3.2x = 3{,}008$, so $x = 940$ glass beads that the jar can hold.

Appendix:
The Optional SAT
Writing Test

INTRODUCTION TO THE SAT WRITING TEST

The final task on the SAT is to write a rhetorical analysis. You will have 50 minutes to read a text and write a logical, well-considered analysis of the author's argument.

According to ETS, the essay will show that:

> *"Students can demonstrate college and career readiness proficiency by producing a cogent and clear written analysis using critical reasoning and evidence drawn from an appropriately challenging text written for a broad audience."*

This really means:

> *Students can read an essay and then explain how the author uses specific aspects of the essay to build his or her argument.*

Even though you won't know what the actual essay will be about, what you're asked to do in it will be the same each time. Because you're tasked with analyzing the author's viewpoint rather than forming your own, you can already start preparing some of the fundamentals you'll need to include and modify them on the day of the test.

Format of the Essay

The prompt will look something like this:

As you read the passage below, consider how the author uses

- evidence, such as facts or examples, to support claims.
- reasoning to develop ideas and to connect claims and evidence.
- stylistic or persuasive elements, such as word choice or appeals to emotion, to add power to the ideas expressed.

The source text will then appear here, followed by directions.

Write an essay in which you explain how [the author] builds an argument to persuade [his/her] audience that [author's claim]. In your essay, analyze how [the author] uses one or more of the features listed above (or features of your own choice) to strengthen the logic and persuasiveness of [his/her] argument. Be sure that your analysis focuses on the most relevant aspects of the passage.

Your essay should not explain whether you agree with [the author's] claims, but rather explain how the author builds an argument to persuade [his/her] audience.

In other words, the essay requires you to

- Carefully read a text
- Understand how an author appeals to a reader's logic, emotions, or morals
- Write a logical analysis of an argument
- Explain how style choices can affect an author's persuasiveness

The essay does NOT require you to

- Give your opinion about a text
- Draw on other examples from literature or history
- Have previous experience with the text

The essay is actually a lot like the Reading section: a sort of open-book test in which you draw on the text that's in front of you to answer a question. Your opinion of the text doesn't matter; your ability to explain how the text works does.

HOW WILL MY ESSAY BE SCORED?

Two graders will each read and score the essay on a 1-4 scale in three different categories: Reading, Analysis, and Writing.

A 4 is Advanced, a 3 is Proficient, a 2 is Partial, and a 1 is Inadequate. The readers' scores will be combined to give you a score from 2-8 in each category.

Because the tasks are scored separately, a high (or low) score in one category does not guarantee a comparable score in another category.

Let's break those categories down.

Subscore #1: Reading

According to ETS, your reading score will be evaluated on your ability to show

- Comprehension of the source text
- Understanding of central ideas, important details, and their interrelationship
- Accuracy in representation of the source text (i.e., no errors of fact or interpretation are introduced)
- Use of textual evidence (quotations, paraphrases, or both) to demonstrate understanding of the source text

This means you need to be an active reader, thinking about how the essay works as you read through it. Though you may not know a great deal about the passage you're given, you do already know a lot about making an argument because most of us make arguments, about things big and small, every day.

SOAPS is a handy acronym to help you identify key elements of an argument.

Speaker: Who is speaking or writing and what qualifications does he or she have to address this topic?

Occasion: What happened that requires this speech or text? What larger historical context might be relevant?

Audience: Who is the intended audience and what relationship does the author have to that audience? What pre-existing ideas might the author and audience have about one another?

Purpose: What is the author's intention? To attack or defend? To persuade, blame, teach, praise? To rally the audience to action? Something else?

Subject: What is the main idea and what are the main lines of reasoning used?

As you read and identify the SOAPS, you should also look for the kind of **Appeals** the text makes.

Mental Sidebars

See this sidebar? That's basically active reading, except you're filling in the asides as you read. You don't have to write anything down, although you're free to jot notes in the margin if it helps. The general idea is that you be flexible and open enough to generate sidebars for each sentence of what you're reading. Once you recognize that you don't have to focus on content alone (there's also style and presentation), you should be finding plenty to put in your mental sidebars.

There are three main types of rhetorical appeals the arguments will use.

> **Appeal to Credibility**: What makes the author someone whose opinion on the subject carries weight? How does the author establish his or her authority to address the subject?
>
> **Appeal to Emotion**: How does the author evoke emotions to affect the audience? Does he or she play on positive (for example, happiness, well-being, love, pride) or negative emotions (for example, fear, distrust, anger, shame)?
>
> **Appeal to Logic**: How is the argument made to seem reasonable? What reasons and/or data are presented and how are they organized to make what the author's argument seem logical and solidly grounded in reasoning?

Subscore #2: Analysis

The second task you'll be evaluated on is the analysis of the text. According to ETS, you will be scored on your ability to

- Analyze the source text and understand the analytical task
- Evaluate the author's use of evidence, reasoning, and/or stylistic and persuasive elements, and/or features chosen by the student
- Support claims or points made in the response
- Focus on features of the text most relevant to addressing the task

This means that you need to point to things the author does—such as using imagery or making a joke—and explain how those things work to achieve an effect. It's not enough to say, "The author uses a quote to appeal to the audience's reason." You have to explain *how* the quote appeals to the audience's reason. The *how* and the *why* matter here, which makes sense, as these specifics are what support your claims. Just as a lawyer stacks up pieces of evidence in order to suggest a motive for the defendant or the accused, so too does an essay reader quote specific and particular elements of an author's work in order to support their own analysis of the author's intentions and overall effect.

Elements of Style

Here are some common style elements that may show up in the passage. You don't need to know or use the specific terms in your essay, but you do need to know their purposes and effects.

Imagery—language that appeals to the senses

Allusion—a brief reference to a person thing or idea from history, literature, politics, or something with cultural significance

Tone—the attitude the author has toward the subject

Syntax—the way in which words are put together to achieve a certain effect

Diction—the particular set of words used

Comparison—the act of taking at least two distinct things and making a connection between them

Juxtaposition—placing at least two ideas side by side in order to better illuminate a difference between them

Repetition—deliberately reusing a letter, word, or phrase to achieve a specific effect

Statistics or quotes—using data or text from a respected/recognized source to add credibility to an argument

Subscore #3: Writing

The final task you'll be evaluated on is the actual writing of the essay. According to ETS, this requires you to

- Use a central claim
- Use effective organization that shows a progression of ideas
- Use varied sentence structures
- Employ precise word choice
- Maintain consistent, appropriate style and tone
- Show command of the conventions of standard written English

Of course, when you write your essay, you are also showing the graders that you have read, understood, and analyzed the text. The writing score you receive reflects not so much what you say, which is covered in the other scores, but how you say it.

WRITING THE ESSAY

Here, we outline a template that shows how this all comes together.

Introduction

Your introduction should do three things.

1. Describe the text. This is where you bring in the SOAPS points. This can be done in one sentence.
2. Paraphrase the argument. Show the graders that you understand the text by concisely summing up the main points and overall message of the text. The Reading score comes from your demonstration of comprehension of the text.
3. Introduce the examples you will be discussing in the body paragraphs. This establishes the framework that the rest of your essay will follow.

Body Paragraphs

Each body paragraph will focus on a different appeal or style element that the author uses effectively to communicate and enhance his or her argument. Each body paragraph should do the following:

1. Name and explain the rhetorical device or appeal. Identify where it is in the text and use short, relevant quotes to show you understand the text and the rhetorical device or appeal. Don't rely on long excerpts—a high score will depend on your using your own words to explain.
2. Identify the effects of the author's use of that device or appeal. Explain the connection between the device or appeal and the author's argument, as well as your own. Use your own words to explain how the device or appeal specifically contributes to the author's argument—this explanation is how you show the graders your ability to analyze the text.

Conclusion

The most significant thing about your conclusion is that it be there, demonstrating your ability to organize and present a complete argument. The conclusion should do two things.

1. Restate the goal of the text and briefly paraphrase the elements you discussed in your essay.
2. Be concise and accurate.

FINAL TIPS

Presentation isn't everything, but it matters. Your argument will get a better chance to shine if the presentation is polished and reflects the sense of occasion that ETS expects of the SAT.

- Maintain formal style and tone. Avoid using "I, " "you," and slang.
- Use varied sentence structure.
- Write neatly.
- Use clear transitions.
- Use short, relevant quotes from the text.
- Use the formal terms for devices if you know them. It's perfectly fine to say that an element "appeals to emotions," but if you happen to know the term "pathos," feel free to use that instead.

About the Authors

Brian Becker is a writer and teacher. He completed a Ph.D. in Literature at Rutgers in 2015. He has worked with The Princeton Review for over 10 years, contributing to various books and testing materials. Brian is an avid traveler, who fills time at home and afar reading and writing. And on the squash court, Brian is a force to reckoned with, as long as his opponent is not very good.

V. Zoe Gannon began her teaching career with The Princeton Review during her sophomore year at Trinity University. Since then, she has worn many hats, working as an instructor and Master Tutor, serving as National Content Director for SSAT & ISEE for The Princeton Review, and overseeing special needs and student accommodations nationwide. She is known for going above and beyond in her dedication to her SAT, ACT, AP, and Early Edge students. In her free time, Zoe enjoys running, playing with her two dogs Arrow and Scout, knitting, sewing, homebrewing, and camping.

Kathryn Menefee is an ACT/SAT instructor, tutor, and project manager with the Princeton Review. She also draws pet portraits and writes half-baked novels in her free time.

Amy Minster has been teaching and tutoring for The Princeton Review since 2004. She is a Master Tutor for the ACT, SAT, and GRE in the western suburbs of Chicago. In addition to tutoring for these tests, Amy tutors for the SAT Subject tests in Math (Levels 1 and 2) and is a certified College Admissions Counselor. Amy also helps with content development for new manuals and tests and trains incoming SAT teachers. Prior to joining The Princeton Review, Amy worked as an art teacher and art therapist in the Chicago Public Schools. Amy has two kids, Annalee and Everett, and one dog, Ringo. She doesn't have much free time, but likes to read, make jewelry, and sew. She often dreams about math.

Elizabeth Owens started her teaching career as a high school English teacher. She then began teaching SAT classes for The Princeton Review in 2004 as a part-time job to make her car payment, and soon realized that she quite liked teaching kids how to beat the SAT. When her first child was born in 2007, she left the public school system for the world of test prep. Over the next couple of years she branched out into ACT, GRE, GMAT, MCAT Verbal, and Early Edge. She is a Premier Tutor, an SAT Uber Trainer, and an ACT and Early Edge Master Trainer. She is very involved with content development for the high school programs, and when she's not eyeball-deep in scantrons and #2 pencils, she enjoys reading, baking things with chocolate in them, and playing princess superheroes with her two kids.

The Princeton Review®

International Offices Listing

China (Beijing)
1501 Building A,
Disanji Creative Zone,
No.66 West Section of North 4th Ring Road Beijing
Tel: +86-10-62684481/2/3
Email: tprkor01@chol.com
Website: www.tprbeijing.com

China (Shanghai)
1010 Kaixuan Road
Building B, 5/F
Changning District, Shanghai, China 200052
Sara Beattie, Owner: Email: sbeattie@sarabeattie.com
Tel: +86-21-5108-2798
Fax: +86-21-6386-1039
Website: www.princetonreviewshanghai.com

Hong Kong
5th Floor, Yardley Commercial Building
1-6 Connaught Road West, Sheung Wan, Hong Kong
(MTR Exit C)
Sara Beattie, Owner: Email: sbeattie@sarabeattie.com
Tel: +852-2507-9380
Fax: +852-2827-4630
Website: www.princetonreviewhk.com

India (Mumbai)
Score Plus Academy
Office No.15, Fifth Floor
Manek Mahal 90
Veer Nariman Road
Next to Hotel Ambassador
Churchgate, Mumbai 400020
Maharashtra, India
Ritu Kalwani: Email: director@score-plus.com
Tel: + 91 22 22846801 / 39 / 41
Website: www.score-plus.com

India (New Delhi)
South Extension
K-16, Upper Ground Floor
South Extension Part-1,
New Delhi-110049
Aradhana Mahna: aradhana@manyagroup.com
Monisha Banerjee: monisha@manyagroup.com
Ruchi Tomar: ruchi.tomar@manyagroup.com
Rishi Josan: Rishi.josan@manyagroup.com
Vishal Goswamy: vishal.goswamy@manyagroup.com
Tel: +91-11-64501603/ 4, +91-11-65028379
Website: www.manyagroup.com

Lebanon
463 Bliss Street
AlFarra Building - 2nd floor
Ras Beirut
Beirut, Lebanon
Hassan Coudsi: Email: hassan.coudsi@review.com
Tel: +961-1-367-688
Website: www.princetonreviewlebanon.com

Korea
945-25 Young Shin Building
25 Daechi-Dong, Kangnam-gu
Seoul, Korea 135-280
Yong-Hoon Lee: Email: TPRKor01@chollian.net
In-Woo Kim: Email: iwkim@tpr.co.kr
Tel: + 82-2-554-7762
Fax: +82-2-453-9466
Website: www.tpr.co.kr

Kuwait
ScorePlus Learning Center
Salmiyah Block 3, Street 2 Building 14
Post Box: 559, Zip 1306, Safat, Kuwait
Email: infokuwait@score-plus.com
Tel: +965-25-75-48-02 / 8
Fax: +965-25-75-46-02
Website: www.scorepluseducation.com

Malaysia
Sara Beattie MDC Sdn Bhd
Suites 18E & 18F
18th Floor
Gurney Tower, Persiaran Gurney
Penang, Malaysia
Email: tprkl.my@sarabeattie.com
Sara Beattie, Owner: Email: sbeattie@sarabeattie.com
Tel: +604-2104 333
Fax: +604-2104 330
Website: www.princetonreviewKL.com

Mexico
TPR México
Guanajuato No. 242 Piso 1 Interior 1
Col. Roma Norte
México D.F., C.P.06700
registro@princetonreviewmexico.com
Tel: +52-55-5255-4495
+52-55-5255-4440
+52-55-5255-4442
Website: www.princetonreviewmexico.com

Qatar
Score Plus
Office No: 1A, Al Kuwari (Damas)
Building near Merweb Hotel, Al Saad
Post Box: 2408, Doha, Qatar
Email: infoqatar@score-plus.com
Tel: +974 44 36 8580, +974 526 5032
Fax: +974 44 13 1995
Website: www.scorepluseducation.com

Taiwan
The Princeton Review Taiwan
2F, 169 Zhong Xiao East Road, Section 4
Taipei, Taiwan 10690
Lisa Bartle (Owner): lbartle@princetonreview.com.tw
Tel: +886-2-2751-1293
Fax: +886-2-2776-3201
Website: www.PrincetonReview.com.tw

Thailand
The Princeton Review Thailand
Sathorn Nakorn Tower, 28th floor
100 North Sathorn Road
Bangkok, Thailand 10500
Thavida Bijayendrayodhin (Chairman)
Email: thavida@princetonreviewthailand.com
Mitsara Bijayendrayodhin (Managing Director)
Email: mitsara@princetonreviewthailand.com
Tel: +662-636-6770
Fax: +662-636-6776
Website: www.princetonreviewthailand.com

Turkey
Yeni Sülün Sokak No. 28
Levent, Istanbul, 34330, Turkey
Nuri Ozgur: nuri@tprturkey.com
Rona Ozgur: rona@tprturkey.com
Iren Ozgur: iren@tprturkey.com
Tel: +90-212-324-4747
Fax: +90-212-324-3347
Website: www.tprturkey.com

UAE
Emirates Score Plus
Office No: 506, Fifth Floor
Sultan Business Center
Near Lamcy Plaza, 21 Oud Metha Road
Post Box: 44098, Dubai
United Arab Emirates
Hukumat Kalwani: skoreplus@gmail.com
Ritu Kalwani: director@score-plus.com
Email: info@score-plus.com
Tel: +971-4-334-0004
Fax: +971-4-334-0222
Website: www.princetonreviewuae.com

Our International Partners

The Princeton Review also runs courses with a variety of
partners in Africa, Asia, Europe, and South America.

Georgia
LEAF American-Georgian Education Center
www.leaf.ge

Mongolia
English Academy of Mongolia
www.nyescm.org

Nigeria
The Know Place
www.knowplace.com.ng

Panama
Academia Interamericana de Panama
http://aip.edu.pa/

Switzerland
Institut Le Rosey
http://www.rosey.ch/

All other inquiries, please email us at
internationalsupport@review.com